Brick *by*
Brick

The **Association of Southeast Asian Nations (ASEAN)** was established on 8 August 1967. The Member Countries of the Association are Brunei Darussalam, Cambodia, Indonesia, Lao PDR, Malaysia, Myanmar, Philippines, Singapore, Thailand and Vietnam. The ASEAN Secretariat is based in Jakarta, Indonesia.

For enquiries, contact:
Public Affairs Office
The ASEAN Secretariat
70A Jalan Sisingamangaraja
Jakarta 12110
Indonesia
Tel: (62 21) 724-3372, 726-2991
Fax: (62 21) 739-8234, 724-3504
E-mail: public@aseansec.org
ASEANWeb: www.aseansec.org

Asia Pacific Press is based in the Crawford School of Economics and Government at The Australian National University. Asia Pacific Press specializes in economics, development, governance and management in the Asia Pacific region.

The **Institute of Southeast Asian Studies (ISEAS)** was established as an autonomous organization in 1968. It is a regional centre dedicated to the study of socio-political, security and economic trends and developments in Southeast Asia and its wider geostrategic and economic environment.

The Institute's research programmes are the Regional Economic Studies (RES, including ASEAN and APEC), Regional Strategic and Political Studies (RSPS), and Regional Social and Cultural Studies (RSCS).

ISEAS Publishing, an established academic press, has issued almost 2,000 books and journals. It is the largest scholarly publisher of research about Southeast Asia from within the region. ISEAS Publishing works with many other academic and trade publishers and distributors to disseminate important research and analyses from and about Southeast Asia to the rest of the world.

Brick *by* Brick

The Building of an ASEAN Economic Community

EDITED BY

DENIS HEW

A collection of economic research on ASEAN integration issues produced
under the ASEAN–Australia Development Cooperation Program —
Regional Economic Policy Support Facility

Australian Government

AusAID

Supported by the Australian Goverment, AusAID

ASIA PACIFIC PRESS
THE AUSTRALIAN NATIONAL UNIVERSITY

INSTITUTE OF SOUTHEAST ASIAN STUDIES
Singapore

First published in Singapore in 2007 by ISEAS Publishing
Institute of Southeast Asian Studies
30 Heng Mui Keng Terrace
Pasir Panjang
Singapore 119614
E-mail: publish@iseas.edu.sg
Website: http://bookshop.iseas.edu.sg

ISEAS ISBN 978-981-230-732-3 (soft cover)
ISBN 978-981-230-733-0 (hard cover)
ISBN 978-981-230-734-7 (PDF)

First published in Australia in 2007 by Asia Pacific Press
Crawford School of Economics and Government
The Australian National University
Canberra ACT 0200
Australia
Tel: 61-2-6125 0178
Fax: 61-2-6125 0767
Website: http://www.asiapacificpress.com

Asia Pacific Press ISBN 978-0-7315-3814-0

Disclaimer
The responsibility for facts and opinions in this publication rests exclusively with the authors and their interpretations do not necessarily reflect the views or the policy of the ASEAN Secretariat and/or the Australian Government, the publishers or their supporters.

ISEAS Library Cataloguing-in-Publication Data

Brick by brick : the building of an ASEAN Economic Community / edited by Denis Hew.
A collection of select policy research on ASEAN integration issues conducted under the Regional Economic Policy Support Facility, ASEAN-Australia Development Cooperation Program.
1. ASEAN.
2. Southeast Asia—Economic integration.
3. Southeast Asia—Foreign economic relations.
4. Southeast Asia—Commercial policy.
5. Free trade—Southeast Asia.
I. Hew, Denis.
II. ASEAN-Australia Development Cooperation Program. Regional Economic Policy Support Facility.
III. Title: ASEAN Economic Community
HC441 B841   2007

Typeset by Superskill Graphics Pte Ltd
Printed in Singapore by Utopia Press Pte Ltd

Contents

Foreword

ASEAN is celebrating its fortieth anniversary in 2007. The usual busy meeting schedule is now spiced up with festivities and exuberance of spirit and colours. It will be an exciting year for ASEAN.

At the same time, the ASEAN Leaders are forging strongly ahead with their plans for the ASEAN Community, especially the effort to integrate the ten ASEAN economies into one single market and regional production base. This is an unprecedented initiative and one which would break the traditional mindset and create a new paradigm of regional cooperation and development. Many partners of ASEAN as well as stakeholders from numerous sectors are involved. Their joint endeavour would establish ASEAN a firm foundation for the intense competition and the complexities of a globalized community.

Over the past five years, the Regional Economic Policy Support Facility (REPSF) under the ASEAN–Australia Development Cooperation Program (AADCP) has supported ASEAN's community-building efforts by providing the ASEAN Secretariat and ASEAN bodies with economic policy analysis and advice to assist them in putting in place measures and actions contributing to achieving economic integration and competitiveness.

This book is a collection of select policy research on ASEAN economic integration issues conducted under the Facility. What are the implications of the goal of a single market? How will integration affect the less developed member countries of ASEAN? What strategies should ASEAN employ to free up trade and facilitate investment? How can ASEAN add value to the economic relations with its dialogue partners? These are just some of the challenging questions examined in this collection of studies by some of the most eminent policy analysts from ASEAN and Australia.

I would like to take this opportunity to express my deep appreciation to ASEAN's strong supporters in neighbouring Australia for instituting such an innovative economic research facility as part of the cooperation programme assisting ASEAN deal with the challenges of integration. I would like to commend the various experts who have been engaged by the Facility over the years. I thank them for sharing their knowledge and unique insights to help ASEAN navigate through the complicated situation. Last but not the least, I would like to thank all the relevant ASEAN sectoral bodies and the ASEAN Secretariat staff who have in one way or another contributed to these research endeavours.

The task at hand is arduous and time consuming. Let us continue to ask the hard questions, engage in informed policy discourse, assess the best available options, and then act decisively towards realizing our goal. Brick by brick, we shall be able to establish the ASEAN Community based on the three pillars of political/security cooperation, economic integration and socio-cultural advancement.

Bravo!

Ong Keng Yong
Secretary-General
Association of Southeast Asian Nations

Foreword

Partnership is fundamental to Australia's relationships with our neighbours. This is no more clearly reflected than in Australia's long-standing development cooperation with ASEAN. For over thirty years, Australia has worked closely with ASEAN to reduce poverty and promote sustainable economic growth in the region. Our shared experience has confirmed not only the centrality of economic growth to poverty reduction, but the importance of close cooperation in driving and sustaining the region's economic prosperity.

ASEAN has become the primary regional organization in Southeast Asia driving closer economic integration. In leading a dynamic and rapidly growing region, it has made significant advances towards closer economic integration. Through the ASEAN–Australia Development Cooperation Program (AADCP) and its predecessors, Australia has been privileged to assist ASEAN in this important goal. In ASEAN's fortieth anniversary year, we remain committed to supporting ASEAN's economic integration and applaud its aspiration to create an ASEAN Economic Community by 2015.

This will be no simple task. It will demand innovative and robust economic policy-making, with high-quality research as an essential ingredient. Under the AADCP's Regional Economic Policy Support Facility (REPSF), the best minds in ASEAN and Australian research institutions have come together to address difficult and sometimes sensitive issues on ASEAN's economic development and integration agenda. Together, they have produced fifty research studies of lasting relevance to the challenges ahead. This book, *Brick by Brick: The Building of an ASEAN Economic Community*, is a fitting tribute to that collaboration.

I would like to thank all the ASEAN and Australian experts who have contributed to the REPSF over the last five years. I appreciate the pivotal role of the ASEAN Secretariat in making this research facility a great success.

I sincerely hope that this book inspires further understanding and informed debate among researchers and policy-makers interested in the region's economic progress. We need to ensure that ASEAN and Australia are well aware of both the opportunities and the risks in a challenging period ahead. In this way, we can continue jointly to shape a sustainable and equitable future for the region.

Bruce Davis
Director-General
Australian Agency of International Development

Acknowledgements by Academic Editor

I would like to thank the chapter writers for their contributions, especially their excellent work in revising their original studies to meet the guidelines of this book project.

I am deeply indebted to Ms Sanchita Basu Das for her editorial assistance without which this book would not be possible. My thanks also to Associate Professor Mely Caballero-Anthony, Dr Ramonette Serafica, Professor Brian Brogan and his associate, Ms Gail Tregear, for their valuable advice.

I would like to thank Ambassador K. Kesavapany, Director of ISEAS, for his support in this book project.

My sincere thanks to the staff of ISEAS Publications Unit, especially Mrs Triena Ong, for their valuable support in getting this book published.

Denis Hew
Academic Editor

Acknowledgements by Technical Director REPSF

The Regional Economic Policy Support Facility (REPSF) has been privileged to have been associated with two ASEAN Secretary Generals, initially with H.E. Rodolfo Severino, whose perceptive vision shaped the reporting lines within ASEC and the broad research priorities which ensured that REPSF would be able to focus on serious economic policy issues and that its work interfaced with the key economic decision-makers within ASEC and ASEAN at large.

His successor, H.E. Ong Keng Yong, has continued that tradition throughout his term of office. His involvement was detailed, enthusiastic, and intellectually rigorous. This book was his idea, and it is dedicated to him.

REPSF has been fortunate to work with two Deputy Convenors, Directors of the Bureau for Economic Integration and Finance, initially Mr Noordin Azhari and subsequently with his successor Mr Sundram Pushpanathan. Both gave freely of their time, their expertise, their commitment and their wisdom. Their involvement has had a major impact on the range of projects undertaken, the quality of the project implementation and the use to which the finished reports were finally put.

REPSF's first point of contact within ASEC has been Mr Rony Soerakoesoemah, now Senior Resource Officer, FTA Unit of the Bureau for Economic Integration and Finance. He has assisted both Deputy Convenors and has been a source of great advice and support. It was he who suggested the title for this book.

Many people have contributed to REPSF's work and its success. They include sponsors and other professional colleagues within ASEC and ASEAN working groups. AusAID, the Managing Contractor (Melbourne Development Institute), as well as current and former REPSF team members who have all played important roles in the smooth running of the project without which none of this would have been possible.

Finally we have to thank the researchers who came from many consulting firms, research institutes and countries and who in the final analysis did the substantive work for which REPSF is noted.

Brian Brogan
Technical Director
Regional Economic Policy Support Facility

The Contributors

Rajenthran Arumugam is former Visiting Research Fellow at the Institute of Southeast Asian Studies (ISEAS), Singapore.

Sanchita Basu Das is Research Associate, Regional Economic Studies, at the Institute of Southeast Asian Studies (ISEAS), Singapore.

Brian Brogan is Technical Director Regional Economic Policy Support Facility (REPSF) and Visiting Fellow at the College of Business and Economics, The Australian National University.

Loreli C. de Dios is an economic consultant based in the Philippines. She is also connected with the Center for the Advancement of Trade Integration and Facilitation.

Ian Farrow is Senior Manager with KPMG Australia's taxation practice with a special focus on taxation policy issues in Australia and within the Asia Pacific.

Christopher Findlay is Professor and Head of School of Economics, University of Adelaide. He is also a member of the Australian Pacific Economic Cooperation Committee.

Denis Hew is Senior Fellow and Coordinator, Regional Economic Studies at the Institute of Southeast Asian Studies (ISEAS), Singapore.

Sunita Jogarajan is Senior Consultant with KPMG Australia's taxation practice and a Lecturer on taxation law at the University of Melbourne.

Habibullah Khan is Associate Professor at the Graduate School of Business, Universitas 21 Global, Singapore.

Peter J. Lloyd is Professor Emeritus in the Department of Economics, Faculty of Economics and Commerce, University of Melbourne, Australia.

Rina Oktaviani is Lecturer and Head of the Economics Department, Bogor Agricultural University, Indonesia.

David Parsons is Executive Director of the Committee on Investment and International Trade Development at the Indonesian Chamber of Commerce and Industry (Kadin Indonesia) based in Jakarta.

Herb Plunkett is a Canberra-based economic consultant and former employee of the Productivity Commission.

Henny Reinhardt is Lecturer in the Economics Department, Bogor Agricultural University, Indonesia.

Amzul Rifin is Lecturer in Agribusiness Department, Bogor Agricultural University, Indonesia.

Rahul Sen is Fellow, Regional Economic Studies at the Institute of Southeast Asian Studies (ISEAS), Singapore.

M. Sornarajah is Professor at the Faculty of Law, National University of Singapore.

Jose L. Tongzon is Professor at the Graduate School of Logistics, Inha University, South Korea.

The Regional Economic Policy Support Facility

Brian Brogan

This collection of studies results from the first five years of operation of the Regional Economic Policy Support Facility (REPSF), a component of the Australian Government's ASEAN–Australia Development Cooperation Program (AADCP). During this five-year period, REPSF produced a total of fifty research papers.

AADCP is the prime vehicle for the Australian Agency for International Development (AusAID) development cooperation activities carried out in collaboration with ASEAN through interaction with the ASEAN Secretariat (ASEC).

AADCP consists of three separately managed streams, namely, the Program Stream (PS), the Regional Partnership Scheme (RPS), and REPSF. The PS and the RPS implement activities of medium to small size in policy and capacity-building.

REPSF was the first stream to be mobilized in January 2002. It conducted a rolling programme of small to medium economic policy research projects. These projects assisted ASEC in its mission to provide ASEAN Working Groups with economic policy and development analysis for working towards the goal of integrating the economies of the ten ASEAN member countries (AMCs) in line with the objectives and priorities of ASEAN Vision 2020, the Hanoi Plan of Action, and the subsequent Vientiane Action Programme (VAP).

In December 2005 Australia's Foreign Minister Alexander Downer announced the funding of a further AUD5 million for joint research examining economic integration between ASEAN nations and the other East Asian nations — Japan, the Republic of Korea, China, India, New Zealand, and Australia. Therefore REPSF was given an extension period from the completion of REPSF I in January 2007 to 30 June 2008 for this East Asia Summit Research Initiative.

REPSF is a funding mechanism which, in consultation with its key stakeholders AusAID, ASEC and ASEAN's Senior Economic Officials Meeting (SEOM), provides ASEC with the capacity to develop and implement a programme of priority economic policy research. It is more specialized than the other two streams of AADCP. Its programme of economic policy research on aspects of ASEAN economic integration is undertaken by researchers selected through either competitive tender or deliberative invitation (depending on the budget level of the study). ASEC personnel and ASEAN sectoral bodies monitor the research in progress. During the project the researchers present drafts of their report to audiences of relevant ASEAN or other experts. On its completion the research report is transmitted to the initial ASEAN or ASEC sponsor and to AusAID and is usually released onto the REPSF and ASEC websites, www.aadcp-repsf.org and www.aseansec.org, respectively. The copyright on the completed reports resides with ASEC.

REPSF is bound by a number of guidelines — mandated modalities for topic and team selection, and for research management. These guidelines give REPSF a high degree of autonomy in operational matters, but research priority setting is in the hands of the three stakeholders. Team selection and research management guidelines mandate conformity with AusAID's financial management and general development criteria (such as AusAID's gender equity goals).

The research team selection guidelines have required a broad regional balance across the ASEAN and CER countries in addition to AusAID's gender balance requirements. Tight deadlines, availability of suitable personnel, and specialist needs of some of the research topics have sometimes made compliance with these criteria difficult to achieve.

REPSF and its ASEC colleagues have consistently striven for high standards in team selection and research management. Not all of the final reports have reached the highest standards but a number of them (including all those collected in this book) have, and the average is high indeed. All finished within budget and most within the agreed time-frame.

In Phase I REPSF's fifty research reports were undertaken by thirty ASEAN-based research organizations/individuals, thirty-six Australian-based research organizations/individuals, and two "others" — one organization from the United States and one from New Zealand. Thirteen research subcontracts have been joint partnerships with two or more organizations/individuals.

REPSF's broad priorities, specific topics included in the rolling programme and other agreed activities are set by the Research Priorities Committee (RPC) which meets usually about every six months at ASEC in Jakarta. The Committee consists of the Co-Chairs (the ASEAN Secretary-General and a senior AusAID official from the Asia Regional Branch) and a representative of the third stakeholder, SEOM. The Secretary-General hosts the meeting.

The RPC set the original operational guidelines. It approves all new topics, research budgets and timetables. It is the RPC which formally accepts completed reports. Those arrangements have made for a very effective working relationship between REPSF staff, ASEC, and AusAID.

In its structures and modalities REPSF has pioneered a number of innovations in development cooperation that are now becoming more common. Key among these is the degree of involvement in priority setting and delegation of implementation to the target agency, ASEC. In the view of REPSF staff this devolution, in addition to the intense commitment it has generated among stakeholders and their officials, has made REPSF the success it is.

REPSF's narrow focus on economic policy research of relevance to ASEAN's economic integration has given it currency and credibility in the ASEAN-CER economic policy research community. As REPSF gained a reputation for quality economic policy analysis and influence, the numbers of leading regional researchers who were keen to undertake REPSF projects grew.

This combination of a relevant work agenda, close involvement in the policy process and intense professionalism of its staff and processes helped establish REPSF as a reputable sponsor of East Asian economic policy research and analysis.

REPSF has accumulated a unique collection of data from all its studies. A number of projects have focussed on fact-finding — 02/001 "Developing Indicators of ASEAN Integration", 03/004 "A Background Paper for the Strategic Plan of Action on ASEAN Cooperation in Food and Agriculture (2005–2010)", and 03/006(e) "The Pattern of Intra ASEAN Trade in the Priority Goods Sectors". Several studies included separate country reports for all ten ASEAN member countries, which also contribute to the voluminous authoritative data on the topics by country.

Other studies have provided useful options for ASEC/ASEAN at seminal moments such as the five 03/006 studies, which provided inputs to ASEC's role in developing the VAP. These included assessments of ASEAN's past effectiveness and future prospects, a framework for future evaluation of progress to the VAP's implementation, and a paper on resourcing models for ASEC's future.

The majority of projects have concentrated on assessments of past performance, prospects for future progress, optional scenarios for integration, and barriers to integration in ASEAN's priority sectors. Papers directly contributing to regional policy development include 02/006 on "Liberalization of Financial Services in the ASEAN Region" which provided key inputs into the development of the Roadmap for ASEAN Financial and Monetary Integration and 02/008 on "Preparing ASEAN for Open Sky" which has become the basis of the Action Plan for ASEAN Air Transport Integration and Liberalization.

REPSF's largest project, 06/001, which was undertaken in six parts, was on measures affecting the integration of ASEAN's priority sectors. This major study, coordinated by a group from the University of Adelaide, was based on the influential Project 03//006(a) by Lloyd and Smith "Global Economic Challenges to ASEAN Integration and Competitiveness: A Prospective Look". The paper by Lloyd and Smith is the most widely read REPSF report as evidenced by the website downloads to date.

In the final months of REPSF I a new paper was developed "A Background Paper on Energy Issues for the 2nd East Asia Summit", which was acknowledged in the Chairman's Statement of the 2nd East Asia Summit.

REPSF stakeholders can be proud of the past and optimistic for the future.

1

Introduction: Brick by Brick — The Building of an ASEAN Economic Community

Denis Hew

1. Introduction

The Association of Southeast Asian Nations (ASEAN) is one of the world's most successful regional organizations. Established on 8 August 1967, ASEAN consists of ten member countries, namely, Brunei, Cambodia, Indonesia, Laos, Malaysia, Myanmar, the Philippines, Singapore, Thailand, and Vietnam.

ASEAN countries combined constitute a population of about 567 million, spanning a total area of 4.5 million square kilometres. In 2006, ASEAN generated a combined gross domestic product of US$1.07 trillion and total trade of US$1.44 trillion, accounting for more than a quarter of Asia's total exports and imports.[1]

Since its inception four decades ago, ASEAN has successfully managed to foster closer political and security cooperation, creating a peaceful and stable region. As a result, ASEAN, especially its original five members (ASEAN-5), i.e., Indonesia, Malaysia, the Philippines, Singapore, and Thailand, has enjoyed impressive economic growth, reduced poverty and improved living standards over the past three decades.

Although many ASEAN countries were severely affected by the 1997 Asian financial crisis, their economies have recovered ten years on. However, during this time the region has begun to face stiff competition from China, particularly in attracting foreign direct investments (FDIs). This has raised serious concerns among ASEAN policy-makers about the longer term economic development and sustainability of this region.

Against this backdrop, ASEAN leaders agreed to embark on a bold project to integrate their economies and establish an ASEAN Economic Community. This ambitious project will clearly require a significantly higher level of economic integration than that which exists today.

2. The ASEAN Economic Community

At the 2003 ASEAN Summit in Bali, Indonesia, ASEAN leaders agreed to integrate their economies by 2020 and establish an ASEAN Economic Community (AEC). The AEC is one of the three components or pillars that make up the ASEAN Community as declared by ASEAN leaders in the ASEAN Concord II (better known as the Bali Concord II).[2] At the ASEAN Summit held in Cebu, Philippines in January 2007, the deadline to realize the AEC was brought forward by five years to 2015.[3]

The end-goal of the AEC is the creation of a single market and production base where there is free flow of goods, services, investments, capital, and skilled labour. Although the approach towards achieving this end-goal was not elaborated in the Bali Concord II, what seemed clear at the start was the need to have a significantly higher degree of regional economic integration and institutional development.

Why an ASEAN Economic Community? The loss of economic competitiveness to emerging markets such as China has been the major driving force in ASEAN's efforts to accelerate economic integration. A study on ASEAN undertaken by McKinsey found that ASEAN had lost its competitive edge in terms of labour costs to China (Schwartz and Villinger 2004). Furthermore, China had overtaken ASEAN as the world's prime location for FDIs. This could have serious repercussions on ASEAN's economic well-being over the medium to long-term as FDI has long played an important role in the region's economic development (Freeman and Hew 2002). See Figure 1.1.

FDI has played an important role in Southeast Asia's economic development. First in Singapore in the 1970s and later by Malaysia, Thailand, and Indonesia in the 1980s, the economic development model adopted by these ASEAN countries was driven by strategies that favoured FDI from

Figure 1.1
FDI Inflows to China and ASEAN, 1980–2005

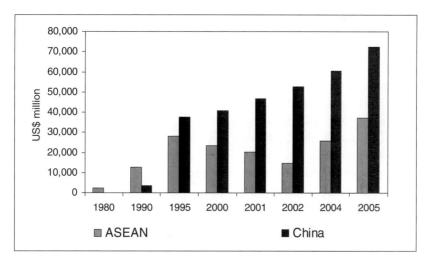

Source: UNCTAD.

multinational corporations (MNCs) and export-orientated domestic industries. More recently, Vietnam and China have adopted similar economic strategies as these countries made the transition to become more market-oriented economies. Over the past two decades, China's high economic growth rates and rapid economic expansion have transformed the country, making it the fifth largest economy in the world (World Bank 2007).

Economic integration could provide the means to revitalize ASEAN's economies. ASEAN countries are currently at very different levels of economic development. This diversity could prove advantageous in maximizing the complementarities among its member countries. An integrated market and production base would clearly boost intra-regional trade and investment flows across the region while ASEAN's consumer market of over half a billion would be a lucrative place for companies to do business.

In 2003, the ASEAN High Level Task Force (HLTF) on Economic Integration recommended a slew of economic initiatives to kick-start the AEC project.[4] These initiatives included:

- Fast-track integration of priority sectors.
- Faster customs clearance and simplified customs procedures.
- Elimination of barriers to trade.

- Accelerated implementation of the Mutual Recognition Arrangements (MRAs) for key sectors (for example, electrical and electronic equipment and telecommunications equipment).
- Harmonization of standards and technical regulations.

Eleven priority sectors were highlighted by the ASEAN HLTF on Economic Integration which are: electronics, e-ASEAN (information and communication technology), healthcare, wood-based products, automotives, rubber-based products, textiles and apparels, agro-based products, fisheries, air travel, and tourism.[5] At the 2007 ASEAN Cebu Summit, a twelfth priority sector was endorsed by ASEAN leaders, which was the logistics sector. These priority sectors were identified based on their potential to maximize the complementarities among ASEAN economies and serve as a catalyst for expediting the integration process.

In the area of trade in goods, ASEAN officials also proposed improving the Common Effective Preferential Tariffs (CEPT) Scheme's rules of origin (ROO). This would include making the ROO more transparent, predictable and standardized and taking into account the best practices of other regional trading arrangements (RTAs) including the World Trade Organization (WTO)'s ROO. To ensure transparency on non-tariff measures (NTMs) and eliminate those that are barriers to trade, the following measures would also be undertaken over the next few years:

- establish an ASEAN Database on NTMs.
- set a clear criteria to identify measures that are classified as barriers to trade.
- set a clear and definitive work programme for the removal of such barriers.
- adopt the WTO agreements on Technical Barriers to Trade; Sanitary and Phyto-Sanitary and Import Licensing Procedures and develop implementation guidelines appropriate for ASEAN.

One of the most important recommendations by the HLTF was to enhance the ASEAN dispute settlement mechanism (DSM). To date, the ASEAN DSM has never been used by any member country. This is not surprising, given ASEAN's consensus-driven and non-confrontational decision-making process as well as the politically charged nature of any trade-related DSMs. Nevertheless, the number of trade disputes will invariably rise as the region undergoes deeper economic integration. Hence, having a workable DSM would be absolutely vital for the successful implementation of the AEC project. The following measures were undertaken to enhance the ASEAN DSM:[6]

- Establish a legal unit within the ASEAN Secretariat to provide legal advice on trade disputes.
- Establish the ASEAN Consultation to Solve Trade and Investment Issues in order to provide quick resolution to operations problems (this would be similar to the EU mechanism).
- Establish the ASEAN Compliance Body.

To effectively implement the AEC, a six-year action plan was launched at the 2004 ASEAN Summit in Vientiane, Laos. This plan, which is known as the Vientiane Action Programme 2004–2010 (VAP), has three broad objectives:

- Intensify current economic cooperation initiatives which are targeted for completion on or before 2010 as well as accelerate the integration of the eleven priority sectors.
- Remove barriers to free flow of goods, services, and skilled labour and freer flow of capital by 2010.
- Develop and implement economic measures that would put in place the essential elements for ASEAN to function as a single market and production base.

3. Building Blocks of the AEC

Achieving a higher level of economic integration may seem daunting at first glance but ASEAN is not starting from scratch. This is because ASEAN has already put in place important building blocks to support the AEC. These building blocks include the ASEAN Free Trade Area (AFTA), the ASEAN Investment Area (AIA), and the ASEAN Framework Agreement on Services (AFAS). These are discussed separately below.

3.1. ASEAN Free Trade Area

AFTA was launched with the signing of a Common Effective Preferential Tariff (CEPT) Scheme on 28 January 1992. The CEPT scheme requires member countries to reduce their tariff rates on a wide range of products traded within the region to 0 to 5 per cent. ASEAN-5 plus Brunei (ASEAN-6) have already complied with the CEPT scheme in 2003. Vietnam achieved its tariff elimination target in 2006, Laos and Myanmar in 2008, and Cambodia in 2010. To date, 99.77 per cent of products in the CEPT Inclusion List of the ASEAN-6 countries have been reduced to 0 to 5 per cent.

In November 1999, ASEAN Economic Ministers went further in their efforts to realize the vision of a regional free trade area by agreeing to adopt a target of zero tariffs by 2010 for the ASEAN-6 and 2015 for the CLMV countries. For products in the priority sectors, tariffs are targeted to be eliminated for the ASEAN-6 by 2007 and 2012 for the CLMV. Hence, having a fully operational AFTA by 2015 should provide a solid foundation for the AEC.

3.2. ASEAN Investment Area

The AIA, signed on 7 October 1998, aims to make ASEAN a highly competitive investment area that will attract FDI flows from ASEAN and non-ASEAN investors. This agreement binds member countries to reduce or eliminate investment barriers and grant national treatment to ASEAN investors by 2010 and to all investors by 2020. The AIA will encourage investors, particularly from ASEAN countries, to adopt a regional investment strategy and to promote regional production networks.

The AIA is thus expected to provide greater scope for division of labour and industrial activities across the region, creating opportunities for greater industrial efficiency and cost competitiveness. Investors can benefit from the AIA through greater investment access to industries and economic sectors, as well as from more liberal and competitive investment regimes that should reduce the transaction costs of doing business in the region.

The AIA currently covers manufacturing, agriculture, mining, forestry, and fishery sectors and services incidental to these sectors. Recognizing that the services sector accounts for a sizeable portion of investment flows to the region, ASEAN policy-makers are considering whether the scope of the AIA should be expanded to include industries in the services sector, viz., education, healthcare, telecommunications, tourism, banking and finance, insurance, trading e-commerce, distribution and logistics, accounting, engineering, and advertising.

It is worth noting that the AIA is supported by the ASEAN Industrial Cooperation (AICO) scheme. AICO, which was launched in 1996, aims to promote closer industrial collaboration through the sharing of resources to manufacture products, which enjoy preferential tariff rates of 0–5 per cent under the CEPT scheme. Clearly, the AIA and AICO provide the necessary foundation to create a single production base (one of the AEC's objectives).

3.3. ASEAN Framework Agreements on Services

AFAS, which was signed on 15 December 1995, aims to enhance cooperation in the services sector among ASEAN countries by eliminating intra-regional trade restrictions and facilitate free flow of services by 2015. Under AFAS, the scope of liberalization in services goes beyond those already undertaken under the WTO's General Agreement on Trade in Services (GATS). In other words, the AFAS is designed to be a GATS-Plus agreement. AFAS uses a positive list approach to services liberalization under a GATS framework. Seven sectors that are covered under AFAS are: air transport, business services, construction, financial services, maritime transport, telecommunications, and tourism.

Presently, ASEAN has concluded five packages of commitments under AFAS. These packages provide details of commitments from each ASEAN country to the other member countries. The ASEAN-X principle is currently being applied as a means to expedite the implementation process. This principle allows member countries that are ready to liberalize to go ahead first with other members joining at a later stage.

Regional cooperation in the services sector took another important step with Mutual Recognition Agreements (MRAs). MRAs will facilitate freer movement of professional services providers in the region. ASEAN will use the value of intra-regional trade, existence of technical barriers, and indication of strong interest from member countries as criteria for identifying the sectors that would be suitable for MRAs. MRAs on engineering services and nursing services haven been concluded in December 2005. ASEAN is also considering having MRAs in architecture, accountancy, surveying, medical practitioners, and tourism.

4. About the Book

Against the significant developments in ASEAN's economic cooperation and integration over the last decade, the main objective of this book is to present some of the key challenges facing the regional organization as it embarks on this major initiative to establish an AEC. Organized under the auspices of the ASEAN Australia Development Cooperation Program's Regional Economic Policy Support Facility (REPSF), the book brings together authoritative studies on the issues and challenges pertaining to building an AEC by 2015. These studies were undertaken over a period of five years (2002–2007) and written by prominent experts and academicians.

Following this introduction chapter, Peter Lloyd in Chapter 2 defines a single market in terms of economic integration. According to him, an area is completely integrated if the Law of One Price holds for all commodity and factor markets. The chapter examines the conditions that are necessary for the Law to hold. First, a single market requires a competition law and other competition policies to promote competition. Second, a single market crossing national borders requires the removal of all border restrictions and full National Treatment with respect to taxes and other state charges and regulations. Third, in the case of services markets, such as Mode 3 (consumption abroad, i.e., tourism) the Law will hold in the country in which the service is delivered. Finally, it implies no tax discrimination against foreign goods or factors or residents.

Lloyd then measures the progress towards this goal in a sample of regional trading agreements (RTAs) like European Union (EU), Closer Economic Relations (CER), and ASEAN. For ASEAN, there is limited progress towards economic integration of the markets as discussions or negotiations on several measures are still in progress. He further suggests the steps ASEAN needs to take if it is to be a single market. These include the ASEAN Framework Agreement for the Integration of Priority Sectors and the Road Map for the Integration of ASEAN. The adoption of a single market will require clarification of the markets included in the ASEAN Single Market and the extent of deep integration envisaged. This will finally require a fundamental change in thinking so that the end-goal can be achieved by adopting a new and bold approach.

Tongzon and Khan (Chapter 3) examine the customs revenue losses of CLMV countries (Cambodia, Laos, Myanmar, and Vietnam) due to the implementation of the CEPT scheme under AFTA. They estimate that while Laos, Vietnam, and Cambodia were likely to lose US$36 million, US$32 million and US$17 million respectively, Myanmar stands to gain US$67 million from ASEAN imports due to the scheme. However, if the economies can maintain healthy economic growth (say 5–7 per cent per annum), the overall government revenue (tax as well as non-tax) is likely to rise substantially in all CLMV countries despite CEPT rate reductions. For this to happen, Tongzon and Khan suggest appropriate policies that could tackle the problems affecting the region. These could be both less complicated (legal, political, or otherwise) or more fundamental changes (reforms) in the governance/corporate structure. The countries should, therefore, stay committed to the full implementation of CEPT scheme despite temporary decline in their revenues.

The next three chapters examine the challenges in expediting the economic integration of ASEAN's priority sectors. As mentioned earlier, ASEAN has earmarked twelve priority sectors for fast-track integration.

Rina Oktaviani, Amzul Rifin, and Henny Reinhardt (Chapter 4) provide an overview of trade performance and tariff rates in the priority sectors of the ASEAN economies. The pattern of trade of all ASEAN countries shows a low degree of interdependence between them. Seven of the ten ASEAN members have negative balances of trade with the other three. This low degree of interdependence is not due to high tariff barriers against fellow ASEAN countries, but could be due to non-tariff barriers against each other.

Oktaviani, Rifin, and Reinhardt also examine the degree of integration in these economies using measures of comparative advantage and intra-industry trade in the priority sectors. It is found that the largest values of intra-ASEAN trade are in electronics, ICT, and automotives. However, for these products the index of Revealed Comparative Advantage (RCA) is relatively low. This suggests that the countries which export these products within ASEAN do not have a comparative advantage (except for Malaysia which has revealed a (small) comparative advantage). As far as the relationship between RCA and IIT is concerned, it does not seem to be the case that countries have RCA in the products for which they conduct a large amount of IIT.

Loreli de Dios (Chapter 5) identifies the non-tariff measures (NTM) affecting trade in goods among ASEAN members in the nine priority goods sectors, namely, fisheries, agro-based, wood-based, textiles and apparel, healthcare, rubber-based, automotive, electronics, and information and communication technology (ICT). Using the ASEAN and UNCTAD TRAINS Databases on NTMs, a wide variety of NTMs is found to be pervasive both across countries and commodities under the Priority Goods Sectors. This is not only hurting the intra-ASEAN trade but also negating the objectives of CEPT.

Loreli de Dios further studies the recent trend in regional and bilateral trade agreements and suggests that these agreements could spur ASEAN members to deliver on their commitments to eliminate NTMs, although there are other considerations influencing this outcome.

Christopher Findlay, David Parsons, and Herb Plunkett (Chapter 6) provide an assessment of ASEAN's priority sectors earmarked for fast-track integration. According to them, ASEAN integration offers significant gains to all member countries. In a dynamic context, economic integration is a process, since as structural changes occur in all economies the adjustments required never stops. The removal of border barriers is a necessary condition for successful economic integration but not sufficient for success. The sectoral cases in this chapter not only identified key border barriers demanding immediate attention, but also highlighted the value of taking a more dynamic perspective to economic integration. The authors further conclude that policy application varies between countries, suggesting there may be value in particular countries adopting a different economic reform path.

The last three chapters before the conclusion examine more specific issues related to ASEAN's economic and business competitiveness.

Ian Farrow and Sunita Jogarajan (Chapter 7) identify generic impediments to ASEAN integration in the absence of a comprehensive network of Double Taxation Agreements (DTAs) between ASEAN member countries (AMCs). They argue that a limited DTA network is an impediment to regional economic integration and development because it increases business tax costs, imposes administrative burdens, creates transaction uncertainties, and provides a general disincentive to regional investment and profit repatriation. They further analyse taxation incentives and impediments in each member country that are specific to the priority sectors.

Farrow and Jogarajan also outline the taxation experience of the EU as the most highly integrated regional economic organization. They conclude by proposing several recommendations that would remove many of the impediments to economic integration resulting from current taxation arrangements. These may include "Agreed Positions" (this could focus on "the easier issues" first, such as income source recognition and transfer pricing allocation), adoption of a non-discrimination principle for AMC resident corporations, and maximum withholding tax rates regime between AMCs.

M. Sornarajah and Rajenthran Arumugam (Chapter 8) on Investment Jurisprudence indicate that ASEAN already has an investment treaty, which aims to liberalize the flow of foreign investment as well as to protect the foreign investment. One would expect that picture to continue in the future. Indeed, the AMCs of the region welcome investments. The existing instruments on investment in ASEAN reflect the trends, policies and laws that existed in the region at the time of their making. But, on the negative side, litigation of disputes has increased and in most of them, the claim to jurisdiction has been based on the dispute settlement provision in the treaties. It is, therefore, necessary to ensure that there are sufficient safeguard measures in the treaties that enable a state leeway to take action when faced with situations that require action in the event of economic necessities justifying interference with foreign investment.

Rahul Sen and Sanchita Basu Das (Chapter 9) focus on "ASEAN Plus 1" free trade agreements (FTAs). They argue that as current FTAs implies liberalization of goods, services and investment, it is imperative that in order to complete successful negotiations ASEAN needs to enter into investment agreements with its five dialogue partners (CER, China, India, Japan, and Korea). This would require an understanding of underlying strengths and weaknesses as these countries differ in terms of their economic structures and extent of economic linkages vis-à-vis ASEAN.

Sen and Das found that ASEAN stands to gain from entering into bilateral FTAs with these five dialogue partners. Although there is limited degree of competition in some areas of manufacturing, there exist far more complementarities. In the area of services, such complementarities abound. However, the challenges ahead for ASEAN relate to both realizing the external opportunities arising from its internal strengths, while concomitantly mitigating the external threats that could aggravate as a result of its internal weaknesses. This would require ASEAN to balance its goals of regional economic integration with that of maximizing economic and strategic benefits in a globalized world from its relations with major external trading partners.

In the conclusion chapter, Hew (Chapter 10) addresses the vision of an AEC by 2015. Will it be a European-style common market or a free trade area? Hew addresses the stumbling blocks to the AEC's building blocks (i.e. AFTA, AIA, and AFAS) as well the challenge of narrowing the economic development divide within ASEAN.

Hew argues that "ASEAN minus X" and the "2 plus X" may be innovative ways to getting round the existing consensus-based decision-making process. But creating a bona fide ASEAN Community will not be possible if ASEAN policy-makers are unable to be more flexible on the concept of national sovereignty which currently undermines greater institutional development. He suggests that the ASEAN Charter should not only provide a more rule-based institutional structure for ASEAN but should also chart out the longer term strategic goals of the AEC beyond 2015.

NOTES

1. Basic ASEAN Statistics, www.aseansec.org/13100.htm.
2. See Declaration of the ASEAN Concord II (Bali Concord II), Bali, Indonesia, 7 October 2003, www.aseansec.org/15159.htm.
3. Cebu Declaration on the Acceleration of the Establishment of an ASEAN Community by 2015, Cebu, Philippines, 13 January 2007, www.aseansec.org/19261.htm.
4. The ASEAN High Level Task Force's Economic Recommendations are annexed to the Bali Concord II.

5. The recommendations of the ASEAN HLTF on Economic Integration were annexed to the Bali Concord II.
6. For more details regarding the enhanced DSM, please see Recommendations of the High Level Task Force on ASEAN Economic Integration (Annex 1: Mechanism of the Dispute Settlement Mechanism).

REFERENCES

ASEAN ISIS. "Towards an ASEAN Economic Community: A Track Two Report to ASEAN Policy Makers". Unpublished manuscript, Jakarta, 2003.

ASEAN Secretariat. *ASEAN Into The Next Millennium: ASEAN Vision 2020, Hanoi Plan of Action*. Jakarta: ASEAN Secretariat, 1999.

————. *ASEAN: An Overview*. Jakarta: ASEAN Secretariat, 2005.

————. *ASEAN Statistical Pocket Book 2006*. Jakarta: ASEAN Secretariat, 2006.

Freeman, N. and D. Hew. "Introductory Overview: Rethinking the East Asian Development Model". *ASEAN Economic Bulletin* 19, no. 1 (Special Focus, April 2002): 1–5.

Hew, D. "Towards an ASEAN Charter: Regional Economic Integration". In *Framing the ASEAN Charter: An ISEAS Perspective*, compiled by R.C. Severino. Singapore: Institute of Southeast Asian Studies, 2005*a*.

————. "Southeast Asian Economies: Towards Recovery and Deeper Integration". In *Southeast Asian Affairs 2005*, edited by Chin Kin Wah and Daljit Singh. Singapore: Institute of Southeast Asian Studies, 2005*b*.

————, ed. *Roadmap to an ASEAN Economic Community*. Singapore: Institute of Southeast Asian Studies, 2005*c*.

———— and R. Sen. "Towards an ASEAN Economic Community: Challenges and Prospects". ISEAS Working Paper on Economics and Finance. Singapore: Institute of Southeast Asian Studies, November 2004.

Institute of Southeast Asian Studies. "ISEAS Concept Paper on the ASEAN Economic Community". Unpublished manuscript, Singapore, 2003.

Schwartz, A. and R. Villinger, R. "Integrating Southeast Asian Economies". *The McKinsey Quarterly*, No. 1, 2004.

Soesastro, H. "Towards an ASEAN Economic Community". In *The 2nd ASEAN Reader*, compiled by Sharon Siddique and Sree Kumar. Singapore: Institute of Southeast Asian Studies, 2003.

World Bank. *2007 World Development Indicators*. Washington D.C.: World Bank, April 2007.

2
What Is a Single Market? An Application to the Case of ASEAN

Peter J. Lloyd

1. Introduction

Until recently, the European Union (EU) was the only major Regional Trading Agreement (RTA) that had formally adopted a Single Market as a goal. Since 2002, the Caribbean Community (CARICOM) has styled itself as a Single Market and Economy. The 2003 Declaration of ASEAN Concord II declared "The ASEAN Economic Community shall establish ASEAN as a single market and production base." Australia and New Zealand are members of the regional trading agreement (RTA) known as the Closer Economic Relations (CER) Agreement. In January 2004 the Australian and New Zealand Prime Ministers announced an intention of creating a "single economic

Reprinted from Peter J. Lloyd, "What is a Single Market? An Application to the Case of ASEAN", *ASEAN Economic Bulletin* 22, no. 3 (2005): 251–65, by permission of the Institute of Southeast Asian Studies.

market" (Prime Ministers Howard and Clark 2004). Thus, there are now four regional groups that are committed to the goal of a single market.

The meaning of the term "single market" is not clearly defined in any of the four RTAs that have adopted this goal but the interpretation of the term will have a vital effect on the evolution of each agreement. The achievement of the declared goal of a single market can be made only if political decision-makers and bureaucrats understand fully the meaning of a single market and the measures required to implement it. The meaning of the term, therefore, requires careful examination.

To clarify the issues, section 2 defines a single market in terms of concepts of economic integration and the Law of One Price. Section 3 discusses the conditions that are necessary for the Law of One Price to hold. Section 4 discusses the progress that has been made towards complete economic integration in a sample of RTAs, including ASEAN and two of the three other RTAs that have adopted the goal of a single market (the EU and CER). Section 5 considers the steps necessary for ASEAN to become a single market.

2. A Single Market = The Law of One Price

The idea of a single market comes of course from the European Economic Community (EEC)/EU. Initially the EEC created by the 1957 Treaty of Rome was a Common Market. This European concept of a common market was expressed in terms of the "four freedoms", that is, freedom of trade in goods, services, capital, and labour. A Common Market required the abolition of all *border* restrictions on the movement of goods, services, capital, and labour. It also required the establishment of "common policies" in four designated areas: external trade, agriculture, transport, and competition.

However, the 1985 White Paper (Commission of the European Communities 1985) identified 280 remaining restrictions on these movements and proposed measures to abolish all of these restrictions. The White Paper did not use the term single market. It spoke instead of a "fully unified internal market". The implementation of these measures and the associated debate soon gave rise to the idea of a Single Market. The Single European Act of 1987 formally created a Single Market that came into operation on 1 July 1987.

The Single Market is something more than the Common Market. The 1985 White Paper began with the statement:

> Unifying the market (of 320 million people) presupposes the member States will agree on the abolition of all barriers of all kinds, harmonisation of rules, approximation of legislation and tax structures, strengthening of

monetary cooperation and the necessary flanking measures to encourage European firms to work together. (Commission of the European Communities 1985, p. 4)

The Single European Act describes the Single Market as "an area without internal frontiers in which the free movement of goods, persons, services and capital is ensured". Both of these descriptions are imprecise.

The central idea of a single market is that there should be *no discrimination* according to source in the regional markets for goods, services or factors, thus creating a market that should be a single market with no geographic segmentation. It was realized that the cross-border freedoms were not sufficient for foreign suppliers to have access equal to that of domestic suppliers.

The elimination of border controls, important as it is, does not of itself create a genuine common market. Goods and people moving within the Community should not find obstacles inside the different member States as opposed to meeting them at the border. (Commission of the European Communities 1985, p. 17)

The restriction of imports by measures applying *beyond-the-border* is usually couched in terms of the principle of National Treatment. National Treatment is the rule that a good or factor that crosses the border should receive the same treatment[1] as a like product produced domestically or a like factor owned by domestic residents with respect to taxes and charges and regulations. Is national treatment enough to ensure a single market? We need to look more closely at the notion of National Treatment.

For goods, the interpretation of this term has been given great precision by the development of the law in the General Agreement on Tariffs and Trade (GATT) and later the World Trade Organization (WTO). In considering whether National Treatment has been granted to an imported good, the WTO considers three elements: it compares "like products"; it considers all government measures in the sense of "a law, regulation, or requirement affecting their internal sale, offering for sale, purchase, transportation, distribution or use"; and it then requires that the treatment of the imported product be "no less favourable" than the treatment of the like domestic product(s). Thus, the scope of the government measures is broad. It applies if the discrimination is implicit rather than explicit, that is, there is no explicit discrimination against foreign goods but, because of some characteristic of the foreign good, it is subject to a higher tax rate. It applies even if the measures are not mandatory or if they result from actions initiated by private parties. The important consideration is that the measure has an effect on decisions of private firms with respect to the sourcing of products. Under the GATT/WTO, National Treatment has been applied to a wide range of government taxes, charges, and product standards that provide discrimination against foreign goods. (For a good introduction to the GATT/WTO interpretation of National Treatment, see Jackson 1997, Chapter 8.)

There are exceptions to the National Treatment rule in the GATT/WTO. The most blatant is subsidies. A subsidy paid to a group of domestic producers is a negative tax and, as such, subsidies should, in principle, be treated in the same way as domestic commodity taxes. Full National Treatment requires the elimination of subsidies restricted to domestic producers. However, all subsidies were exempted from the National Treatment requirement. The second notable exception is government procurement of goods. At the time GATT was negotiated, subjecting these measures to National Treatment was regarded as an unacceptable restriction on national sovereignty, and consequently they were exempted and continue to be so. The term *full National Treatment* is used in this paper to cover National Treatment as in the WTO plus the areas which are exceptions in the WTO, that is, National Treatment with no exceptions.

The principle of National Treatment was not stated in the Treaty of Rome, though there was a general prohibition in Article 30 preventing members from applying "measures having equivalent effect" to quantitative restrictions. Standards relating to health and safety, the environment, the workplace, and consumers were all regarded by the EEC as technical barriers to trade. This term covered such areas of goods standards as chemicals, pharmaceuticals, food, and construction and construction products. However, Article 36 of the Treaty of Rome allowed derogations to protect the health and life of humans, animals or plants. Consequently, there was some ambiguity and a lack of a general Community approach to these barriers to trade. (See Pelkmans 1990.) The idea of a Single Market introduced into the EU a new approach to standards, based on minimum essential standards and using new modalities such as mutual recognition.

Other early RTAs, such as the 1960 European Free Trade Area (EFTA) and the 1983 CER Agreement between Australia and New Zealand did not contain provisions guaranteeing National Treatment for goods.[2] The North American Free Trade Agreement (NAFTA), signed in 1993, does, however, contain the principle of National Treatment for goods (and for investment), in accordance with GATT Article III and its interpretation in the GATT. (The Canada–U.S. Free Trade Area, signed in 1988, contained the same National Treatment provisions.) Post-NAFTA, many RTAs have provided for National Treatment for goods (and in some cases for services and investments).

Increasingly, it has been realized that even full National Treatment is not enough to remove all measures which inhibit cross-border trade or factor movements. With some exceptions, standards for industrial products, the environment and other areas are not discriminatory; they apply equally to goods produced domestically and goods imported. However, in some cases, to meet these standards, foreign producers have to modify their products or incur extra costs. A simple case is one in which one member uses metric standards for goods sold within its jurisdiction and another uses non-metric, say Imperial, standards. Another way of expressing this point is to note that, in such cases, there is no question of a violation of National Treatment yet there is a barrier to trade. The same result may apply where there are differences in business laws.

The solution to these barriers to trade is the harmonization across member countries of the relevant laws or regulations. To distinguish this set of policies from other policies intended to eliminate discrimination the term *across-borders* measures is used. They are an extension of beyond-the-border measures.

Harmonization of laws and regulations across member countries has become more common in RTAs. Examples are the harmonization of standards such as those relating to industrial products, food, health and safety, and conformity assessment. However, any regulatory policies used in common by member countries are candidates for possible harmonization. Areas of business law are being incorporated in the harmonization of regional policies. These include competition law, securities law, corporation law, and intellectual property rights. Most of these areas relate to goods markets but some concern services or capital markets; for example, securities law. Labour market standards may also be harmonized. The list of regulations that are being subject to provisions in new RTAs continues to grow.

The literature on harmonization tends to emphasize that harmonization of any standards or policies should not be regarded as an end in itself. (See the papers in Bhagwati and Hudec 1996.) Harmonization should be adopted only if it confers net benefits on the countries concerned. In fact, in the general literature on harmonization, there are two opposing views, one favouring policy harmonization and one favouring competition among jurisdictions; for example, the literature on tax competition versus the tax harmonization (see Genser and Haufler 1996 and Sykes 2000). The strand of the literature that questions the economic benefits of harmonization focuses on the difficult problem of determining the optimal standards. Differences in national circumstances and priorities may dictate differences in national standards. It is also difficult for members to agree on the single standard: should this be the standard of one of the members or new agreed standards?

These views are reflected in the many approaches to harmonization. Harmonization can mean common standards, that is, a single area-wide standard. But it can also mean minimum standards. The EU 1992 measures introduced another approach based on the mutual recognition of each other country's standards. The EU used this approach for some product standards and for labour market standards such as the recognition of labour market qualifications. Mutual recognition has the considerable advantages of allowing each nation to retain its own national standards and thereby avoiding negotiation of common or minimum standards, and requiring little bureaucracy and enforcement via courts. National Treatment is achieved by the mutual recognition of the distinct national standards. With several approaches, harmonization is best described as a convergence of standards rather than the establishment of single standards.

Thus, three sets of policies are involved in the process of economic integration:

(i)   the elimination of border measures applying to imports into one member country from another member country;
(ii) full National Treatment of beyond-the-border measures applying to imports into one member country from another member country; and
(iii) harmonization of measures across member countries.

Lawrence (1996) made a distinction between "shallow" and "deep" integration. Shallow integration refers to the elimination of the traditional border measures, tariffs and non-tariff measures for goods trade, and other border barriers to trade in services and factors. Deep integration refers to the elimination of measures that are beyond-the-border. This terminology has been widely adopted in the literature on regionalism. As used by Lawrence and others, the term deep integration seems to cover both the second and third sets of measures. It is probably better to use the threefold classification as the second and third sets specify distinct modalities.

To give precision to the concept of a single regional market, economists have defined a single market as one in which the Law of One Price must hold in all goods, services and factor markets; see, for example, Lloyd (1991) and Flam (1992). That is, there should be a single price in the regionwide market for every tradable commodity and factor, expressing all prices in a common currency and adjusting for the real costs of moving goods or factors between locations.[3] This definition allows for the real costs of moving goods or factors from one location to another.

This definition of a single market can be applied to any set of countries. This may be a region comprising several countries as above or just one country or the whole world economy. (Cooper (1976) first gave the interpretation of a single market in terms of the Law of One Price holding at the global level.)

The establishment of a single market, therefore, is much more demanding than the establishment of a common market. The next section considers the conditions necessary for the Law of One Price to hold.

3. What Is Required for the Law of One Price to Hold?

The conditions for the Law of One Price to hold in one market are much more demanding than is generally recognized. These conditions are relevant to regional trading agreements as they show what policies must be in place if a region is to be a single market.

The Law of One Price has been extensively discussed in relation to individual markets in the theory of spatial arbitrage for commodity markets, the literature on the nature of competition and the literature on foreign exchange markets. It is useful to begin with this discussion. It gives us a number of conditions that are additional to the straightforward removal of border restrictions on trade.

Consider a commodity market which is a national market or a part of a national market. By restricting one's attention at the moment to trade within a nation, one is abstracting from international trade aspects of the Law of One Price. These non-trade aspects are more basic than the traditional focus on trade aspects.

First, a single market requires a competition law and other competition policies to promote competition. In the absence of perfect competition, markets will be segmented by having different prices in different segments of a market which will not equalize prices across segments. Second, a single market also requires full information for buyers and sellers, or less demanding, for arbitrageurs. Positive costs of gathering information lead to deviations from the Law. If these two conditions are met, spatial arbitrage will establish a single price within the nation, adjusting for the costs of transport between locations.

One must be careful with the definition of price. Transport takes time and some commodities require costly storage. With non-instantaneous transport and positive storage costs, commodity spot prices will deviate from the Law of One Price even if there is perfect arbitrage and no barriers to trading. The law should be interpreted in terms of the equality between the spot price in one location and the expected future price minus storage costs in another location. (See Williams and Wright 1991.)

When a single market crosses national borders other conditions are required.

A single market crossing national borders requires the removal of all border restrictions and full National Treatment with respect to taxes and other state charges and regulations. These steps may need to be supplemented by the harmonization across national borders of laws and regulations which otherwise prevent a single price from ruling among the countries. In goods markets, these standards include industrial products, health and safety of persons, and the environment, policies relating to particular sectors such as industry or transport. The laws include business laws that differentiate between foreign and domestic supplies. In labour markets, full National Treatment requires measures such as the recognition of foreign labour market qualifications. In capital markets, it requires full National Treatment with respect to taxes and business laws and regulations. It implies the absence of such measures as performance requirements that apply to foreign-owned enterprises but not like domestic enterprises.

If all of these conditions are met, there are no impediments to the sale or purchase of commodities and factors imported from other countries. Perfect arbitrage will then establish a single price for a like product or factor that can be traded across borders.

In the markets for services, some services can be traded across borders. Those covered by GATS Modes 1 (Cross-border Movement) and 4 (The Movement of Natural Persons) are inherently tradable. In these markets, the Law of One Price will hold if all of the conditions are met. In services markets supplied by Mode 3 (Consumption Abroad) such as international tourism, the Law will hold in the country in which the services is delivered. Other services cannot be traded in a way in which arbitrage can establish one price; for example, those supplied by the mode of commercial presence. In these cases, however, there will be a tendency towards convergence of price across borders due to factor price equalization in a single market and to competition from substitutes supplied by other modes; for example, financial services supplied by the mode of commercial presence in the country in which the consumer is located compete increasingly with financial services supplied by Mode 1, especially services provided to business customers.

What does a single market imply with respect to taxes on goods and services? Here, a distinction is sometimes made between a "fiscal union" and a "unified fiscal system". A fiscal union is the weaker arrangement. It does not entail a single set of tax rates and tax laws within the area. Rather, it entails equal tax treatment within a member country of all taxpayers in the sense that there is no geographic discrimination among member citizens or corporations paying taxes *in one country*. This is National Treatment in the fiscal area. Tax rates and other provisions affecting tax liability may still be different among member countries. A "unified fiscal system" goes further: there is no discrimination against foreigners within each country and *all* tax rates and other aspects of tax treatment are equal across countries. Thus, with respect to the treatment of domestic taxes, a fiscal union stands in relation to a unified fiscal system in the same way, with respect to border taxes, as a free trade area stands in relation to a customs union.

A single market certainly implies no tax discrimination against foreign goods or factors or residents. It, therefore, excludes tax breaks and other incentives which go to domestic investors but not to foreign investors in the same country and the converse, tax breaks which go to foreign investors but not to domestic investors. A single market also implies a unified fiscal system with equal tax rates across countries and other provisions that determine effective tax rates. It also requires no double taxation of corporate income earned in one member country and paid to shareholders in a second member country, but this is usually taken care of by a Double Taxation Treaty or a Bilateral Investment Treaty. Thus a single market goes beyond the removal of tax discrimination against foreigners in all markets. It requires no discrimination within countries plus the harmonization of effective tax rates. Differences in tax rates across member countries may be regarded as another form of discrimination; they discriminate against agents operating in the higher tax jurisdiction. A single market requires the removal of all discrimination in tax regimes.[4]

If the locations are in different countries and the bilateral exchange rates vary, one must also take account of behaviour by risk-averse agents in foreign exchange markets. It is usually assumed that a single market does not imply a common currency. However, there is substantial evidence from foreign exchange markets that, in the presence of exchange rate uncertainty and aversion to exchange rate risk, the pass-through of foreign prices to domestic markets is incomplete. (See, for example, Maloney 1999 and Menon 1995.) Hence, there will be less than full price equalization if two countries do not share a common currency.

This definition of a single market in terms of the Law of One Price might be regarded as too strict. It is very difficult to meet. Some countries with a federal structure would not be regarded as a single market in this sense because state or provincial laws, regulations, taxes and charges create price differences among the states or provinces. This strict definition is, however, required for two reasons. First, it provides a precise standard against which one can measure the degree of market integration and progress over time towards a single or completely integrated market. For example, there have been numerous studies of the Law of One Price in the EU, including those by the European Commission (2001). Second, a single market is important for a set of countries because any discrimination in goods and factor markets against foreign goods and factors suppliers creates inefficiencies in these markets (See Lloyd and Smith 2004, section 2.2 for discussion.) Of course a single regional market in this sense does not mean complete *laissez-faire*. It may be compatible with major distortions of prices away from real costs due to tax-subsidy wedges; for example, the EU Common Agricultural Policy distorts prices of many goods markedly from world prices because of border tariffs and domestic (EU-wide) subsidies.[5]

4. Progress Towards Economic Integration in RTAs

No two RTAs are identical in all of their features. In fact, there is great variation among them in their features. A few RTAs have achieved free trade in goods in the traditional sense of removing all border restrictions on goods trade but most have not. Some RTAs have progressed to removing some or all beyond-the-border measures that discriminate against foreigners. Some have progressed to liberalizing trade in factors. The latest agreements, such as the U.S.–Singapore Agreements and the Australia–U.S. Free Trade Agreement, contain provisions relating to even more areas. (For a description of the changing nature of RTAs generally, see Crawford and Fiorentino 2005.)

Tables 2.1A to 2.1E set out the progress for a representative sample of RTAs. The EU and NAFTA had to be included because of their importance in international markets and the precedents they have set. (For this purpose the EU is the EU-15, excluding the ten new member states for which transitional arrangements still apply.) MERCOSUR is one of the largest RTAs and serves as an example of Latin American regional trading arrangements. In the Asia-Pacific region, ASEAN and CER are older agreements. As a sample of "New Age" agreements, the Agreement between Japan and Singapore and that between New Zealand and Singapore have been included.

The measures reported in Tables 2.1A to 2.1D distinguish between measures that apply to goods markets, services markets, capital markets, and labour markets respectively. Within each set of markets, we also distinguish between measures that apply at borders, beyond-the-border, and across-borders as appropriate. However, by convention, National Treatment is not applied to labour markets. There is a final category titled "Multi-market measures" (see Table 2.1E), which apply to all markets or to

Table 2.1A
Progress Towards Economic Integration in Seven RTAs: Goods Markets

	EU	NAFTA	CER	MERCOSUR	ASEAN	Japan-Singapore	NZ-Singapore
Border measures							
Elimination of industrial tariffs	✓	✓	✓	✓	*	✓	✓
Elimination of industrial NTBs	✓	✓	✓	✓	*	*	✓
Elimination of agriculture trade-distorting measures	✓	*	✓	*	*	*	✓
Elimination of government procurement barriers	✓	✓	✓	✗	✗	*	✓
Prohibition of export incentives	✓	✗	✓	✗	✗	✗	✓
Prohibition of anti-dumping actions	✓	✗	✓	✗	✗	✗	*
Beyond-the-border measures							
National Treatment	✓	✓	*	*	✗	✓	*
Prohibition of trade-distorting production subsidies	*	✗	✓	✗	✗	✗	✓
Across-borders measures							
Harmonization of product standards – convergence of product standards	✓	✗	✓	✗	*	✗	*
– mutual recognition of product standards	✓	✗	✓	✗	*	✗	*

Table 2.1B
Progress Towards Economic Integration in Seven RTAs: Services Markets

Border measures	EU	NAFTA	CER	MERCOSUR	ASEAN	Japan-Singapore	NZ-Singapore
Market access	✓	✓	✓	*	*	*	*
Temporary movements of business persons	✓	✓	✓	*	✗	✓	✓
Beyond-the-border measures							
National Treatment	✓	✓	✓	✓	*	✓	✓
Across-borders measures							
Mutual recognition of labour standards	✓	✗	✓	✗	✗	✗	✓

Table 2.1C
Progress Towards Economic Integration in Seven RTAs: Capital Markets

	EU	NAFTA	CER	MERCOSUR	ASEAN	Japan-Singapore	NZ-Singapore
Border measures							
MFN treatment	✓	✓	✓	✓	✓	✗	✓
Rights of establishment	✓	✗	✗	✓	*	✗	✗
Repatriation of capital and profits	✓	✓	✓	✓	✓	✓	✓
Beyond-the-border measures							
National Treatment	✓	✓	✗	✓	✓	✓	✓
Prohibition of performance requirements	✓	✓	✓	✗	✗	✓	✗
Prohibition of incentives to foreign investors	✓	*	✗	✗	✗	✗	✗
Investor protection	✓	✓	✗	✓	✓	✓	✗
Across-borders measures							
Harmonization of business laws	✓	✗	*	✗	✗	✗	✗
Taxes – double tax treaty/bilateral investment treaty	✓	✓	✓	✓	✓	✓	✓
– harmonization of taxes on business	*	✗	*	✗	✗	✗	✗

Table 2.1D
Progress Towards Economic Integration in Seven RTAs: Labour Markets

Border measures	EU	NAFTA	CER	MERCOSUR	ASEAN	Japan-Singapore	NZ-Singapore
Temporary movement of natural persons	✓	✓	✓	*	✗	✓	✓
Permanent movement of natural persons	✓	✗	✓	✗	✗	✗	✗
Across-borders measures							
Mutual recognition of labour standards	✓	✗	✓	✗	✗	✗	✗

Table 2.1E
Progress Towards Economic Integration in Seven RTAs: Multi-Market Measures

Border measures	EU	NAFTA	CER	MERCOSUR	ASEAN	Japan-Singapore	NZ-Singapore
Regional competition law							
– convergence of competition laws	✓	✗	✓	✓	✗	✗	✗
– bilateral cooperation agreement(s)	✓	✓	✓	✓	✗	*	*
Intellectual property	✓	✓	✗	✓	✓	✗	✗
Monetary union	✓	✗	✗	✗	✗	✗	✗
Unified fiscal system	*	✗	✗	✗	✗	✗	✗

two or more sets of markets. These include monetary unions and unified fiscal systems as they are a major step by themselves and mark further progress towards a single economy.

Within each market category, the choice of features reported in Tables 2.1A to 2.1D is designed to measure key stages in the progress towards complete economic integration in these markets. Thus, in relation to goods trade, provisions that prohibit anti-dumping action against imports sourced from member countries or prohibit export incentives affecting intra-region trade or grant mutual recognition of product standards are all milestones in this progress. Trade in agricultural goods is distinguished from trade in industrial goods because there is a clear division in the rates of progress in lowering border barriers to trade in these two categories of goods in many RTAs. The features listed do not cover all features included in RTAs. Some minor features and some features which are not related to the degree of integration of markets have been omitted: for example, provisions in some agreements concerning state-to-state and investor-to-state dispute settlement procedures and e-commerce. There are fewer measures listed for services markets than for goods markets because service delivered by Mode 3, "Commercial Presence", are also affected by the measures affecting FDI that are listed under the measures applying to capital markets.

Each box has been scored by giving one of three scores — all, some, or none. These are denoted by the symbols ✔, *, and ✘ respectively. For example, with respect to industrial tariffs, "all" means that all industrial tariffs (on intra-area trade) have been removed; that is, the commodity coverage is 100 per cent and the percentage cut is 100 per cent. If there are very minor exceptions only to a measure, the score will be taken to be "all". Everything between all and none is "some". Thus "some" indicates that some steps have been taken by the members towards the implementation of this measure but it is incomplete. For example, in the Singapore–New Zealand Closer Economic Partnership Agreement, for the line "Prohibition of anti-dumping action", the agreement does not prohibit anti-dumping action against imports originating from the partner country but it introduces higher thresholds at which such action might be triggered and thereby reduces the likely incidence of such actions. As a second example, MERCOSUR has a National Treatment provision for goods, but it is confined to taxes and charges only and does not include regulations. In one case, that of monetary union in the EU, the entry is scored "some" because not all of the members have adopted the measure.

These scores are based on the actual progress as at March 2005. Where an RTA has a long-term goal for some border and beyond-the-border measures, the level of achievement at March 2005 has been assessed. For example, in AFTA, for the line "Elimination of industrial tariffs", the items of the Temporary Exclusion List of each country and the items on the Inclusion List that have tariffs above zero mean that intra-area trade in these items is not yet free. Hence the entry is rated "some". In a number of cases for ASEAN (and for other agreements) discussions or negotiations on measures are in progress but these cannot be recognized as they have not yet been agreed and implemented; for example, there are discussions on mutual recognition of labour standards in service industries. The Agreement that took effect most recently, the Japan–Singapore Economic Partnership Agreement, has not had time to implement the commitments made in the initial agreement; the timetable for tariff reductions extends to 2010. In this case, we have accepted the agreed timetable of tariff reductions as a commitment that will be implemented.

The scoring is based on an examination of the agreements and related documents for each of the RTAs. In recording the achievements of each RTA, account has been taken of some agreements among the members of an RTA which are not part of the agreement establishing the RTA. In a few cases, members have reached a separate agreement on particular aspects, either before or after the agreement establishing the RTA. For example, many pairs of countries which are members of RTAs have double taxation agreements outside the agreements. As another example, Australia and New Zealand have an arrangement that allows free movement of persons in the CER area but it predates the CER Agreement and is not part of it. However, in such cases, what matters is the totality of commitments towards integrating the economies of the area. Consequently, all binding agreements have been recognized in compiling the tables.

Using this typology and scoring, we can compare the progress towards complete integration of the major RTAs. From Tables 2.1A to 2.1E, the EU is clearly the RTA that has progressed the furthest towards complete integration. This is not surprising as it has had the policy of no discrimination against goods or persons coming from other members and the goal of a Common Market since 1957 and the goal of a single market since 1987.

The EU has completed the elimination of all border measures in all four markets and almost all the beyond-the-border and across-borders measures. The exceptions to beyond-the-border measures are a limited restriction of production subsidies and limited harmonization of business taxes. With regard to the production subsidies, Article 92 of the original Treaty of Rome forbade "state aids" which distort trade between member states but in practice a number of EU countries give a variety of subsidies to ailing or to high-tech industries (see the discussion on State Aids in the annual report of the European Commission Directorate-General IV). Harmonization of tax rates has been limited. Despite these exceptions, the EU can be regarded as the only RTA to approach the status of a single market.

By comparison with the EU, all other agreements have made selective progress beyond the liberalization of border measures. The items in which progress has been made vary greatly among the RTAs. CER and NAFTA rank after the EU in terms of general progress towards the integration of the economies of the member countries. The two "New Age" agreements are broadly similar in their pattern of progress and general level of integration. There are, however, some significant differences between the provisions which integrate the Singapore economy with that of Japan compared to those which integrate it with that of New Zealand. Although both have been put forward as model new style agreements, the measures they incorporate are in fact a long way from complete integration. ASEAN and MERCOSUR are the least integrated of these RTAs.

5. Steps Necessary for ASEAN to Become a Single Market

The emphasis in ASEAN has been on border measures. In the first three decades of ASEAN, there was no mention of economic integration. However, attention has been switching to deep integration measures.

The landmark ASEAN Vision 2020 statement, made in 1997, declared that "we commit ourselves to moving towards closer cohesion and economic integration". It announced a number of measures to pursue this new goal. The First Plan of Action, the Hanoi Plan of Action, the following year reaffirmed the goal of "closer economic integration". Significantly, it expanded on this goal by declaring an intention:

> To create a stable, prosperous and highly competitive ASEAN Economic Region in which there is *a free flow of goods, services and investments, a freer flow of capital,* [italics added] equitable economic development and reduced poverty and socio-economic disparities.

The 2003 Declaration of ASEAN Concord II went further. In the section on the ASEAN Economic Community, it reiterated the "end-goal of economic integration as outlined in the ASEAN Vision". It then declared:

> The ASEAN Economic Community shall establish ASEAN as a single market and production base.

The Tenth ASEAN Summit in Vientiane in November 2004 reaffirmed the ASEAN Concord II Declaration. The Vientiane Action Programme (VAP) replaces the Hanoi Plan of Action. It is to be implemented over the six years 2004–2010.

How far ASEAN has progressed in 2005 towards an EU-style Single Market is examined by using Tables 2.1A to 2.1E. (Detail of ASEAN programmes and measures are available on the ASEAN website.) For ASEAN, the boxes showing no or limited progress towards economic integration of the markets involved indicate what measures will need to be adopted before a single market is achieved.

With regard to border measures, ASEAN has not completed the process of economic integration for any of the six border measures for goods markets listed in Table 2.1A, and it has not begun the process for three of these; elimination of government procurement barriers, prohibition of export incentives, and prohibition of anti-dumping actions (though few, if any, anti-dumping actions have been taken on imports from fellow ASEAN member countries). For services trade (Table 2.1B), it completed the fourth round of negotiations in 2004 and has adopted new modalities, such as the ASEAN minus-X formula, to extend the coverage of Market Access. In 2001 AFAS was extended to include services delivered by Mode 4, the Movement of Natural Persons. The Vientiane Action Plan agreed to facilitate the movement of business people, skilled labour and talents in the region and currently ASEAN is exploring Mutual Recognition of some professional qualifications such as those in engineering and architecture.

With regard to beyond-the-border measures, there is no ASEAN commitment to National Treatment for goods, but National Treatment under Article III of GATT 1947 applies to goods imported by ASEAN members who are members of the WTO. Progress in the beyond-the-border measures affecting services trade to the individual national commitments are listed in their national schedules.

With regard to across-borders measures, progress in the harmonization of standards and other laws and regulations affecting goods trade has been accelerating. Under the provision in CEPT regarding non-border areas of co-operation to complement trade liberalization, ASEAN standards were developed initially for twenty priority products and in 2004 for safety of electrical products and electronic compatibility. ASEAN adopted in 1998 the Framework Agreement on Mutual Recognition Arrangements (MRAs). Under this scheme, three sectoral MRAs have been concluded and are being implemented by member countries: those for electrical and electronic equipment, telecommunications, and cosmetics. MRAs are being developed for the pharmaceuticals, prepared foods, equipment and automotive sectors. Conformity assessment standards have been harmonized for the twenty priority products.

With regard to capital markets, the progress is more substantial. Two of the three border measures listed in Table 2.1C have been achieved (MFN treatment and repatriation of capital and profits) and two of the four beyond-the-border measures have been achieved substantially. There is National Treatment though exceptions were permitted in the ASEAN Investment Area (AIA) via a Temporary Exclusion list, a Sensitive List, and a General Exceptions List; seven of the countries have no Temporary Exclusion List. With regard to investor protection, there is full protection from expropriation and nationalization. Apart from double taxation treaties, there has been no harmonization of business laws and taxes distorting intra-ASEAN investment.

With regard to the labour markets and the multi-market measures (Tables 2.1D and 2.1E), no progress towards integration has been made with one exception. The exception is intellectual property where some initial steps have been taken: ASEAN countries have adopted a common domestic filing form and an ASEAN Common Form for trademarks and preparatory work in other areas.

How far has the VAP advanced ASEAN towards a single market? First, it is not clear exactly what the end objective of an ASEAN "single market" is. Section 2 above provided a definition of a single market. This is the commonly used definition based on the EU. Although ASEAN uses the term in apparently the same way, the Vientiane Plan of Action committed to a "free flow of goods, services and skilled labour and a freer flow of capital". The overall strategy for realizing the ASEAN Economic Community "involves deepening and broadening economic integration in the product and factor markets and accelerating the integration process towards a single market and production base".

The main vehicles to promote integration are the ASEAN Framework Agreement for the Integration of Priority Sectors and the Road Map for the Integration of ASEAN. Both of these existed before the Summit but they are being developed and fast tracked. There are eleven priority sectors at present but more will be added. The commitment is to remove barriers to the free flow of goods, services and skilled labour and freer flow of capital by 2010 "to the extent feasible and agreeable to all member countries" (ASEAN 2004, section 2). A goal of National Treatment for all service sectors is stated in the Road Map for the Integration of ASEAN. Regarding harmonization of standards and technical regulations, working groups have been established in four priority sectors to implement standard-related measures and a survey is being conducted to identify more standards for harmonization in the priority sectors. Regarding the multi-market measures, initial steps have been taken to set up a common intellectual property regime, and in Vientiane, the Finance Ministers agreed to establish an ASEAN Single Currency or ASEAN Currency Cooperation by 2010.

The adoption of a single market is a large step in the evolution of ASEAN. It will require clarification of the markets included in the ASEAN Single Market and the extent of deep integration envisaged. To be an EU-style Single Market, it will require all measures set out in Tables 2.1A to 2.1E.

The adoption of the objective of a single market will require a fundamental change in thinking. The objective of a free trade area with limited commitments to removing beyond-the-border measures that inhibit cross-border trade is a much more limited goal with no definite end-point in terms of the coverage of measures. This objective can be pursued through modalities based on consensus. However, the objective of a single market is quite definite in terms of the ultimate coverage of measures, namely, all measures required to remove discrimination against other ASEAN suppliers of goods, services, and factors. Consequently, modalities must be found in subsequent negotiations to include all of the measures required and to achieve this for all of the member countries. A far-sighted end-goal can be achieved only by adopting a new and bold approach.

NOTES

This paper is a revised version of part of a longer report, Lloyd and Smith (2004), prepared for the ASEAN Secretariat. The full report is available on the website, http://www.aadcp-repsf.org/publications.html. I would like to acknowledge the financial support and assistance provided by the ASEAN–Australia Development Cooperation Program — Regional Economic Policy Support Facility, and the many helpful comments provided on drafts of this report by personnel in the ASEAN Secretariat and by two referees. The views expressed in this paper are the views of the author and not necessarily those of the ASEAN Secretariat and/or the Australian government.

1.　In the WTO and in many treaties, National Treatment is couched in terms of treatment that is "no less favourable" than the treatment accorded national products or corporations or persons.

2.　EFTA did have a provision relating to Internal Taxation that prevented the use of internal taxes for protective purposes.

3.　Alternatively, we can say that a single market is synonymous with complete economic integration of the area. Dixit and Norman (1980, pp. 108–109) identified an integrated equilibrium for the world economy as one in which the Law of One Price held for goods and factor markets.

4. Alternatively, the definition of the equality of prices across countries could be stated in terms of pre-tax prices. This separation treats taxes-subsidies in effect like the costs of transporting goods between nations. Arbitrage will then equate pre-tax commodity and factor prices. However, this alternative hides the differences in prices due to non-uniform tax rates and the associated economic inefficiencies.

5. This test looks only at individual markets. One referee pointed out that the government of one member country may lower the market price of some good (or service) by subsidizing an input, perhaps the education of key skilled workers used in its production. In such a case the Law of One Price may hold in the goods market but competition is hardly equal. However, this could not arise in a Single Market which held for all commodity and factor markets as this requires equality of prices for such inputs throughout the region.

REFERENCES

Association of Southeast Asian Nations (ASEAN). "Vientiane Action Programme", available on the ASEAN website, www.aseansec.org, 2004.

Bhagwati, J. N. and R. E. Hudec. *Fair Trade and Harmonization: Prerequisites for Free Trade?* Cambridge, MA: MIT Press, 1996.

Commission of the European Communities. *Completing the Internal Market: White Paper for the Commission to the European Council.* Luxembourg: Office for Official Publications of the European Communities, 1985.

Cooper, R. "Worldwide Regional Integration: Is There an Optimal Size of the Integrated Area?". In *Economic Integration Worldwide, Regional and Sectoral*, edited by F. Machlup. New York: Macmillan, 1976.

Crawford, J. and R. V. Fiorentino. "The Changing Landscape of RTAs". WTO Discussion Paper No. 8, 2005.

Dixit, A. K. and V. Norman. *Theory of International Trade.* Welwyn: Cambridge University Press, 1980.

Estevadeordal, A. "Traditional Market Access Issues in RTAs: An Unfinished Agenda in the Americas?". Paper presented to the WTO Seminar on Regionalism and the WTO, Geneva, 26 April 2002.

European Commission. "Price Levels and Price Dispersion in the EU". *European Economy*, Supplement A. Brussels: European Commission, 2004.

Flam, H. "Product Markets and 1992: Full Integration, Large Gains". *Journal of Economic Perspectives* 6 (1992): 7–30.

Genser, B. and A. Haufler. "Tax Competition, Tax Coordination and Tax Harmonization: The Effects of EMU". *Empirica* 23 (1996): 59–89.

Howard, Prime Minister John and Prime Minister Helen Clark (2004). "Australia

Keen to Develop Single Market with New Zealand". Press Statement, 3 March 2004.

Jackson, J. H. *The World Trading System: Law and Policy of International Economic Relations.* 2nd ed. Cambridge, MA: MIT Press, 1997.

Jones, R. W. *Globalization and the Theory of Input Trade.* Cambridge, MA: MIT Press, 2000.

Lawrence, R. Z. *Regionalism, Multilateralism and Deeper Integration.* Washington, D.C.: Brookings Institution, 1996.

Lloyd, P. J. *The Future of CER: A Single Market for Australia and New Zealand.* Wellington, New Zealand: Institute of Policy Studies, 1991.

———— and Penny Smith. "Global Economic Challenges to ASEAN Integration and Competitiveness: A Prospective Look". A report prepared for the ASEAN Secretariat. Available on the ASEAN Australia Development Cooperation Programme — Regional Economic Policy Support Facility website, http://www.aadcp-repsf.org/publications.html. 2004.

Maloney, W. F. "Exchange Rate Uncertainty and the Law of One Price". *Review of International Economics* 7 (1999): 328–41.

Menon, J. "The Relationship between the Law of One Price and Exchange Rate Pass-through". *Economic Internazionale* 48 (1995): 551–68.

Ohyama, M. "The Economic Significance of the GATT/WTO Rules". In *Economic Theory and International Trade. Essays in Honour of Murray C. Kemp*, edited by A. D. Woodland. Cheltenham: Edward Elgar, 2002.

Pelkmans, J. "Regulation and the Single Market: An Economic Perspective". In *The Completion of the Internal Market*, edited by H. Siebert. Tübingen: J.C.B. Mohr, 1990.

Productivity Commission. *The Trade and Investment Effects of Preferential Trading Arrangements — Old and New Evidence.* Staff Working Paper. Canberra: Productivity Commission, 2003.

Salazar-Xirinachs, J. M. "Proliferation of Sub-regional Trade Agreements in the Americas: An Assessment of Key Analytical and Policy Issues". *Journal of Asian Economics* 13 no. 2 (2002): 181–212.

Sykes, A. O. "Regulatory Competition or Regulatory Harmonization? A Silly Question?". *Journal of International Economic Law* 3 (2000): 257–64.

Williams, J. and B. D. Wright. *Storage and Commodity Markets.* Cambridge: Cambridge University Press, 1991.

3

The Challenge of Economic Integration for Transitional Economies of Southeast Asia

Jose L. Tongzon and Habibullah Khan

1. Introduction

One of the difficult challenges facing Cambodia, Lao PDR, Myanmar, and Vietnam (usually referred to as CLMV) as new members of ASEAN is how to implement their commitments and obligations as signatories of the ASEAN Free Trade Area (AFTA). There is a real concern that, as they reduce their tariffs in accordance with the AFTA guidelines, they will suffer significant revenue losses with adverse economic and social implications. Revenues from import tariffs in these countries constitute a sizeable proportion of their government revenues (for example, the share of import tariffs in total revenue among CLMV countries has ranged between 7 per cent and 25 per cent).

Reprinted from "The Challenge of Economic Integration for Transitional Economies of Southeast Asia: Coping with Revenue Losses", *ASEAN Economic Bulletin* 22, no. 3 (2005): 266–83, by permission of the Institute of Southeast Asian Studies.

In light of this concern, this study aims to investigate if there is any empirical basis of this concern and to draw out some policy implications. Except for the studies made by Fukase and Martin (1999*a–d*) for the World Bank and by Lao-Araya (2002), no in-depth study has yet been undertaken to assess the tariff revenue implications as a result of their participation in AFTA. Fukase and Martin (1999*a–d*) used a static computable general equilibrium model (CGE) based on a full market equilibrium assumption. Lao-Araya (2002) used a partial equilibrium approach but her estimates due to the lack of disaggregated data were highly aggregative and did not take into account the growth of imports. This paper uses a partial equilibrium approach and takes into account the growth of imports. Its estimates are also derived from disaggregated data which have become available.

The rest of the paper is organized as follows: section 2 provides a brief review of the major aspects of AFTA and the trade liberalization commitments made by CLMV countries as new members of ASEAN; section 3 discusses the revenue structure in CLMV countries; section 4 briefly presents the theoretical basis and the methodology used for this study; section 5 discusses the revenue impact; section 6 suggests a set of policy recommendations followed by some concluding remarks in section 7.

2. AFTA and the CLMV Countries

The old members of ASEAN at the 1992 Summit agreed to establish a free trade area in the region. The 1992 AFTA was a watershed, as it represented a significant change in the economic policy orientation of the ASEAN countries. A number of internal and external developments have made free trade politically acceptable for these countries.[1]

Vietnam became officially the first Southeast Asian transitional economy to become a member of ASEAN on 28 July 1995. At about the same time Myanmar, emerging from its self-imposed isolation, ceded to the ASEAN Treaty of Amity and Co-operation and opened up to join the rest of Southeast Asia in terms of economic orientation and objective. At the Thirtieth Annual Ministerial Meeting in Kuala Lumpur in July 1997, Lao PDR and Myanmar were admitted as full members of ASEAN. The admission of Cambodia to ASEAN in 1999 marked the fulfilment of the ASEAN founding fathers' long-cherished dream to establish an ASEAN-10, a group covering all countries in Southeast Asia.

The main objective of AFTA is to increase the international competitiveness of ASEAN industries and the ASEAN region as an investment location. Specifically, the objectives are to increase intra-ASEAN trade by abolishing intra-regional trade barriers while allowing member countries to keep their respective trade policies towards the rest of the world, to attract local and foreign investors to invest in the region and to make their manufacturing sector more efficient and internationally competitive within a liberalizing global market.

To realize these benefits, the ASEAN Free Trade Agreement (AFTA) seeks to reduce tariffs on all commodities traded within the member countries to between 0 and 5 per cent *ad valorem* and eliminate all trade restrictions under the Common Effective Preferential Tariff (CEPT) — the main instrument of AFTA. The agreement also lays down the rules for fair competition and identifies a number of measures to enhance economic co-operation such as harmonization of standards, macroeconomic consultations, and improved reciprocal recognition of product testing and certification, co-ordination of foreign investment policies, joint investment promotion strategies, and co-operation in transport systems. To ensure that the benefits of the scheme are restricted within the member countries a minimum of 40 per cent of value must originate within AFTA, if the products are not wholly produced within AFTA countries.

Under the CEPT scheme, the CLMV member countries are required to allocate their products among the four agreed lists: the Inclusion List (IL), the Temporary Exclusion List (TEL), the Sensitive List (SL), and the General Exception List (GEL). The Inclusion List includes those products that will be subjected to tariff reductions which are agreed to be at the maximum of 5 per cent by 2006 for Vietnam, by 2008 for Lao PDR and Myanmar, and by 2010 for Cambodia. It is germane to mention here that the long-term vision of ASEAN is to eliminate the tariff completely in two phases — by 2010 for old ASEAN members and by 2015 for the new members of ASEAN.

A key feature of the CEPT is that the concessions are granted on a reciprocal, product-by-product basis. There are two conditions for a product to be eligible for concessions under the CEPT, apart from the local content requirement: the product has to be included by both the importing and the exporting countries; and to receive all concessions, the product must have a CEPT tariff of 20 per cent or below. If the tariff on a product that a country has included in the CEPT is above 20 per cent, then it is eligible for concessions only in those member countries that also impose a CEPT rate that is higher than 20 per cent. In the short-run, the reciprocal nature of the CEPT scheme provides incentives for the member countries to include their commodities in the Inclusion List (IL) and to reduce tariffs below 20 per cent to receive concessions.

Another important feature of the CEPT is that the member countries are required to eliminate quantitative restrictions on products immediately upon receiving CEPT concessions on that product and eliminate other non-tariff barriers (NTBs) within a period of five years after the enjoyment of the concessions. Based on the UNCTAD classification of NTBs, a working definition of NTBs has been agreed upon in ASEAN. This covers para-tariff measures, price control measures, finance measures, monopolistic measures, and technical measures (ASEAN Secretariat 1995).

3. Overview of Revenue Structure in CLMV

Before discussing the revenue implications of CEPT implementation in CLMV, it would be useful to present a brief picture of government revenue structure in these countries. Not unlike other developing countries, CLMV governments also require substantial resources to finance their activities and use a number of tax as well as non-tax measures to raise the required funds.

Tables 3.1–3.4 show recent trends (past four to five years depending on data availability at the time of study) in overall revenue collection, and several common features can be discerned from the data. In all cases, tax revenue is relatively more important than non-tax revenue. Non-tax revenue is defined as revenue earned by government departments and state enterprises from entrepreneurial and property income and various other administrative charges and fees. As these countries are committed to implement various market reforms including privatization of public enterprises, the scope for further increase in non-tax revenue is also limited. Tax revenue registered significant rise in all countries and the role of indirect taxes (vis-à-vis direct taxes such as income tax) remain predominant as is usually observed in developing countries characterized by large-scale poverty and non-monetary activities. The importance of trade taxes, particularly customs duties, is also evident from the data. For example, customs duties (import tariffs or trade taxes) accounted for roughly 11 per cent to 35 per cent of total tax revenue in CLMV in 2001 (or the latest available year). Export tariffs are rather very small and often not separated from the aggregate trade revenue.

Total revenue in Cambodia rose from 943 billion riel in 1998 to 1,520 billion riel in 2001, but the share of tax revenue to total revenue remained virtually stagnant at 72 per cent over the period. One remarkable feature of Cambodia's revenue collection that can be gleaned from the data is the overwhelming importance of trade taxes (particularly customs duties) as a source of government tax revenue. Trade taxes constituted 55 per cent of total tax revenue in 1998 and then declined over the years and currently hovering around 35 per cent (or roughly one-third) of total tax revenue.

Table 3.1
Cambodia's Central Government Revenue, 1998–2001

	1998	1999	2000	2001
	(in billions of riels)			
Total revenue	**943**	**1,316**	**1,409**	**1,520**
Tax revenue	**679**	**948**	**1,026**	**1,087**
Share of tax revenue in total revenue	*72%*	*72%*	*73%*	*72%*
Direct taxes	56	83	136	140
Indirect taxes of which:	248	432	500	571
Excise taxes (including on imports)	76	92	113	155
Domestic	16	16	19	20
Import	60	76	94	135
VAT (including on imports)	—	315	371	403
Domestic	—	43	73	85
Import	—	286	313	327
Refund	—	14	14	9
Trade taxes	**376**	**433**	**391**	**376**
Share of trade taxes in tax revenue	*55%*	*46%*	*38%*	*35%*
Share of trade taxes in total revenue	*40%*	*33%*	*28%*	*25%*
Non-tax revenue	**230**	**355**	**353**	**424**
Share of non-tax revenue in total revenue	*24%*	*27%*	*25%*	*28%*
Timber royalties	23	36	41	29
Enterprises and immobile leases	27	20	27	28
Civil aviation	18	19	25	38
Tourism income	1	1	6	14
Royalties (mining, etc.)	4	2	0	2
Royalties (casino)	—	0	12	22
Post and telecommunications (PTT)	87	109	92	122
Passports and visa	7	13	20	36
NBC profit	—	10	13	15
Quota auction	—	87	22	32
Garment licences	—	21	43	39
Others	42	27	29	47
Capital revenue	**33**	**14**	**29**	**9**

Note: Totals may not add due to rounding errors.
Source: IMF Country Report, latest available year.

Tax revenue in Lao PDR has shown a phenomenal rise from 290 billion kip in 1997/98 to 2,043 billion kip in 2001/02, and currently it constitutes more than 80 per cent of total revenue. The share of import duties in tax revenue has gradually declined from 17 per cent in 1997/98 to 11 per cent in 2001/02, though the revenue from this source has been steadily rising in absolute terms, from 50 billion kip to 229 billion kip in the same period.

Table 3.2
Lao PDR's General Government Revenue, 1997/98–2001/02

	1997/98	1998/99	1999/00	2000/01	2001/02
	(in billions of kip)				
Tax revenue	**290**	**745**	**1,367**	**1,742**	**2,043**
Share of tax revenue in total revenue	*79%*	*80%*	*81%*	*79%*	*82%*
Profit tax	33	80	187	316	362
Income tax	19	70	117	182	190
Agriculture/land tax	3	5	7	13	21
Business licences	0	0	1	3	3
Turnover tax	63	160	290	379	452
Excise tax	51	157	226	336	362
Import duties	**50**	**88**	**135**	**192**	**229**
Share of import duties in tax revenue	*17%*	*12%*	*10%*	*11%*	*11%*
Share of import duties in total revenue	*14%*	*9%*	*8%*	*9%*	*9%*
Export duties	8	24	41	62	62
Registration	2	5	7	9	15
Other fees	19	33	47	104	111
Natural resource tax	0	5	14	11	17
Timber royalties	37	89	273	115	165
Hydropower royalties	4	17	22	21	55
Non-tax revenue	**77**	**184**	**324**	**452**	**438**
Share of non-tax revenue in total revenue	*21%*	*20%*	*19%*	*21%*	*18%*
Leasing	10	11	15	20	57
Concession	0	1	2	3	3
Fines	11	9	14	22	31
Administrative fees	0	11	17	19	62
Depreciation/dividends	8	22	42	212	89
Interest	15	89	79	40	42
Overflight	33	40	123	125	153
Irrigation, etc.	0	0	33	11	1
Total revenue	**367**	**929**	**1,691**	**2,194**	**2,481**

Note: Totals may not add up due to rounding errors.
Source: IMF Country Report, latest available year.

Tax revenue in Myanmar rose from 20.9 billion kyat in 1995/96 to 35.1 billion kyat in 1998/99, accounting for 44 per cent of total revenue. One distinctive feature of Myanmar's revenue system is her greater reliance on non-tax sources, particularly on transfers from her State Economic Enterprises or SEEs, for revenue collection and the share of non-tax revenue rose from 46 per cent to 56 per cent during 1997/98 to 1998/99. Customs duties collected

Table 3.3
Myanmar's Government Revenues, 1995/96–1998/99

	1995/96	1996/97	1997/98	1998/99
	(in billions of kyats)			
Total revenue and grants	**40.2**	**53.8**	**88.3**	**80.4**
Tax revenue	**20.9**	**28.9**	**45.9**	**35.1**
Share of tax revenue in total revenue	*53%*	*54%*	*53%*	*44%*
Taxes on Income	7.6	9.2	15.3	12.3
Income Tax	4.2	6.2	11.1	—
Profit tax	3.3	3	4.2	—
Commercial tax	7.1	9.5	18.1	13.9
Taxes on property use	0.8	1	1.6	1.4
Land tax	0.1	0.1	0.1	0.1
Extraction of forestry products	0.3	0.4	0.7	0.7
Fisheries Tax	0.4	0.4	0.7	0.6
Customs duties	**4.5**	**7.8**	**8.6**	**5.5**
Share of customs duties in tax revenue	*22%*	*27%*	*19%*	*16%*
Share of customs duties in total revenue	*12%*	*15%*	*10%*	*7%*
Excise duties	0.1	0.1	0.2	0.1
Other	0.9	1.4	2.3	1.9
Import licence fee	0.2	0.2	0.2	0.2
Motor vehicle tax	0.1	0.2	0.8	0.4
Stamp duties	0.5	0.9	1.3	1.3
Non-tax revenue	**18.2**	**24.2**	**40.7**	**44.7**
Share of non-tax revenue in total revenue	*47%*	*45%*	*47%*	*56%*
Transfers from SEEs	10.5	15.4	26.9	34.2
Others	7.7	8.8	13.9	10.5
Registration fees	0	0.1	0.1	0.1
School fees	0.3	0.4	0.2	0.9
Mechanized Agricultural Department receipts	0.7	2.2	1	1.9
Union Government capital receipts	0.9	0.8	0.8	0.8
Other Union Government Receipts	3.9	2.9	7.8	3.2
Representative Bodies receipts	0.1	0.1	0.1	0.1
Public Debt Account receipts	0.2	0.2	0.1	0.1
State lottery	1.5	2.2	3.7	3.5
Foreign grants	**1.1**	**0.6**	**1.6**	**0.6**

Note: Totals may not add due to rounding errors.
Source: IMF Country Report, latest available year.

increased from 4.5 billion kyat in 1995/96 to 5.5 billion kyat in 1998/99 though its proportion to tax revenue fell from 22 per cent to 16 per cent in the same period.

Table 3.4
Vietnam's Government Revenue, 1995–2001

	1995	1996	1997	1998	1999	2000	2001 Budget
				(in trillions of dong)			
Total revenue and grants	**53.4**	**62.4**	**65.4**	**73.6**	**78.5**	**90.7**	**86.3**
Tax revenue	**40**	**50.3**	**49.7**	**55.7**	**60.3**	**64.1**	**65.9**
Share of tax revenue in total revenue	*77%*	*83%*	*79%*	*78%*	*79%*	*72%*	*78%*
Corporate income tax	7.4	10.1	11.6	13.1	14.5	19.8	20.8
Individual income tax	0.5	1.4	1.5	1.8	1.9	1.9	1.8
Capital user charge	1.3	1.5	1.5	1.7	1.5	1.4	1.5
Land and housing tax	0.3	0.4	0.3	0.3	0.3	0.4	0.3
Licence tax	0.2	0.3	0.4	0.3	0.4	0.4	0.4
Tax on the transfer of properties	—	1.1	1	1	1	0.9	0.9
Tax on land use right	—	0.3	0.3	0.4	0.3	0.2	0.2
Value added tax (VAT)	7.8	11.1	11.8	11.8	17.2	17.1	17.6
Excises	2.5	4.5	4.6	5.6	4.5	5.3	5.7
Slaughter tax 3/	0.1	0.1	0.1	0	0	0	0
Agricultural tax	1.6	1.9	1.7	2	2	1.8	1.5
Import and export taxes	**13.3**	**15.1**	**13.5**	**14.9**	**14.4**	**13.5**	**15**
Share of import and export taxes in tax revenue	*33%*	*30%*	*27%*	*27%*	*24%*	*21%*	*23%*
Share of import and export taxes in total revenue	*26%*	*25%*	*21%*	*21%*	*19%*	*15%*	*18%*
Other taxes on trade	0	1.2	0	1.5	1	0.1	0.2
Other taxes	4.9	1.3	1.4	1.4	1.2	1.4	0.1
Non-tax revenue	**11.8**	**10.6**	**13.1**	**15.2**	**15.8**	**24.7**	**18.5**
Share of non-tax revenue in total revenue	*23%*	*17%*	*21%*	*21%*	*21%*	*28%*	*22%*
Fees and charges	—	3.3	3.9	4.1	3.6	5.1	4.6
Rental of land	—	0	0.5	0.5	0.6	0.5	0.4
Income from natural resources	2.4	3.1	3.4	3.3	4.6	6.7	6.1
Net profit after tax	—	2.1	2.4	2.1	2.9	8.7	5.2
Capital revenues	—	0.3	0.8	0.8	0.8	0.8	0.4
Other	—	1.8	2.1	4.3	3.4	2.8	1.7
Grant	1.6	1.5	2.6	2.1	2.4	1.9	1.9

Source: IMF Country Report, latest available year.

Tax revenue in Vietnam currently accounts for roughly 75 per cent of total revenue, and it rose from 40 trillion dong in 1995 to nearly 66 trillion dong in 2001 budget year. Revenue collected from import and export taxes jointly (export taxes are very small and virtually negligible) ranged from 13 to 15 trillion dong during 1995–2001 and its share as a percentage of total tax revenue presently hovers around 23 per cent.

4. Theoretical Basis and Methodology Used

The revenue implications of trade liberalization are in general uncertain. Blejer and Cheasty (1990) and Tanzi (1989) concluded that ultimately the net impact of trade reform on revenue is an empirical issue. Greenaway and Milner (1991) in a case study analysis of the revenue implications of World Bank-supported structural adjustment loans concluded that a range of outcomes is possible, depending on the country's initial conditions and the components of the reform package.

The effect of tariff reductions on revenue depends on the levels and coverage of tariffs in effect before the reduction and on the extent to which they are then reduced. The precise impact is difficult to estimate because it depends on complex economic responses. If import values are unchanged, the immediate effect of a reduction in tariff rates is to lower revenue. If goods subject to trade taxes are included in the base of domestic taxes on imports, this reduction in trade taxes will also be accompanied by a reduction in excise and value-added tax collections levied on imports (Ebrill, Stotsky, and Gropp 1999, p. 5). The value of imports, however, can be expected to change in response to tariff reductions. If the price elasticity of net demand for imports is greater than one, the revenue gain due to increased demand for the now-cheaper imports may compensate for or even outweigh the revenue loss due to the tariff cut itself. The value of imports can also increase in response to increases in income. The extent of this income-induced increase in imports depends on the income elasticity of demand for imports. Another offsetting factor that could compensate or even outweigh the revenue loss due to tariff reductions is the impact on the incidence of illegal trading. Smuggling, which is a major source of import duty leakages, is likely to decline when the cost (premium) of smuggling no longer exceeds the cost of paying for the import taxes. Formally, smuggling occurs if $s < t(1)$, i.e. $P(1 + s) < P(1 + t(1))$, where P is the marginal cost of the import, $t(1)$ the original or pre-AFTA tariff rate plus the tariff equivalent of non-tariff barriers and s is the smuggling premium. See Menon (1996) for more explanation. It should, however, be noted that the above offsetting factors which work through quantity changes are only relevant as long as the post-trade liberalization tariffs remain greater than zero.

The response of import values also depends on the price elasticity of supply of import substitutes. The less elastic this supply, the smaller is the reduction in output for a given fall in price and hence the smaller is the increase in import values. Moreover, since price elasticities of demand and supply typically are not constant over the entire range of prices, the starting point for tariff reduction is also likely to affect the economic response. Indeed, if protectionist motives have dominated the setting of tariff rates, tariffs may be above their revenue-maximizing levels (Ebrill, Stotsky, and Gropp 1999, p. 5).

The impact of tariff reduction is analysed in a simple partial equilibrium setting with the following assumptions made regarding the tariff rates, proportion of import values represented by different categories, intra-ASEAN trade, and growth of imports.

The average tariff rates are computed for each category of products from the disaggregated data provided by the CLMV countries. For base year revenue calculation (before the implementation of CEPT), the average MFN rates are applied and these rates are also assumed to be valid for non-ASEAN countries.

The shares of IL, TEL, SL, and GEL in import values are calculated from the disaggregated import values collected from the respective countries' Customs Departments. It is assumed that each country transfers 20 per cent of its TEL products each year to IL, and the transfer is completed in five years from the start. In the spirit of ASEAN co-operation and to expedite the benefits of trade liberalization, the countries are assumed to complete the process of phasing-in as early as possible and avoid last-minute bunching of products for the sake of smooth transfer and efficiency.

Since SL constitutes a very small portion of total products (for example, in Cambodia, only 0.73 per cent of the products are included in this category) and they are scheduled to be transferred to IL on a much later date (tariff reduction on SL goods begins in 2008 in Cambodia, for example), it is assumed that the short-run revenue impact comes from only IL and TEL.

Intra-ASEAN trade values are assumed to represent 53.2 per cent, 82.7 per cent, 41.0 per cent, and 24.9 per cent for Cambodia, Lao PDR, Myanmar, and Vietnam respectively in line with recent available data. We also assume that these proportions remain constant until the process of phasing-in is completed.

For projecting import growth rate, two methods are adopted depending on data availability: (a) the average rate of growth of imports for the past ten years or so; and (b) the results of regression based on 1995–2000 data. Several regression models are experimented with and the one with most robust results is applied for forecasting the year to year growth in imports.

For projecting economic growth rate, the average real GDP growth rate is used, published in Country Reports by the International Monetary Fund of the past five years or so. It is assumed that all other revenues (tax and non-tax) grow by the rate of economic growth over the years. It is also assumed that the overall import patterns do not change and no major tax reforms are implemented during the implementation of CEPT.

5. Revenue Impact

As can be gleaned from Tables 3.5 and 3.6, all CLMV countries, with the notable exception of Myanmar, stand to lose substantial amounts of customs revenue from ASEAN imports due to the implementation of CEPT scheme.[2] The losses are quite substantial given the overall size of total government revenue and they account for 3 to 15 per cent of total government revenue.

For Lao PDR, the results, quite ironically, convey the negative revenue outcome of CEPT, and Lao PDR is likely to lose US$36 million that amounts to more than 83 per cent of total ASEAN customs revenue, which is equivalent to nearly 16 per cent of her total government revenue.

For Myanmar, results were positive for the predicted outcome of CEPT. It stands to gain US$67 million (more than 93 per cent of total ASEAN customs revenue) in terms of customs revenue despite CEPT rate reductions. These gains are, however, quite small with respect to the size of Myanmar's

Table 3.5
Revenue Impact Assessment for CLMV

CLMV	CEPT Schedule	Customs Revenue from ASEAN (US$ million)	Customs Revenue from non-ASEAN (US$ million)	Total Revenue (US$ million)
Cambodia	2002	123	122	427
	2010	106	340	729
Lao PDR	2002	43	14	233
	2008	7	48	303
Myanmar	1999	72	115	18,371
	2008	139	430	30,622
Vietnam	2001	376	1,867	5,582
	2006	344	5,369	10,352

Note: Estimations based on regression analysis (price and income effects).

Table 3.6
Change in ASEAN Customs and Total Revenue Due to CEPT

CLMV	Change in ASEAN Customs revenue due to CEPT (US$ million)	Change in total revenue after CEPT implementation (US$ million)	Change in customs revenue as % of total ASEAN customs revenue	Change in customs revenue as % of total revenue	% Change in total revenue due to CEPT implementation
Cambodia	-17	+302	-13.8%	-3.4%	+70.7%
Lao PDR	-36	+70	-83.7%	-15.5%	+30.0%
Myanmar	+67	+12,251	+93.1%	+0.4%	+66.7%
Vietnam	-32	+4,770	-8.5%	-0.6%	+85.5%

Note: Plus (+) and minus (−) signs indicate revenue gains and losses respectively. All percentage changes are computed with reference to data reflecting the start of CEPT scheme (i.e., base year).

overall revenue and accounts for less than 1 per cent of total government revenue.

Vietnam's loss of revenue from CEPT rate reductions is estimated to be US$32 million, which is equivalent to roughly 9 per cent of her total customs revenue from ASEAN imports.

The revenue earned from non-ASEAN imports seem to provide a strong cushion against any fall in overall customs revenue. If the economies can maintain healthy economic growth (say 5–7 per cent per annum) as they experienced in the recent past, the overall government revenue (tax as well as non-tax) is likely to rise substantially over the years despite CEPT rate reductions, and this observation is found to be consistently true for all CLMV countries. For example, Cambodia's total revenue can rise by US$302 million (more than 70 per cent), though it faces short-run decline in its customs revenue. Lao PDR which stands to suffer badly in terms of short-term decline in customs revenue will also see substantial increase in the overall revenue amounting to US$70 million (accounting for 30 per cent change in total revenue). Myanmar's total revenue is predicted to increase by almost 67 per cent due to CEPT implementation. Vietnam is also likely to see a big rise in its total revenue (by US$4,770 million accounting for nearly 86 per cent increase in total revenue) due to the implementation of CEPT scheme.

Over the past few years since they started to implement their tariff reduction commitments, their overall revenues did not show any decline but rather showed some increase particularly for Cambodia and Vietnam. As Figure 3.1A shows, Cambodia's total imports have been rising since the 1997/98 Asian crisis. Except for a slight decrease in total revenues from US$1,726 million to US$1,694 million in 2003, its total revenue has been steadily increasing. A look at the share of trade taxes and non-tax revenues shows us that Cambodia's reliance on trade tariffs may have been overcome by developments in other forms of tax or other sources of revenue. Thus, the trend of the non-tax revenue to total revenue ratio seems to be on the rise from the year 2000, as Figure 3.1B shows.

Lao PDR's total imports have also been rising since 2001/02, as Figure 3.2A shows; however, unlike Cambodia the share of tax revenue in total revenue rose after 2001/02 due to the rise in revenue from import duties while the share of non-tax revenue declined, as can be gleaned from Figure 3.2B.

Figures 3.3A and 3.3B illustrate the revenue and import performance of Vietnam in the last decade. Similarly, it can be observed that total level imports, except for a sluggish performance during the Asian financial crisis of

Figure 3.1A
Cambodia's Total Imports, 1995–2003
(In US$ million)

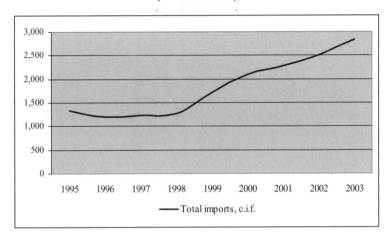

Source: International Monetary Fund (IMF) Country Reports, various issues.

Figure 3.1B
Cambodia's Selected Revenue Ratios, 1995–2003
(In Percentages)

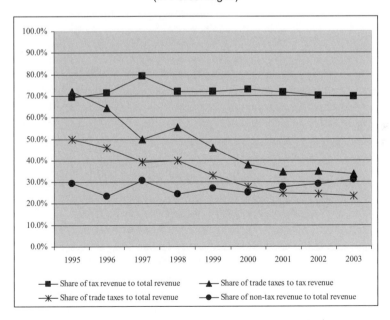

Source: International Monetary Fund (IMF) Country Reports, various issues.

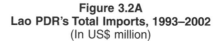

Figure 3.2A
Lao PDR's Total Imports, 1993–2002
(In US$ million)

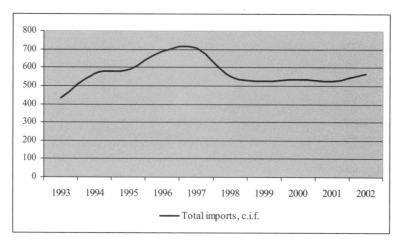

Source: International Monetary Fund (IMF) Country Reports, various issues.

Figure 3.2B
Lao PDR's Selected Revenue Ratios, 1993/94–2002/03
(In Percentages)

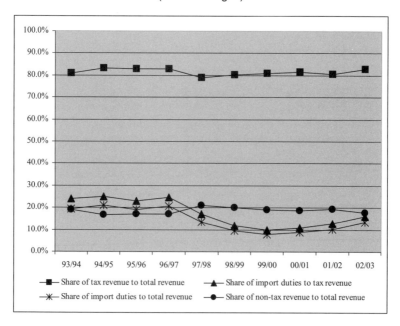

Source: International Monetary Fund (IMF) Country Reports, various issues.

Figure 3.3A
Vietnam's Total Imports, 1992–2002
(In US$ million)

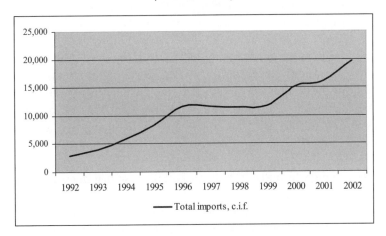

Source: International Monetary Fund (IMF) Country Reports, various issues.

Figure 3.3B
Vietnam's Selected Revenue Ratios, 1992–2002
(In Percentages)

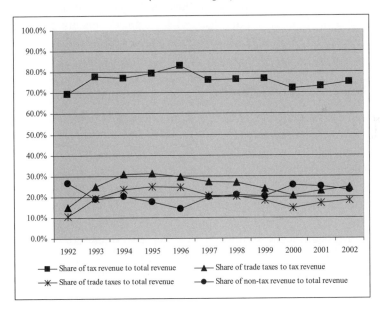

Source: International Monetary Fund (IMF) Country Reports, various issues.

1997–98, has been increasingly rising. The shares of tax and trade tax revenues displayed an increasing trend which can be attributed to the heavy tax reforms taken by the Vietnamese government during this period.[3]

Since there should be no fear of any reduction in overall government revenue due to CEPT, the countries should meticulously follow the schedule and complete the process of phasing-in TEL to IL by the deadline. Myanmar can perhaps consider expediting the process (including the transfer of SL to IL) and bring the deadline forward so as to reap the full benefits of liberalization earlier than schedule. The realization of the long-term objective of converting CLMV into a full-fledged "free trade zone" by reducing the tariff rates to zero by 2015 or 2017 seems to be achievable. It is germane to mention here that CLMV should make additional efforts to reduce various non-tariff barriers (seemingly formidable) that currently exist so that they cannot impede the process of liberalization.

What happens to imports from non-ASEAN countries as tariff rates within ASEAN fall eventually to zero? Will CLMV switch to their ASEAN neighbours for all of their import needs? This is unlikely to happen as the imports from non-ASEAN constitute mainly machines and equipments (as well as industrial raw materials) essential for industrialization that the neighbouring countries are unable to supply. Moreover, CLMV will continue to depend on Western countries for aid, grants and investments, and imports from those countries are likely to flow in larger quantities under such commitments. Besides, import demand for superior quality goods usually produced by the West is likely to rise as people's affordability continue to improve due to sustained economic growth in the region.

6. Policy Recommendations

Although the estimated revenue losses can only inflict temporary injuries to CLMV countries as their overall revenue position is likely to remain strong in the long-run, it is essential that certain measures of fiscal reform are undertaken to optimize revenue collection and enhance the revenue-raising capacity of CLMV governments. Some of these measures that entail relatively less complications (legal, political, or otherwise), are less expensive in terms of resources and can be quickly applied (say, in a couple of years) without causing any significant spillover (negative) effects are considered "short term" (interim) in nature. On the other hand, the measures that require fundamental changes (reforms) in the governance/corporate structure, more extensive use of resources, and are likely to have far-reaching (permanent) consequences across the economy are usually referred to as "long term" (or sometimes "medium term" depending on ease of implementation) measures. The implementation of such measures could be a long-drawn-out process (ten years or more) but their importance remains paramount as their impacts are long-lasting and they are indispensable tools for achieving growth and efficiency objectives.

The sequencing of measures is another important consideration and before setting a definite timeline for implementing any particular measure, costs as well as benefits of such measure discounted over the time horizon (vis-à-vis other alternatives) should be meticulously reviewed. Some long-term measures may be considered more urgent and should be given priorities if funding (as well as the required skills) is available from international sources. There are also issues related to efficiency (growth) and equity and at times efficiency may have to be sacrificed to achieve equity. Attempts should, however, be made to strike a balance between the two objectives and we believe the following measures would satisfy that requirement.

6.1. Short-term Policies

- Customs and tax exemptions as well as deductions except those stipulated by international conventions and agreements or contractual obligations should be immediately withdrawn;

- All exemptions and deductions should be closely monitored so as to avoid any possible abuse of the system or revenue loss;

- Tax incentives (tax holidays, exemptions, etc.) provided to foreign investors should be reviewed so as to keep them in line with all other ASEAN countries. The prevailing investment incentives are too generous in CLMV vis-à-vis other ASEAN countries. Further, a number of empirical studies (for example, Shah and Toye 1978 and Lim 1983) have shown that tax incentives *per se* do not encourage a higher level of foreign direct investment (FDI) and that there are other factors more important than tax incentives in determining FDIs such as quality of institutions and political stability;

- Liberalization of export-oriented sectors should be carried out from the domination of state-owned enterprises and from export and import licensing requirements;

- There should be transparent and consistent laws and regulations on land ownership and tenure to provide more security and incentives for the private sector;

- The existing customs classification and valuation systems need to be reformed so as to conform to the agreed ASEAN tariff classification nomenclature and valuation system. Simplification of the customs procedures and overhauling of the by-law regulations should be completed; and

- Upgrading and modernizing vocational training is required to meet the growing skill needs of these economies.

6.2. Long-term Policies

- The prevailing revenue system in CLMV is at its infancy and comprehensive reforms should be undertaken to modernize the entire system. Assistance should be sought from international agencies (ADB, World Bank, IMF) and developed ASEAN countries (Singapore and Malaysia in particular). Cambodia, for example, has undertaken a project for long-term capacity-building of tax revenue as well as tax administration with the help of the IMF. Similar projects should be undertaken in other CLMV;
- Non-compliance rather than tax avoidance or tax evasion is a major problem in CLMV, and the problem is compounded by inefficiency and alleged corruption in tax administration. Although inefficiencies are visibly present at all levels due mainly to the lack of proper education and trained manpower, the level of corruption is hard to document due to its diverse meaning and sensitivity. A recent report however confirms that "Poor governance and corruption are systematic features of communist-ruled Vietnam and Lao PDR, the transitional economy of Cambodia and military-ruled Myanmar" (Transparency International 2003, p. 140). While the level of efficiency is likely to improve with continued growth and modernization, the eradication of corruption will take time as it requires fundamental changes in many institutional and cultural factors (such as good government, tough laws, impartial judiciary, informed middle class, strong private sector, transparency and accountability at all levels of administration, strong civil society, and so on). It is, however, heartening to note that anti-corruption efforts in some of these countries (for example, Cambodia) have received momentum in recent years by collaboration between NGOs and multilateral organizations, as claimed by the above Report;
- Smuggling and informal trade must be reduced in order to raise the revenue earnings from trade (import duties and export taxes). The speedy implementation of CEPT scheme is likely to be helpful as tariff rates would be substantially lowered, making such activities less attractive. The price as well as perceived quality gap between smuggled goods and the locally produced goods should also be minimized in order to reduce

the incentives for smuggling. The various measures such as improvement of transportation and communication facilities, training of local workers, higher productivity and efficiency, dissemination of correct information on product quality as well as characteristics should be taken to make domestically produced goods more competitive with their imported counterparts;

- The demand for imported goods (so as to earn additional import revenues) should be generated by accelerating the process of economic growth (income effect) and not by leaving the domestic goods uncompetitive vis-à-vis foreign imports. Imported goods are seemingly cheaper than local goods in these countries, and if such a trend is allowed to persist, they may not be able to realize their growth potential (through industrialization) that may impinge upon the fulfilment of revenue targets;

- Exemptions and deductions to various taxes (such as turnover tax, VAT, and import duties) that are seemingly overwhelming should be continuously reviewed in order to determine their justification and effectiveness in the face of changing needs of these countries as time evolves. Only those found to be consistent with their overall growth strategy should be retained and implemented with utmost care and efficiency so as to avoid any possible revenue leakage;

- Information and data gathering system should be improved so as to conduct regular surveys pertaining to the fiscal system and its efficiency. The profile of the statistical agency should be lifted and inter-Ministerial co-ordination is necessary to produce a consistent set of data that will be useful for monitoring and evaluation. Assistance should be sought from developed ASEAN members (such as Singapore and Malaysia) and international agencies (such as ADB and World Bank) for computerization of the Statistics Departments (or agencies) and other supporting units and training the critical pool of statistical manpower needed for that purpose. The ASEAN Secretariat should continue to oversee the process of statistics compilation in all member countries and provide necessary logistics support so as to generate a useful database for various types of policy research in the region;

- Infrastructure and human resource investments should be intensified. These investments are not only essential for sustainable economic development but are also the key to long-term international competitiveness;

- Policies of foreign trade liberalization, financial sector reforms, private sector development, privatization of state-owned enterprises and domestic savings mobilization should be adopted;

- The activities of existing NGOs should be co-ordinated and integrated to achieve greater efficiency in the delivery of welfare assistance to the poor and structurally unemployed;
- Adjustment assistance programmes in the form of subsistence allowance provision and re-training for relevant skills and/or establishing income-generating activities should be adopted to deal with the negative implications of trade liberalization at the industry level; and
- The experiences of the older ASEAN countries in dealing with the adjustment costs from the recent Asian crisis can provide useful and valuable lessons for the CLMV countries. Provision of micro-credits and small- and medium-sized enterprises (SME) credit programmes, human resource development, strengthening of existing safety nets, public employment information services, and training programmes for the structurally unemployed will help mitigate the short-run costs of trade liberalization.

7. Conclusion

Although the results of revenue analysis tend to vary widely across methods of estimation employed and sources of data, the general trend is very clear. All CLMV countries, with the notable exception of Myanmar, stand to lose substantial amounts of customs revenue from ASEAN imports due to the implementation of the CEPT scheme. The revenue earned from non-ASEAN imports seem to provide a strong cushion against any fall in overall customs revenue, and if the economies can maintain healthy economic growth as they did in the recent past, the overall government revenue (tax as well as non-tax) is likely to rise substantially over the years despite CEPT rate reduction. This observation is found to be consistently true for all CLMV countries.

Generally, the people in the region are optimistic about the long-term benefits of AFTA and the results of our study also subscribe to such optimism. The CLMV governments are very much aware of substantial declines in customs revenue in the short-run, and measures for compensating the loss of customs revenue are already underway. If the countries continue to grow positively as they did in the recent past, import demand will surge along with demand for other goods and services and total government revenue (tax and non-tax) is likely to increase. The region is currently afflicted with problems such as communication and language barriers, multiplicity of rules and regulations inconsistent with WTO standards, existence of numerous non-tariff barriers, rudimentary system of tax collection, non-compliance of tax rules and inefficient tax administration, and the lack of political will to reduce the power of state enterprises. If appropriate reforms are taken to tackle these problems, the long-term growth prospects of CLMV remain bright.

NOTES

This paper draws heavily on a research project commissioned by the ASEAN Secretariat under the ASEAN–Australia Development Cooperation Programme — Regional Economic Policy Support Facility (AADCP-REPSF) for the governments of the CLMV countries as part of the Initiative for ASEAN Integration (IAI) to narrow the development gaps within ASEAN. The authors would like to express their gratitude to the ASEAN Secretariat and to all those people who have helped in various ways in making the project a success. Thanks are also due to two anonymous referees of *ASEAN Economic Bulletin* for their valuable comments on an earlier version of this paper. Needless to say, the errors that still remain are the sole responsibility of the authors.

1. See Tongzon (2002) for the number of reasons behind the older ASEAN countries' decision to deepen their level of economic integration.
2. This is based on the assumption that the data are generally reliable.
3. See IMF Country Report No. 03/380 for a discussion of the tax reforms and revenue structure of Vietnam.

REFERENCES

ASEAN Secretariat. *AFTA Reader*. Jakarta: ASEAN Secretariat, 1995.
Blejer, M. and A. Cheasty. "Fiscal Implications of Trade Liberalization". In *Fiscal Policy in Open Developing Economies*, edited by V. Tanzi, pp. 66–81. Washington, D.C.: International Monetary Fund, 1990.
Ebrill, L., J. Stotsky, and R. Gropp. *Revenue Implications of Trade Liberalization*. Washington, D.C.: IMF, 1999.
Fukase, E. and W. Martin. *Evaluating the Implications of Cambodia's Accession to the ASEAN Free Trade Area: A General Equilibrium Model (CGE) Approach*. Development Research Group, Washington: World Bank, 1999*a*.
————. *Economic effects of joining the ASEAN Free Trade Area (AFTA): The case of the Lao People's Democratic Republic*. Development Research Group, Washington: World Bank, 1999*b*.
————. *Evaluating the Implications of Myanmar's Accession to the ASEAN Free Trade Area: A Simple General Equilibrium Model (CGE) Approach to Assessing the Effects of RIAs for Small Countries*. Development Research Group, Washington: World Bank, 1999*c*.
————. *Evaluating the Implications of Vietnam's Accession to the ASEAN Free Trade Area (AFTA): A Quantitative Evaluation*. Development Research Group, Washington: World Bank, 1999*d*.

Greenaway, D. and C. Milner. "Fiscal Dependence on Trade Taxes and Trade Policy Reform". *Journal of Development Studies* 27 (1991): 95–132.

International Monetary Fund. *Myanmar: Recent Economic Developments*. IMF Country Report No. 99/134, November 1999, Washington, D.C.

———. *Lao People's Democratic Republic: Selected Issues and Statistical Appendix*. IMF Country Report No. 02/207, September 2002, Washington, D.C.

———. *Vietnam: Selected Issues and Statistical Appendix*. IMF Country Report No. 02/5, January 2002, Washington, D.C.

——— *Cambodia: Selected Issues and Statistical Appendix*. IMF Country Report No. 03/59, March 2003, Washington, D.C.

———. *Vietnam: 2003 Article IV Consultation*. IMF Country Report No. 03/380, 2003, Washington, D.C.

Lao-Araya, Kanokpan. *How Can Cambodia, Lao PDR, Myanmar and Vietnam Cope with Revenue Lost Due to AFTA Tariff Reductions?* ADB ERD Working Paper Series No. 29, Economics and Research Department, November 2002.

Lim, D. "Fiscal Incentives and Direct Foreign Investment in Less Developed Countries". *Journal of Development Studies* 19 (1983): 207–12.

Menon, J. "Transitional Economies in Free Trade Areas: Lao PDR in AFTA". *Journal of the Asia Pacific Economy* 4, no. 2 (1999): 340–64.

Shah, S.M.S. and J. Toye. "Fiscal Incentives for Firms in Some Developing Countries: Survey and Critique". In *Taxation and Economic Development*, edited by S.M.S. Shah and J. Toye. London: Frank Cass, 1978.

Tanzi, Vito. "Impact of Macroeconomic Policies on the Level of Taxation and the Fiscal Balance in Developing Countries". *Staff Papers* 36 (1989): 633–56.

Tongzon, J. L. *The Economies of Southeast Asia: Before and After the Crisis*. U.K.: Elgar Publishers, 2002.

———, H. Khan, and D. D. Le. *Options for Managing Revenue Losses and Other Adjustment Costs of CLMV Participation in AFTA*. REPSF Project 02/022. Jakarta: ASEAN Secretariat, 2002.

Transparency International. *Global Corruption Report 2003*. Washington, D.C., 2003.

4

A Review of Regional Tariffs and Trade in the ASEAN Priority Goods Sector

Rina Oktaviani, Amzul Rifin, and Henny Reinhardt

1. Introduction

In 2003 the ASEAN Concord II (also known as the Bali Concord II) established the ASEAN Economic Community with a view to integrate the economies of the ASEAN countries. This is outlined in the document, ASEAN Vision 2020. To this end, there is to be a free flow of goods, services, investment and skilled labour, and freer flow of capital in order to promote economic growth and development and reduce socio-economic disparities within the region. Further details on the background to the Agreement can be found in Lloyd and Smith (2004).

The Framework Agreement for the Integration of Priority Sectors was signed at the Tenth ASEAN Summit which was held in Vientiane, Laos on 29–30 November 2004. This Agreement outlined the steps to be taken to accelerate the integration of eleven major sectors in the ASEAN economies: agro-based products, air travel, automotive products, e-ASEAN, electronics, fisheries, healthcare, rubber-based products, textiles and apparel, tourism, and wood-based products.

A number of previous studies have examined the impediments to the integration of the ASEAN economies. This chapter contains an overview of trade performance and tariff rates in the priority sectors of the ASEAN economies. It also seeks to measure the degree of integration in these economies using measures of comparative advantage and intra-industry trade in the priority sectors.

To give a background, Table 4.1 compares the structure of the various ASEAN economies. In Cambodia, Laos, and Myanmar, the dominant sector is agriculture. Except for Singapore whose dominant sector is services, manufacturing is the dominant sector in the other countries.

2. Methodology

2.1. Data Sources

Trade flows. The source of data is Comtrade (www.unstats.un.org) for the period 2002–2004 and ASEAN Secretariat (www.aseansec.org) for 2005. Trade flows are analysed for nine of the eleven priority sectors: agro-based products, automotive products, electronics, fisheries, healthcare, information and communication technology (ICT), rubber-based products, textiles and apparel, and wood-based products. Some commodities are included in more than one sector.

Reporting by some countries is incomplete. For example, Singapore does not report all its trade flows with Indonesia. This can be overcome to some extent by examining the trade flows that are reported by the partner country. However, in some cases, goods passing through Singapore are simply re-exported. Data from Laos, Myanmar, Cambodia, and Vietnam are also problematic.

CEPT and MFN tariff rates and intra-industry trade index. Tariff data are from the ASEAN Secretariat and are classified by the eight-digit ASEAN Harmonized Tariff Nomenclature (AHTN). The intra-industry trade index is calculated from the four-digit HS code. This is calculated by summing the six-digit HS code from products within the priority sectors. However, some products within this code are not within the priority sectors.

2.2. Method of Constructing Trade Matrices

The priority sectoral trade matrix is constructed from each country's exports to and imports from each of the other countries. For example, the value of agro-based exports by Brunei is derived from the total exports of Brunei to

Table 4.1
Composition of GDP by Economic Sectors, 2000–2004

Country	2000			2002			2003			2004		
	Agriculture	Industry	Services	Agriculture	Industry	Services	Agriculture	Industry	Services	Agriculture	Industry	Services
Brunei Darussalam	1.6	59.5	38.9	1.9	58.7	39.4	2.1	58.4	39.5	—	—	—
Cambodia	39.6	23.3	37.1	35.6	27.9	36.5	36.8	27.9	35.4	—	—	—
Indonesia	15.6	45.9	38.5	15.5	45.4	39.1	15.4	45	39.6	15.2	44.5	40.3
Laos	52.1	22.7	25.2	50.2	24.6	25.1	—	—	—	—	—	—
Malaysia	8.4	44.2	47.4	8.1	41.6	50.4	8.1	42.1	49.8	7.9	42.5	49.6
Myanmar	42.9	17.3	39.7	—	—	—	—	—	—	—	—	—
Philippines	19.9	34.7	45.4	19.7	34.5	45.8	19.8	33.5	46.7	19.6	33.2	47.2
Singapore	0.1	33.8	66.1	0.1	31.3	68.6	0.1	31.1	68.8	0.1	31.6	68.3
Thailand	10.3	44.4	45.3	10	44.8	45.2	10.2	45.8	44	9.2	46.8	44
Vietnam	23.3	35.4	41.3	21.8	37.4	40.8	21.1	38.5	40.5	—	—	—

Source: ASEAN Secretariat, 2005.

each ASEAN country. This step is followed for all countries and all commodities within the priority sectors.

These trade flows for each country are then expressed as a share of her total trade flows to the world as a whole. For example, in the case of Brunei, the total agro-based exports of Brunei to ASEAN countries is divided by Brunei's total exports of these products to all countries.

2.3. Method of Measuring Tariff Barriers

a. Total tariff lines: the number of tariff lines for each country and each priority sector using the CEPT (Common Effective Preferential Tariff) and MFN (most-favoured nation) tariff rates.
b. *Ad valorem* tariff lines: the number and proportion of *ad valorem* tariffs in the total number of tariff lines.
c. Average tariff rates: the arithmetic mean of CEPT and MFN tariff rates.
d. Dispersion of tariff rates around the mean tariff rate: the standard deviation of CEPT and MFN tariff rates.
e. Dispersion of tariff rates by range: the proportion of per cent tariff rates which are within the ranges of zero to 0.1, 0.11 to 5, 5.1 to 10, 10.1 to 20, 20.1 to 30, more than 30.
f. Dispersion of tariff rates by tariff spikes: the proportion of tariff rates which are higher than three times the average tariff rate.
g. Specific tariffs: the number and proportion of specific tariffs.

2.4. Intra-industry Trade Index

Intra-industry trade (IIT) index is calculated from the four-digit HS code. The four-digit HS code is calculated from the six-digit HS code from products included in the priority sectors. However, not all products in the six-digit HS code are included in the priority sectors.

The formula for the Grubel-Lloyd IIT index is:

$$[1 - \text{Sum}|(X - M)|/\text{Sum }(X + M)]\ 100$$

where X is exports and M is imports, and $|\quad|$ signifies absolute value. If there is no IIT, which means that the country only imports or exports the product, and does not both import and export the product, so that either $X = 0$ or $M = 0$, the value of the index will be $[1 - 1/1]\ 100 = \text{zero}$.

On the other hand, if there is the highest possible degree of IIT, so that the country both exports and imports equal values of the product, say $N/2$, so that $X - M = 0$, then the value of the index will be $[1 - 0/N]\ 100 = 100$.

Where the country both exports and imports the product, but not in equal values, so that $|(X - M)| = Z > 0$, the value of the index will be $[1 - Z/N]$ 100, $Z < N$. This is more than zero but less than 100. In general, the greater the difference between X and M, the greater the value of Z and Z/N, and the smaller is the value of the index of IIT.

The IIT index in this report is calculated as Vertical IIT and Horizontal IIT. The formula for Vertical IIT is as follow.

$$IIT_{vp} = \frac{\sum\limits_{i=1}^{n}(X_i + M_i) - \sum\limits_{i=1}^{n}|X_i - M_i|}{\sum\limits_{i=1}^{n}(X_i + M_i)} \; x \, 100 \;\; \text{or} \;\; 1 - \frac{\sum\limits_{i=1}^{n}|X_i - M_i|}{\sum\limits_{i=1}^{n}(X_i - M_i)} \; x100$$

where
IIT_{vp} = IIT vertical for priority sectors
X_i = six-digit HS export
M_i = six-digit HS import

Meanwhile, the formula for Horizontal IIT is as follow.

$$IIT_{hj} = \frac{\sum\limits_{j=1}^{n}(X_j + M_j) - \sum\limits_{j=1}^{n}|X_j - M_j|}{\sum\limits_{j=1}^{n}(X_j + M_j)} \; x \, 100 \;\; \text{or} \;\; 1 - \frac{\sum\limits_{j=1}^{n}|X_j - M_j|}{\sum\limits_{i=1}^{n}(X_j - M_j)} \; x100$$

$$IIT_{hp} = \frac{\sum\limits_{j=1}^{n} IIT_{hj}}{n}$$

where
IIT_{hj} = IIT horizontal for four-digit HS
X_j = six-digit HS export which sum in the four-digit HS
I_j = six-digit HS import which sum in the four-digit HS
IIT_{hp} = IIT horizontal for priority sectors which is average from IIT horizontal for four-digit HS

3. Trade Performance

3.1. Overall Trade Performance of the Priority Sectors

The export trade of all ASEAN countries is far more intensive with non-ASEAN economies than it is with ASEAN itself. As shown in Table 4.2, less

Table 4.2
ASEAN Countries' Total Exports by Priority Sector in 2005
(In US$ million)

| Country | Destination | | | | Total |
| | ASEAN | | Rest of the World | | |
	Value	% from Total	Value	% from Total	
Brunei	112.2	31.3	245.7	68.7	357.9
Cambodia	43.8	1.8	2,346.1	98.2	2,389.9
Indonesia	10,607.5	23.4	34,629.9	76.6	45,237.4
Laos	60.4	0.6	10,547.6	99.4	10,608.0
Malaysia	36,499.6	28.3	92,653.4	71.7	129,153.0
Myanmar	204.0	16.2	1,057.5	83.8	1,261.5
Philippines	6,919.1	20.2	27,319.8	79.8	34,238.9
Singapore	52,328.3	27.2	139,762.9	72.8	192,091.2
Thailand	15,475.7	20.0	61,822.9	80.0	77,298.6
Vietnam	1,758.3	12.7	12,088.6	87.3	13,846.9

than 32 per cent of each country's priority exports are sold to ASEAN customers, and for Cambodia and Laos, this figure is less than 2 per cent. The countries with the highest dependence on ASEAN export markets are Brunei, Malaysia, and Singapore with respective intensities of 31.3, 28.3, and 27.2 per cent.

Likewise, the priority import trade of ASEAN countries has a similarly low intensity with ASEAN (Table 4.3). Apart from Myanmar which imports 90 per cent of its priority requirements from ASEAN, the highest import intensity is 33 per cent. On the other hand, the degree of import intensity is more uniform between countries than is the degree of export intensity: the lowest degree of import intensity is 19 per cent for Cambodia and the Philippines. It follows that for priority products the degree of intra-ASEAN import intensity is higher than the degree of intra-ASEAN export intensity: on average, ASEAN countries are more dependent on each other as sources of their imports of priority products than they are as destinations for their exports of those products.

This asymmetry in export and import dependence of priority products leads to trade imbalances in those products within ASEAN (Table 4.3). With the exception of Brunei and the Philippines, all ASEAN countries have an overall trade surplus with the world as a whole in priority trade products. However, the only countries in trade surplus in priority trade with ASEAN

Table 4.3
ASEAN Countries' Total Imports by Priority Sector in 2005
(In US$ million)

Country	Destination				Total
	ASEAN		Rest of the World		
	Value	% from Total	Value	% from Total	
Brunei	326.97	33.2	656.9	66.8	983.9
Cambodia	408.46	18.9	1,751.4	81.1	2,159.9
Indonesia	3,427.23	20.9	12,989.9	79.1	16,417.1
Laos	61.68	23.3	203.3	76.7	265.0
Malaysia	27,308.22	28.9	67,130.1	71.1	94,438.3
Myanmar	289.46	89.6	33.5	10.4	323.0
Philippines	6,684.45	19.4	27,728.8	80.6	34,413.2
Singapore	54,691.15	32.6	112,837.2	67.4	167,528.4
Thailand	17,446.81	26.5	48,392.9	73.5	65,839.7
Vietnam	3,354.98	31.3	7,357.1	68.7	10,712.1

Source: ASEAN Secretariat, 2006.

Table 4.4
ASEAN Countries' Trade Balances in Priority Trade in 2005
(In US million)

Country	Destination		Total
	ASEAN	Rest of the World	
Brunei	−214.8	−411.2	−626.0
Cambodia	−364.7	594.7	230.0
Indonesia	7,180.2	21,640.0	28,820.2
Laos	−1.3	10,344.3	10,343.0
Malaysia	9,191.4	25,523.3	34,714.7
Myanmar	−85.5	1,024.0	938.5
Philippines	234.7	−409.0	−174.3
Singapore	−2,362.9	26,925.7	24,562.8
Thailand	−1,971.1	13,430.0	11,458.9
Vietnam	−1,596.7	4,731.5	3,134.8

Source: ASEAN Secretariat, 2006.

itself are Malaysia, Indonesia, and the Philippines, in that order, so that the remaining seven are in deficit with these three.

3.2. Intra-ASEAN Trade Performance

The dominant ASEAN exporters of priority products to ASEAN in 2005 are Singapore (US$52 billion), Malaysia (US$36 billion), Thailand (US$15 billion), and Indonesia (US$11 billion), although ASEAN countries take less than 20 per cent of Singapore's total exports. The dominant export products for all of these countries in 2005, as well as Cambodia (the smallest total exporter), the Philippines and Vietnam were ICT and electronics, while automotives were the third most important export by Indonesia, Thailand, and the Philippines. For Singapore, Malaysia, Indonesia, and Thailand, the respective shares of ICT and electronics in 2005 exports were 95, 93, 69, and 66 per cent. Automotives accounted for 21 per cent of Indonesian exports, 20 per cent of Thai exports, and 11 per cent of Philippine exports.

On the import side, the dominant importers from ASEAN are Singapore (US$55 billion), Malaysia (US$27 billion), and Thailand (US$17 billion), while the least active importers are Laos (US$62 million) and Cambodia (US$408 million). For all those countries whose exports are dominated by ICT, electronics, and automotives — Singapore, Malaysia, Indonesia, Thailand, Vietnam and the Philippines — these sectors are also dominant in their imports.

Myanmar is a relatively new member of ASEAN and now sources over 90 per cent of its imports from ASEAN, although the share of its exports going to ASEAN is much less than this. Likewise, Vietnam, another new member, is interesting because ICT, electronics, and automotive now dominate its import and export trade with ASEAN.

4. Review of Tariff Data

4.1. Tariff Rates

The average CEPT rate in the priority sectors is 3.71 per cent, while the average MFN rate is 10.52 per cent in 2005. The difference between these averages indicates the average degree of ASEAN preference for products originating within ASEAN.

For individual sectors, the automotive sector has the highest average CEPT rate of 5.72 per cent, while the average MFN rate is 19.17 per cent, more than three times higher in 2005. This relatively high MFN average tariff reflects a desire to develop the domestic automotive industries at the expense of imports from outside ASEAN under the "infant industry" argument. This argument justifies consumers being temporarily burdened with high domestic prices to subsidize domestic producers who, it is hoped, can eventually compete with foreign producers when the local industry achieves economies of scale and has learned how to make cheaper cars as a result of the experience obtained from making them ("learning by doing"). For a country such as Thailand, which seeks to develop a car assembly industry particularly for Japanese cars, the tariff structure would involve low tariffs on imported components and high tariffs on fully assembled vehicles. On the other hand, for a country such as Malaysia, which seeks to develop its own national car industry, there would be a more extensive system of tariffs.

The lowest average tariff rates are in the healthcare sector where the respective CEPT and MFN rates are 2.12 and 5.08 per cent. These low rates reflect a desire to give some help to local industries with minimal impact on consumers' costs of healthcare.

Cambodia is the country with the highest average CEPT rate at 9.3 per cent, and Vietnam has the highest average MFN rate at 21.98 per cent. Singapore has zero CEPT and MFN tariff rates, reflecting its government's desire to maximize opportunities for international trade arising from its strategic geographical location.

For the agro-based sector, Laos has the highest average CEPT rate at 7.54 per cent. Thailand has the highest average MFN rate at 26.8 per cent, with an average CEPT rate of only 4.38 per cent. Despite this high margin of preference for imports from ASEAN, the share of ASEAN in Thai imports is less than 6 per cent.

For the automotive sector, Vietnam has the highest average CEPT rate at 9.8 per cent, and an average MFN rate of 39.86 per cent. Vietnam was required to reduce its highly protective CEPT rate against ASEAN countries in 2006.

4.2. Margins of Preference

The preferential trade agreement diverts import trade to members of ASEAN from non-members. Therefore, a great deal of interest is attached to the amount of preference that the tariff structure provides. The margin of preference is measured by the difference between the MFN and the CEPT rates. These margins are illustrated in Table 4.5.

Because it has zero tariffs, Singapore offers no margin of preference to ASEAN members. At the other end of the spectrum, Indonesia has the largest number of tariff lines in which the margin of preference is 10 per cent, while Malaysia has the largest number in which the margin of preference is more than 15 per cent. (Malaysia has 827 tariff lines that have a margin of preference of more than 15 per cent, while Thailand has only 365 tariff lines and Philippines 562 tariff lines, see Table 4.5.)

Rina Oktaviani, Amzul Rifin, and Henny Reinhardt

Table 4.5
Margins of Preference (MFN – CEPT) in 2005 by Priority Sector and Country Number of Tariff Lines

Sectors	Brunei		Cambodia		Indonesia		Laos		Malaysia	
	MFN-CEPT=10	MFN-CEPT≥15	MFN-CEPT=10	MFN-CEPT≥15	MFN-CEPT=10	MFN-CEPT≥15	MFN-CEPT=10	MFN-CEPT≥15	MFN-CEPT=10	MFN-CEPT≥15
Agro-based	0	0	0	0	3	0	80	28	0	2
Fisheries	0	0	0	0	0	4	0	29	0	0
Healthcare	0	4	0	0	3	0	0	0	0	0
Rubber-based	32	29	0	15	107	23	0	0	7	124
Wood-based	0	0	0	22	44	0	0	72	0	8
Textiles and garments	4	0	0	0	402	0	0	16	97	63
ICT	0	101	76	90	79	2	44	0	22	30
Electronics	0	107	83	126	170	15	48	0	28	136
Automotives	165	671	0	1	248	496	177	63	158	464
Total	201	912	159	254	1,056	540	349	208	312	827

continued on next page

Table 4.5 — *Continued*

Sectors	Myanmar		Philippines		Singapore		Thailand		Vietnam	
	MFN-CEPT=10	MFN-CEPT≥15	MFN-CEPT=10	MFN-CEPT≥15	MFN-CEPT=10	MFN-CEPT≥15	MFN-CEPT=10	MFN-CEPT≥15	MFN-CEPT=10	MFN-CEPT≥15
Agro-based	0	0	16	2	0	0	0	9	1	54
Fisheries	0	0	41	0	0	0	0	6	0	126
Healthcare	0	0	3	1	0	0	7	14	13	47
Rubber-based	3	0	50	0	0	0	7	14	13	102
Wood-based	2	0	51	0	0	0	0	9	4	41
Textiles and garments	115	0	537	51	0	0	12	252	12	959
ICT	32	0	62	0	0	0	5	10	35	129
Electronics	52	0	121	0	0	0	9	42	64	325
Automotives	154	125	49	508	0	0	0	9	270	378
Total	358	125	930	562	0	0	40	365	412	2,161

The industries that are the most favoured by high margins of preference are automotives in Brunei, Indonesia, Laos, Malaysia, Myanmar, and the Philippines, electronics in Cambodia, textiles in Thailand, and textiles, automotives, and electronics in Vietnam. Based on margins of preference, protection for the automotive industry is clearly important in ASEAN.

4.3. Description of Each Country's Tariff Rates by Sector

Brunei. As a result of its high revenues from oil, Brunei does not need tariffs to generate government revenue. At the same time, Brunei desires to minimize the cost of living for its people. Accordingly, there are no significant tariffs on agricultural, fishery and healthcare products, and textiles. Of the other priority sectors, the highest tariff rates are in the automotive sector, with average CEPT and MFN rates at 5.73 and 18.14 per cent, respectively, leading to a high margin of preference. Wood-based products comes next with respective rates of 3.9 and 13.6 per cent, and rubber-based and ICT products with respective rates less than 3 per cent and less than 10 per cent.

Cambodia. This country has the highest average CEPT rate among the ASEAN countries at 9.3 per cent, while the average MFN rate is 16.23 per cent. Cambodia has relatively high MFN tariffs in the agro-based sector, with 21 per cent of tariff lines in this sector exceeding 30 per cent. Likewise, in the automotive sector, over 37 per cent of MFN tariff lines exceed 30 per cent. In electronics, Cambodia has the highest CEPT and MFN rates in ASEAN, with almost 24 per cent of MFN tariff lines having rates greater than 30 per cent. In fisheries, there is also a relatively high average CEPT rate of 14.83 per cent. Compared with other sectors, the healthcare sector in Cambodia has the lowest average CEPT and MFN rates — 82 per cent of tariff lines have zero CEPT and MFN rates. In the case of ICT, the average CEPT and MFN rates are 9.3 per cent and 18.31 per cent respectively. A similar picture exists for rubber-based products where the average CEPT rate is 8.53 per cent and the average MFN rate is 18.57 per cent. In the textile sector the number of tariff lines is greater than for any other sector, with respective average tariff rates being 11.36 and 16.46 per cent. For wood-based products, the average CEPT rate is almost as high as the average MFN rate of 14.32 per cent, with 95 per cent of CEPT tariff lines being in the range of 10 to 20 per cent.

Indonesia. The average CEPT rate is only 1.76 per cent while the average MFN rate is 8.52 per cent. The lowest average CEPT and MFN rates are for agro-based products, while the highest CEPT rate is for rubber-based products at only 3.95 per cent. By contrast, the highest MFN rate is for automotives at nearly 25 per cent, with 28 per cent of tariff lines exceeding 30 per cent. For electronic products, the average CEPT rate is less than two per cent because 67 per cent of the CEPT tariff lines have zero rates, but there are tariff spikes on 32 per cent of the tariff lines. The average MFN rate is 5.79 per cent with no tariff spikes. In the case of fisheries, the average CEPT rate is less than 1 per cent, but there is high variability due to tariff spikes on some items protected from other ASEAN suppliers. The average MFN rate is also relatively low at 5.03 per cent, with much less variability. There is also a similar pattern for healthcare and ICT. In the case of rubber-based products, the average CEPT rate is nearly 4 per cent, while the average MFN rate is over 11 per cent. The textile industry is characterized by the highest number of CEPT and MFN tariff lines. Average CEPT rates are less than 2 per cent, but highly variable due to tariff spikes in 32 per cent of tariff lines. Average MFN rates are close to 11 per cent with much less variability. Likewise, for wood-based products, there is a low but variable CEPT rate with 68 per cent of tariff lines having a zero tariff, and a less variable MFN rate averaging 11 per cent.

Laos. The average CEPT rate is 5.29 per cent, while the average MFN rate is 14.44 per cent. The highest CEPT rate is on automotives, while the lowest is on textiles. The highest average MFN rate is on wood-based products at 27.68 per cent, while the lowest is on ICT products at 7.76 per cent. Laos has the smallest number of zero CEPT rates in ASEAN, and is required to reduce all its CEPT rates to zero by 2008. In the agro-based sector the average CEPT rate is 7.54, with 63 per cent of the tariff lines less than 5 per cent. The average MFN rate is 22 per cent with most tariff lines in excess of 30 per cent. In the automotive sector most CEPT rates are less than 10 per cent, while the average MFN rate is 22 per cent, with 31 per cent of tariff lines attracting a rate of 40 per cent. In the case of electronics, the average CEPT rate is only 4 per cent, with 79 per cent of tariff lines around the average. The average MFN rate is 8 per cent, with 60 per cent of tariff lines being less than 5 per cent. Since Laos is land-locked, the CEPT rate on fisheries is low at an average of 4.5 per cent, while the MFN rate is 14 per cent. In the case of healthcare, the CEPT average is 4.69 per cent while the MFN average is 9.34 per cent. However, there are four products where there is a tariff spike. For ICT, the average CEPT rate is 3.9 per cent, with the average MFN being twice as high at 7.8 per cent. A similar picture exists for rubber-based products, with the respective averages being 4.6 and 8.7 per cent. For textiles, the respective averages are both higher at 2.9 and 9.6 per cent, with MFN tariff spikes for sixteen tariff lines. In the case of wood-based products there is a very large gap between the CEPT and MFN average tariff rates: 6.6 per cent and 27.7 per cent, with 36 per cent of MFN tariff lines being 40 per cent.

Malaysia. The Malaysian tariff is not high by ASEAN standards — the average CEPT is at 2.4 per cent and the average MFN is at 8.5 per cent. However, the MFN tariffs on agro-based, automotives, and rubber-based products are high at 22.4, 21.1, and 19.2 per cent respectively. In the first case, the high tariff is intended to divert imports to ASEAN countries because the CEPT rate is less than 1 per cent. In the second two cases, these tariffs are used to protect the domestic car industry, which manufactures the well-known Proton, and the domestic natural rubber industry, which faces competition from imported synthetic rubber. There are also an unusually high number of spikes in the CEPT rate. The Malaysian electronics industry assembles imported parts, so there are relatively low tariffs on these parts with the average CEPT rate being 1.3 per cent, with some significant tariff spikes, and the average MFN rate being 5.1 per cent. There are also low tariff rates on fisheries products, 0.83 and 2.6 per cent respectively, although there are significant tariff spikes in both CEPT and MFN rates, with a higher proportion of spikes in the former. Healthcare products also have low tariff rates with some spikes, as is also the case in ICT. In common with other ASEAN countries, there are a large number of tariff lines in the textile industry, with average CEPT and MFN rates being 3.98 and 13.1 per cent, respectively. Wood-based products have respective average CEPT and MFN rates of 2.1 and 8.7 per cent, with a high degree of variation due to some tariff spikes.

Myanmar. The level of per capita GDP and rate of economic growth in this country have been reduced by ongoing political conflict. Previously a rice exporter, Myanmar no longer exports rice. Membership of ASEAN provides an opportunity to help solve these problems. By ASEAN standards, the average level of tariffs is not high — the CEPT average is 5.25 per cent and the MFN rate is 7.23 per cent. The wood-based sector enjoys the highest average CEPT and MFN tariffs, while the ICT and healthcare sectors have the lowest respective CEPT and MFN tariffs. The agro-based sector enjoys tariffs slightly less than the average for all sectors, with 24 per cent of tariff lines having tariff spikes. On the other hand, the automotive sector has average tariffs about 50 per cent higher than the average for all sectors, with 11 per cent of tariff lines having spikes in MFN rates. The electronics sector has average tariffs less than that for all sectors, but there are no tariff lines with zero tariffs. The fisheries, healthcare, ICT, and rubber-based sectors all have tariffs close to or below the average for all sectors. On the other hand, the textile and wood-based sectors have average tariffs above the sectoral average, indicating that the tariff structure is intended to protect these domestic industries against other ASEAN as well as non-ASEAN suppliers.

The Philippines. The average CEPT and MFN tariff rates are 2.9 and 8.2 per cent, respectively. The highest CEPT rate is on textiles at 4.1 per cent, while the lowest is on ICT at 1.3 per cent. The highest MFN rate is on automotives at 16.7 per cent, and the lowest is on ICT at 2.97 per cent. These low tariffs on ICT reflect a desire to develop this industry by keeping the cost of its imported components low. The agro-based, fisheries, healthcare, ICT, rubber-based, and wood-based sectors have average tariff levels close to the sectoral average whereas, as already noted, the automotives and textile sectors have relatively high MFN tariffs.

Singapore. The country is considered to be the trading centre of Southeast Asia or even in Asia. In order to accelerate the flow of goods to this country, the government apply zero per cent tariff on all products for ASEAN and non-ASEAN countries. This will facilitate goods entering the country more freely and accelerate the development of the country.

Thailand. The two priority sectors that Thailand has succeeded in developing are the agricultural sector, predominantly rice and tropical fruits, and the assembly of mainly Japanese automobiles. Malaysia, on the other hand, has developed its own national car. The Thai tariff system is also distinguished by the high proportion of specific tariffs, as opposed to *ad valorem* tariffs, so that the average tariff rate has less meaning than for other countries. In any case, the average CEPT and MFN rates are 3.02 and 13.04 per cent, respectively. The sectors with the highest average respective CEPT and MFN rates are fisheries (4.8 per cent) and agro-based (26.8 per cent), with some tariffs in the latter sector going as high as 60 per cent. Likewise, in the automotive sector, two products have rates of 80 per cent. Textiles are also a relatively high-tariff sector with an average MFN rate of 20.4 per cent, with many specific tariff spikes and specific tariffs. By contrast, tariffs in the other sectors — electronics, healthcare, ICT, rubber and wood-based — are closer to the sectoral average.

Vietnam. Vietnam has followed a policy of attracting foreign investment and one of the instruments of this policy is high MFN tariffs for relatively labour-intensive industries such as agro-based products (23.8 per cent), automotives

(39.9 per cent), fisheries (32.7 per cent), rubber-based products (18.6 per cent), and textiles (37.4 per cent). These relatively high MFN rates are responsible for the large difference between the average CEPT rate of 5.1 per cent and the average MFN rate of 21.98 per cent. It follows that the tariff rates in the other sectors — electronics, healthcare, ICT, and wood-based — are at or below average.

4.4. Commitments to Tariff Reduction under AFTA

Under the ASEAN agreement, CEPT tariffs are to be reduced on all products in the inclusion list, which includes all of the products of the priority sectors as well as other specified products. For the ASEAN-6 (Brunei, Indonesia, Malaysia, the Philippines, Singapore, and Thailand) these CEPT rates should have been reduced to a band between zero and 5 per cent by 2003. In case of Vietnam, the target date is in 2006 (should be 0–5 per cent by 2006), Laos and Myanmar in 2008, and Cambodia in 2010. Furthermore, by 2010, all the products in the inclusion list must be tariff-free for the ASEAN-6, and for the other countries by 2015.

The ASEAN-6 commitment to maximum CEPT rates of 5 per cent on priority products by 2003 had not been met in 2005, Singapore excepted. In the particular case of automotive products, 36.59 per cent of tariff lines in Brunei remain in the range of 5.1 to 10 per cent, and in Malaysia 25.05 per cent of tariff lines are in the range 10.1 to 20 per cent. Similarly, in textiles, 27 per cent of Vietnam's tariff lines are more than 5 per cent. In wood-based products, 61 per cent of Thailand's tariff lines exceed 30 per cent, and in the agro-based sector Cambodia, Myanmar, Laos, and Vietnam levy tariffs in excess of 5 per cent.

5. Revealed Comparative Advantage and Intra-industry Trade

5.1. Why Do Countries Trade?

In the absence of resistance to trade, such as ignorance of trading opportunities, distance, transport costs, and tariffs, countries trade because of differences in prices at home and abroad. These price differences can reflect economies of scale, by which a country has a lower cost of production simply because its domestic market is larger than that of its trading partners. Price differences can also reflect differences in the opportunity costs of production, and a country is said to have a comparative advantage in the production of a commodity if its opportunity costs of production are lower than that of its trading partners. This difference in opportunity costs may reflect international differences in factor endowments, so that a country with a high endowment of natural resources or capital relative to labour will be a low-cost producer and exporter of natural resource or capital-intensive goods, such as agro-, wood- or rubber-based products, and a high-cost producer and importer of labour-intensive goods such as textiles. This phenomenon is called inter-industry trade.

Within ASEAN, Brunei provides an example of a country with large natural endowments of oil, which it exports in such quantities that it needs to import only a few commodities and has a comparative advantage in only one of the nine priority sectors — textiles. A less extreme example is Indonesia, whose oil exports and its endowments of agricultural land, timber and fisheries allow her to avoid the need for a comparative advantage in textiles, normally associated with low-wage countries.

Similarities between countries can also generate opportunities for trade between them. This provides the second reason why countries trade, and this is that they have similarly high levels of income and real wages. This leads them to have a similar industrial structure and an income-led high demand for different varieties (models) of the same commodity (e.g., cars) in their consumption patterns. However, economies of scale do not allow them all to produce something of each variety: they specialize in producing different varieties, and this causes them to have a high level of trade in different varieties or models of the same commodity. That is, a given country exports one variety or model and imports another variety or model of what is essentially the same commodity. This phenomenon is called intra-industry trade.

5.2. Revealed Comparative Advantage

Commodity prices tend to be equalized as a result of trade. Consequently, when trade takes place, we may not observe significant differences in prices and opportunity costs. As a result, we are forced to deduce the pattern of comparative advantage from the actual trade pattern. A country is said to have revealed a comparative advantage in producing a given commodity if the share of that commodity in her total exports is higher than the share of that commodity in total world exports by all countries. And the higher the ratio of the share of that commodity in her exports to the share of that commodity in total world exports, the greater is the degree of revealed comparative advantage (RCA).

Table 4.6 illustrates the RCA in the nine priority sectors for the ASEAN countries in 2005. It shows that no country has RCA in automotive products and healthcare. For agro-based products, the countries with RCA (in order of RCA) are Myanmar, Indonesia, Malaysia, and the Philippines. For each commodity, the countries with RCA are as follow:

- electronics: Malaysia, Singapore, Thailand, and Indonesia;
- fisheries: Vietnam, Myanmar, Thailand, Indonesia, and the Philippines;
- ICT: Malaysia, Singapore, Thailand and the Philippines;
- rubber-based products: Vietnam, Indonesia,Thailand and Laos;
- textiles: Cambodia, Brunei, and Thailand;
- wood-based products: Laos, Indonesia, Vietnam, Myanmar, Malaysia, and Thailand.

Brunei's and Cambodia's RCA are in textiles only. Indonesia's RCA is in agro-based, wood-based products, fisheries, rubber-based products, and electronics, in that order. Other countries' RCA in each commodity, in that order, are as follow:

- Laos: wood-based, rubber-based, and agro-based products;
- Malaysia: agro-based products, electronics, wood-based products and ICT;
- Myanmar: fisheries, agro-based, and wood-based products;
- Philippines: agro-based products, fisheries, and ICT;
- Singapore: electronics and ICT;
- Thailand: fisheries, electronics, rubber-based products, textiles, wood-based products, and ICT;
- Vietnam: fisheries, rubber-based, and wood-based products.

The largest values of intra-ASEAN trade are in electronics (US$57 billion), ICT (US$52 billion), and automotives (US$7 billion) (ASEAN Secretariat 2006). However, for these products the RCA index is relatively low (a maximum of 2.8 in the case of Malaysian electronics, and 2 for Malaysian ICT) and, in the case of automotives, less than unity for all countries. This suggests that the countries that export these products within ASEAN do not have a comparative advantage by world standards, and are being enabled to export to other ASEAN countries by the preferential trading agreement and other close ties between them.

Table 4.6
Revealed Comparative Advantage Index (RCA) by Priority Sector and ASEAN Country in 2005

Sector	Brunei	Cambodia	Indonesia	Laos	Malaysia	Myanmar	Philippines	Singapore	Thailand	Vietnam
Agro-based	0.001	0.321	7.398	1.117	4.628	9.188	1.905	0.126	0.970	0.221
Automotive	0.001	0.024	0.383	0.059	0.114	0.000	0.286	0.217	0.880	0.132
Electronics	0.004	0.007	1.092	0.030	2.809	0.015	0.926	2.331	2.096	0.350
Fisheries	0.019	0.635	3.563	0.012	0.618	9.801	1.505	0.267	5.689	11.047
Healthcare	0.015	0.019	0.324	0.073	0.240	0.010	0.097	0.422	0.350	0.188
ICT	0.003	0.003	0.729	0.093	1.976	0.011	1.197	1.647	1.218	0.207
Rubber-based	0.002	0.168	1.804	1.219	0.852	0.649	1.000	0.270	1.684	8.033
Textile	1.665	15.609	0.277	0.406	0.486	0.687	0.128	0.309	1.563	0.830
Wood-based	0.004	0.430	5.026	18.092	2.665	3.642	0.060	0.087	1.292	3.754

5.3. Vertical and Horizontal IIT

The vertical index sums the six-digit HS to derive an index of IIT for each sector. These indices are shown in Table 4.7.

The horizontal IIT index for a priority sector is derived from averaging the IIT index for four-digit HS for each priority sector. Because the horizontal measure is based on averaging, sectors with zero IIT will reduce the average. These indices are shown in Table 4.8.

As far as IIT in products are concerned, we expect a low level of IIT for products in which there is intrinsically less variety or less opportunity to develop new varieties, as in the case of agro-based products and textiles. By contrast, there are intrinsically many varieties of fish. As far as IIT by countries is concerned, we expect a high level of IIT between higher wage countries because of their high income, which creates similar demand for variety in their consumption patterns.

These expectations are consistent with the data from Table 4.8. The lowest levels of IIT are in more or less uniform products such as agro-based and textiles, while the highest levels are in products where there is more scope for variety as in ICT, rubber-based products, electronics, automotives, and fisheries. Likewise, the highest levels of IIT by country are in the relatively high-wage countries of Malaysia, Singapore, and Thailand, and to a lesser extent Indonesia.

The level of IIT can also be used as an indicator of the degree of integration between economies. A high degree of integration between economies means that trade and factor mobility have caused income per head to converge. In turn, this convergence of incomes causes a convergence of domestic demand and production patterns. Although the pattern of production is similar, it is not identical, because economies of scale cause each variety of a given commodity to be produced in only one country. A high level of IIT ensues, because a given country is simultaneously exporting one variety and importing another variety of the same commodity. By this logic, there is a high degree of integration between Malaysia, Singapore, and Thailand, and very little between these economies and those of Cambodia, Laos, and Myanmar, which are also not highly integrated with each other.

5.4. Intra-industry Trade by Country

Because of the dominance of oil in Brunei's production of traded goods, we do not expect a high level of IIT. The average IIT index for the priority sectors is 12.87, which is low by the integration standards of the OECD (2002).

Table 4.7
Vertical Intra Industry Trade Index

Sector	Brunei	Cambodia	Indonesia	Laos	Malaysia	Myanmar	Philippines	Singapore	Thailand	Vietnam
Agro-based	0.29	4.02	7.27	0.87	11.10	0.03	0.24	23.66	20.68	1.92
Automotive	29.71	6.74	48.34	1.45	39.26	0.20	30.36	44.49	39.94	19.06
Electronics	16.65	25.37	18.79	0.51	66.25	4.50	32.30	72.62	59.78	19.08
Fisheries	5.99	7.68	15.56	0.00	50.51	0.03	34.91	35.81	26.72	35.41
Healthcare	3.26	1.40	25.37	1.18	59.04	1.28	26.96	39.60	26.85	22.07
ICT	16.88	3.86	18.04	0.01	67.45	7.09	32.96	74.54	64.91	21.51
Rubber-based	11.12	0.70	34.44	0.56	48.34	0.12	33.84	60.98	50.62	29.42
Textile	19.16	7.24	18.15	0.26	30.78	0.20	12.27	30.02	22.67	17.80
Wood-based	4.93	20.30	19.98	0.49	48.03	0.20	3.87	20.07	17.35	9.03

Table 4.8
Average Horizontal Intra Industry Trade Index by Sector and Country

Sector	Brunei	Cambodia	Indonesia	Laos	Malaysia	Myanmar	Philippines	Singapore	Thailand	Vietnam	Sector Average
Agro-based	1.43	5.33	16.61	5.29	26.33	0.04	3.52	28.90	14.66	9.42	11.15
Automotive	26.06	11.19	39.86	2.28	39.30	0.61	19.60	40.05	34.68	15.91	22.96
Electronics	24.51	6.03	28.87	0.34	48.09	1.94	22.40	44.34	40.78	16.37	23.37
Fisheries	3.83	12.21	24.19	0.00	44.16	0.02	21.04	33.97	35.36	22.66	19.74
Healthcare	6.84	0.30	23.98	1.02	53.34	2.74	19.68	39.70	29.06	19.30	19.59
ICT	21.86	5.99	29.77	0.06	51.37	2.27	27.23	47.81	45.18	15.40	24.70
Rubber-based	11.37	3.39	37.98	0.04	45.80	0.01	24.98	46.76	47.14	23.12	24.06
Textile	9.61	5.11	17.40	1.16	31.91	0.06	11.46	33.73	20.45	16.57	14.75
Wood-based	10.31	11.79	26.79	10.49	33.50	1.01	16.23	24.58	34.31	32.26	20.13
Country Average	12.87	6.82	27.27	2.30	41.53	0.97	18.46	37.76	33.51	19.00	

Among the priority sectors, there is a moderate degree of IIT in automotives (26.1), electronics (24.5), and ICT (21.9).

As measured by the index of IIT, Cambodia's integration with the rest of ASEAN is weak. The average for the priority sectors is 6.8, the highest being the fisheries sector in which there is more intrinsic variety.

The Indonesian economy is mildly integrated with ASEAN as a result of significant levels of IIT in the automotive (39.9) and rubber-based (38) sectors. Indonesia needs to import many components for its car industry. There are mild levels of IIT in the ICT (29.8), electronics (28.9), and wood-based (26.8) sectors. There is very low IIT in the agro-based sector (16.6), which is the dominant employer of labour. This is to be expected, since there is low intrinsic variety in this sector.

The degree of integration of Laos with the rest of ASEAN is weak, since the average index is only 2.3. The wood-based sector has the highest value in excess of 10, and this is due to two-way trade in cases, boxes and drums (HS4415) where the index is 70.3. Because Laos is land-locked, there is zero IIT in fisheries, where there is high degree of intrinsic variety.

Excluding Singapore, Malaysia has the highest IIT for seven of the nine priority sectors. It also has the highest country average IIT of 41.5. The products which are responsible for this are healthcare (53.3), ICT (51.4), electronics (48.1) and rubber-based (45.8). Within the healthcare sector, there are four products for which Malaysia has an IIT index exceeding 90: perfumes and toilet paper (HS3303), sanitary towels and tampons (HS4818); contact lenses (HS9001); and mechanical therapy devices (HS9019).

The average IIT index for Myanmar is less than unity. The only products with significant IIT are in the healthcare sector, liquorice root (25.5) (HS1211), lipsticks (24.9) (HS3304), and in the electronics sector, apparatus less than 100 volts (HS6537).

The Philippines is weakly integrated with ASEAN because the average IIT index is only 18.5. The ICT sector exhibits mild integration with an index of 27.2, the most prominent component being aerial and aerial reflectors (88.7) (HS8529). These are followed by rubber-based products (25), and electronics (22.4).

Singapore is a special case because so much of its trade comprises re-exports. A hypothetical entrepôt economy that re-exported all its imports after adding 20 per cent value to them would have an IIT index of 90.1. Singapore's actual index is 37.8. When we exclude sectors based on natural resources (agro, fisheries, rubber and wood-based), of which Singapore has very little, the index rises to 41. The corresponding index for Malaysia is 45. This suggests that there is a similar degree of integration of Singapore and Malaysia with ASEAN.

Thailand has an average IIT index of 33.5. The sector with the highest index is rubber-based products at 47.1. Within this sector, rubber parts (HS8437) has an index of 98.2, close to its maximum value. The agro-based sector has a low value of 14.7 because Thailand is a major exporter, but not importer, of rice.

Vietnam has a similar IIT index to the Philippines, at 19. The sector with the highest index is wood-based, 32.3, the most significant component being cases, boxes and crates (96) (HS4415).

5.5. Intra-industry Trade by Priority Sector

It should be noted that if an economy does not possess the capacity to produce a given product, its exports of that product will be zero, and its index of its IIT will also be zero. Accordingly, we expect the least developed members of ASEAN to engage in low levels of IIT in those sectors dominated by manufacturing.

As expected, agro-based and textiles sectors have the lowest levels of IIT because their products have the least intrinsic variety. Their indices are also the lowest in each country.

The countries with significant IIT in the automotive, electronics, and ICT sectors will be those with both the relevant domestic industry to generate the ability to export, and high incomes to generate the demand for imports: Singapore, Malaysia, Indonesia, Thailand, Brunei all figure prominently in these three sectors.

There is high intrinsic variety in fisheries and a high demand for fish as a source of protein in ASEAN. We expect a low level of IIT in Laos, which has no access to the sea and must rely on imports, and Brunei, which has high real wages supported by exports of oil which generates a high demand for net imports of fish products.

There is a universal demand for healthcare, and we expect low levels of IIT in those countries with low capacity for domestic manufacture. Cambodia, Laos, and Myanmar fall into this category.

ASEAN countries are traditional sources of natural rubber. Natural rubber is combined with imported synthetic rubber to produce many products. We expect a high level of IIT for rubber-based products by those countries that are both a source of natural rubber and that have the manufacturing capacity to make rubber products from natural and imported synthetic rubber. This includes Thailand, Singapore, Malaysia, and Indonesia.

As in the case of rubber products, we expect IIT for wood-based products to be important in countries with timber resources and the manufacturing capacity to process them using imported components. This includes Thailand, Malaysia, Vietnam, and Indonesia.

5.6. The Relationship between RCA and IIT

Table 4.9 relates the index of RCA to the index of horizontal IIT for each sector in which each country has an RCA greater than unity. It is based on a combination of Tables 4.6 and 4.8. This comparison excludes Brunei and Cambodia, because these two countries have RCA in only one product, textiles. The table shows that there is no consistent relationship between the ranking of the RCA of a priority sector and the ranking of the amount of IIT in that sector. This relationship is measured by Spearman's Formula for the Co-efficient of Rank Correlation. It is appropriate to correlate the rankings because the measures of RCA and IIT are necessarily inexact.

For example, in the case of Indonesia, the rank order for RCA is Agro 1; Wood-based 2; Fisheries 3; Rubber-based 4; Electronics 5. The rank order for IIT is Agro 5; Wood-based 3; Fisheries 4; Rubber-based 1; Electronics 2. The correlation co-efficient for these rank orders is −0.8.

Table 4.9 shows that in only three of the eight countries which have RCA in more than one sector is there a positive correlation between the relative strength of RCA and the relative index of IIT in that sector.

6. Conclusion

ASEAN countries trade more with the rest of the world than they do with each other. This is to be expected since the natural resource base and level of industrial development of many ASEAN countries is the same. Seven of the ten ASEAN members have negative balances of trade with the other three, but this is not a matter of concern, given the importance of the rest of the world in their total trade.

This low degree of interdependence is not due to high tariff barriers against fellow ASEAN countries. This is because the average tariff rate on goods from other ASEAN countries (the average CEPT rate) is only 3.71 per cent, while the average rate on goods from non-ASEAN countries enjoying MFN status is 10.52 per cent. The average quoted tariffs might considerably understate the true average tariffs. The non-tariff barriers must be taken into account.

Table 4.9
The Ranking of Priority Sectors by RCA and IIT for ASEAN

Country	Sectoral Rank of RCA, IIT					Rank Correlation
Indonesia	A 1,5	W 2,3	F 3,4	R 4,1	E 5,2	−0.8
Laos	W 1,1	R 2,3	A 3, 2			+0.5
Malaysia	A 1,4	E 2,2	W 3,3	I 4,1		−0.8
Myanmar	F 1,2	A 2,1	W 3,3			+0.5
Philippines	A 1,3	F 2,2	I 3,1			−1
Singapore	E 1,2	I 2,1				−1
Thailand	F 1,4	E 2,3	R 3,1	T 4,6	W 5,5	I 6,2 +0.3
Vietnam	F 1,3	R 2,2	W 3,1			−1

Notes: A = Agro-based; E = Electronics; F = Fisheries; I = ICT; R = Rubber-based;
T = Textiles; W = Wood-based.
Source: Tables 4.6 and 4.8.

For the priority sectors, the automotive sector has the highest CEPT and MFN tariff rate, at 5.72 and 19.17 per cent, respectively. The sector with the lowest tariff rates is the healthcare sector, with respective rates of 2.12 and 5.08 per cent.

The country with the lowest tariff is Singapore, which has zero CEPT and MFN tariffs, and thus a zero margin of preference for ASEAN countries. In the case of textiles and garments, Indonesia has the highest margin of preference of 10 per cent for ASEAN countries. In the case of automotive products, Malaysia has the highest margin of preference of 15 per cent.

Singapore's zero tariff regime causes its economy to be highly integrated with the world and ASEAN economies. This and the country's high wages and absence of natural resources lead to a high degree of intra-industry trade (highest for electronics and ICT). Reflecting low tariffs on healthcare and ICT, Malaysia also has a high degree of intra-industry trade in these products. As a result of their low incomes and state of industrial development relative to the rest of ASEAN, the countries with the lowest levels of intra-industry trade are Myanmar and Laos.

The largest values of intra-ASEAN trade are in electronics (US$57 billion), ICT (US$52 billion), and automotives (US$7 billion). However, for these products the index of RCA is relatively low (a maximum of 2.8 in the case of Malaysian electronics, and 2 for Malaysian ICT) and, in the case of automotives, less than unity for all countries, indicating no RCA. This suggests that the countries that export these products within ASEAN do not have a comparative advantage by world standards, and are being enabled to export to other ASEAN countries by the preferential trading agreement and other close ties between them. In particular, relatively new members of ASEAN, Brunei and Cambodia, have RCA in only one product — textiles.

As far as the relationship between RCA and IIT is concerned, it does not seem to be the case that countries have RCA in the products for which they conduct a large amount of IIT.

NOTE

This chapter is a summarized version of the REPSF Project Report 06/001a entitled "An Investigation into the Measures Affecting the Integration of ASEAN's Priority Sectors (Phase 2): Review of Regional Trade and Available Tariff Rate Data".

REFERENCES

ASEAN Secretariat. *ASEAN Statistical Yearbook 2005*. Jakarta: ASEAN Secretariat, 2005.

———. *ASEAN Statistical Yearbook 2006*. Jakarta: ASEAN Secretariat, 2006.

Austria, Myrna. "The Pattern of Intra-ASEAN Trade in The Priority Goods Sectors. REPSF Project No 03/006e". Jakarta: ASEAN Secretariat, 2004.

Krugman, Paul R. and Maurice Obstfeld. *International Economics, Theory and Policy*. 6th ed. Boston: Addison Wesley, 2003.

Lloyd, Peter and Penny Smith. "Global Economic Challenges to ASEAN Integration and Competitiveness: A Prospective Look". REPSF Project No. 03/006a. Jakarta: ASEAN Secretariat, 2004.

OECD. "Intra-industry and Intra-firm Trade and the Internalization of Production". www.unstats.un.org. 2002.

5

Non-tariff Barriers to Trade in the ASEAN Priority Goods Sectors

Loreli C. de Dios

1. Background

Non-tariff barriers (NTBs)[1] have been acknowledged by ASEAN members to be as critical as tariffs in the pursuit of regional trade and integration objectives. Members first committed to their minimization alongside tariffs in the 1977 Agreement on ASEAN Preferential Trading Arrangements. This was reiterated in the 1987 Memorandum of Understanding on the Standstill and Rollback on Non-Tariff Barriers, and again upon the creation of the ASEAN Free Trade Area (AFTA), when a 2003 deadline for elimination was set. Under the broader objective of an ASEAN Economic Community, declarations by the AFTA Council and ASEAN Economic Ministers were reinforced by the recommendation of the High-Level Task Force (HLTF) on ASEAN Economic Integration for members "to ensure transparency on non-tariff measures (NTMs) and eliminate those that are barriers to trade". Accordingly, the Roadmap for Integration of ASEAN specified that NTBs are to be eliminated by 2010 for the ASEAN-5, 2012 for the Philippines, and 2015/2018 by CLMV.

A work programme for this purpose has largely been implemented: (a) an ASEAN Database of Non-Tariff Measures was established based on members' notifications; (b) clear criteria were set to identify measures that are classified as barriers to trade; (c) a clear and definitive work programme for the removal of the barriers by 2005 was set; (d) the WTO Agreements on Technical Barriers to Trade, Sanitary and Phyto-Sanitary Measures, and Import Licensing Procedures were adopted and implementation guidelines were developed. A mechanism for addressing complaints was also instituted. Although it is unclear whether the work programme envisioned the actual removal of trade barriers within its defined time-frame, it has produced another work programme for the removal of trade barriers. Working definitions of NTM types were adopted from the UNCTAD Coding Scheme for Trade Control Measures,[2] consisting of the following:

- Para-tariff measures: customs surcharges, additional taxes and charges, decreed customs valuation
- Price control measures: administrative pricing, voluntary export restraint, variable charges
- Finance measures: advance payment requirements, regulations concerning terms of payment for imports, transfer delays and queueing
- Quantity control measures: non-automatic licensing, quotas, prohibitions, export restraint arrangements, enterprise-specific restrictions
- Monopolistic measures: single channel for imports, compulsory national services
- Technical measures: technical regulations, pre-shipment inspection, special customs formalities

Excluded are internal charges on imports, anti-dumping and countervailing measures, foreign exchange allocation, and automatic licensing.

There is no evidence of compliance under the 1977 and 1987 accords, and no detailed implementation plan except in the case of customs procedures and technical standards. However, there is agreement on the broad process of NTM elimination. Decisions taken in ASEAN Meetings on Non-Tariff Barriers from 1999 to 2004 included the verification of information on NTMs, review of working definitions, prioritizing products and NTMs, design of a work programme, and obtaining a mandate from the ASEAN Economic Ministers to implement it.[3] Several approaches to NTM elimination were suggested.

In February 2004 the Senior Economic Officials Meeting proposed the drafting of a roadmap for the elimination of NTMs in the eleven priority sectors. A definitive work programme for eliminating "unjustifiable and unnecessary" NTMs was designed, based on criteria endorsed by the Nineteenth AFTA Council in 2005 as follows:

(i) NTMs that are non-transparent, discriminatory in application, without scientific basis, and where an alternative less restrictive measure is available, would require immediate elimination (red box).

(ii) NTMs that are transparent but discriminatory in application which nullify or impair some benefits or obligations of the country, that affect highly traded products in the region or under the nine priority sectors, that cannot be clearly justified or identified as a barrier, would be subject to negotiation (amber box).

(iii) NTMs that are transparent, non-discriminatory in application, have no alternative measure, have scientific basis, are imposed for public health and safety or religious or national security reasons, are WTO-consistent and reasonable such as sanitary and phytosanitary and environment regulations, are justified and could be maintained (green box).

2. Objectives

This chapter thus seeks to identify the non-tariff measures affecting trade in goods among ASEAN members in the nine priority goods sectors, namely fisheries, agro-based, wood-based, textiles and apparel, healthcare, rubber-based, automotive, electronics, and information and communication technology or ICT.[4] To gauge the significance of NTMs, price impact estimates from various analysts using both the econometric and price differential approaches were assembled. Some implications of an increasing regionalism and bilateralism on ASEAN liberalization commitments were also considered.

3. Methodology

The commodities covered in each priority sector[5] are classified using the 2002 version of the Harmonized Commodity Description and Coding System (HS), an international product nomenclature used for national customs tariff and statistics by government contracting parties to the HS Convention. ASEAN adopted a common scheme at the eight-digit level of the HS, referred to as the ASEAN Harmonized Tariff Nomenclature (AHTN). Commodity coverage in the priority sectors was defined by the members and excludes a substantial number of AHTN lines in such sectors as the agro-based, wood-based, and information and communication technology (ICT), for example, sensitive agricultural products.

Using the latest available NTM inventories from both the ASEAN NTM Database and UNCTAD Trade Analysis Information System (TRAINS), NTM incidence is estimated through a frequency count of the number of eight-digit AHTN commodity lines on which an NTM is imposed. These are expressed as percentages of the total number of eight-digit AHTN lines per sector. The frequency estimates basically assume that NTMs can be discretely counted and are of equal weight or impact, the eight-digit AHTN line is one single commodity, and the databases are accurate and current. Used goods are considered new, and selective NTMs are treated as general in application. In many cases, the AHTNs were not specified or were inaccurately described, or only the four-digit AHTN was given. Several goods were affected by multiple NTMs, while certain commodities were classified under more than one sector.

The ASEAN NTM Database is based on official notifications by member countries to the ASEAN Secretariat. Essential details such as the intent or manner of implementation, which are crucial to validating which are "unjustifiable and unnecessary", are however not always provided. Since the classifications were assigned by the members themselves, in a number of cases they are ambiguous, while in other instances more than one NTM is imposed by the same official issuance. The UNCTAD TRAINS collates information from numerous sources of about 119 countries. Some NTMs were applied at a level not entirely coinciding with a tariff line, while others only partially covered the tariff line. Other drawbacks (Ando and Fujii 2004) are that: (1) underlying information is reported by governments but not confirmed; (2) reported NTM types are inconsistent between countries; and (3) no information is given on the types of technical measures.

The ASEAN NTM Database covers twenty-four NTM types that are characterized more generally and for disaggregated commodity headings, in contrast to the UNCTAD TRAINS that covers ninety highly disaggregated NTM types for commodities at the two-digit AHTN level, yielding a larger number of measures that appear to be more encompassing.

4. Estimates of NTM Incidence

The ASEAN NTM Database revealed the following NTMs in the nine priority sectors, based on the UNCTAD Coding Scheme for Trade Control Measures.[6]

1400	Tariff quota duties
2200	Additional taxes and charges
2290	Additional charges n.e.s.

2300	Internal taxes and charges on imports
3100	Administrative pricing
5100	Automatic licensing
6100	Non-automatic licensing
6110	License with no specific ex-ante criteria
6170	Prior authorization for sensitive products
6200	Quotas
6240	Quotas linked with export performance
6270	Quotas for sensitive products
6300	Prohibition
6310	Total prohibition
6710	Selective approval of importers
7100	Single channel for imports
7120	Sole importing agency
8100	Technical regulations
8110	Product characteristic requirements
8120	Marking requirements
8130	Labelling requirements
8140	Packaging requirements
8150	Testing, inspection, quarantine reqs.
8200	Pre-shipment inspection

Frequency tabulations for each sector are found in the Appendix.[7] Prevalent or extensive (i.e., geographically widespread or applied by several members) and sector-intensive (i.e., affecting the majority of eight-digit AHTN lines classified in each priority sector) NTMs pervade the fisheries, agro-based, automotive, and ICT sectors which are restricted by non-automatic licensing and technical regulations; electronics which is ruled by non-automatic licensing, prohibitions, and technical regulations; and healthcare on which non-automatic licensing, prohibitions, technical regulations, and labelling, testing and inspection are imposed. NTMs such as technical regulations are geographically widespread but not line-intensive in the rubber-based sector. The opposite is seen in wood-based and textiles and apparel, where NTMs are not widespread but affect substantial proportions of AHTN lines in each sector. Curiously, pre-shipment inspection is still implemented in Indonesia, which contravenes WTO rules. Myanmar subjects all commercial imports to non-automatic licensing and exacts quotas linked with export performance on all goods, while the Philippines requires imports of government agencies and goods under government loans and credit to be shipped on national flag vessels. Vietnam imposes tariff quota duties.

Frequency estimates using the 2004 ASEAN NTM Database (excluding Lao PDR which did not submit its list at the time) enable a comparison with the 2006 inventory, although the former covered products that were excluded from the priority sector listing, i.e., sensitive agricultural commodities. The comparisons generally show that: (1) technical regulations are not as pervasive in fisheries; (2) quotas and prohibitions in the agro-based sector are more widespread and pervasive, and NTMs are more varied, mainly because the product coverage is also more wide-ranging and includes sensitive agricultural products; (3) the same NTMs affect wood-based products despite the wider product coverage in 2004; (4) very few NTM types characterize rubber-based products; (5) except for the absence of prohibition, there was little difference in the textiles and apparel sector; (6) quotas and prohibitions were less pervasive in healthcare; (7) prohibitions and technical regulations were less widespread for the automotive sector, but this is probably because of the much narrower product coverage in 2004; (8) non-automatic licensing and prohibitions were also less prevalent in electronics, owing also to limited product coverage; (9) technical regulations were less common in ICT also for the same reason. Thus, highly similar NTM types and roughly the same number are evident, which is expected in view of the small number of revisions to the members' notifications. The same 100 per cent coverage by the same countries was also evident.

The only available ASEAN-wide documentation of NTMs prior to the NTM Database was a commissioned survey[8] in 1988 of company officials in leading industries in Brunei, Indonesia, Malaysia, Philippines, Singapore, Thailand, and Vietnam to identify non-tariff and customs procedural barriers. The industries covered were processed food, healthcare, textiles, chemicals, automotive, oil and gas, iron and steel, machinery, and electronics, which largely conform to the priority sectors. The results indicate poor compliance with the 1977, 1987, and other similar accords to remove NTMs. Respondents' main concerns were in the area of permits and licences (39.5 per cent), compliance with regulations (24 per cent), and monopolistic measures (21 per cent). In the majority of cases, companies were subject to heavy health and safety regulatory requirements. The issues with customs procedures were inconsistency in the application of tariff classifications (33 per cent), cumbersome and unclear declaration and clearance procedures (23 per cent), inconsistent valuation (24 per cent), facilitation fees for a normal service (18 per cent), and lack of transparency in policy and procedures. These attest to numerous regulatory and procedural barriers to trade.

5. Estimates of NTM Impact

A literature search yielded NTM impact estimates obtained either through econometric or gravity models or the calculation of price differentials per commodity. Dean et al. (2006) focused on core NTMs consisting of import quotas, prohibitions, import licences, and voluntary export restraints. From a simple differentiated product model that specifies a direct relationship between NTMs and retail prices, a price gap specification was derived to explain the observed price gaps given observed differences in local mark-ups (proxied by wage and rent), transport costs (proxied by distance), tariffs and non-tariff trade barriers. The coefficient of the last variable was the estimate of the average price premium due to restrictive NTMs. Least squares estimates using pooled cross-city, cross-product data showed that except for apparel where the impact was negative, NTMs in five ASEAN countries (Indonesia, Malaysia, Philippines, Singapore, and Thailand) pushed prices upward by 73 per cent to 205 per cent in fruits and vegetables, 82 per cent to 109 per cent in bovine meat, and 93 per cent to 112 per cent in processed food. The authors conclude that endogeneity of NTMs, which understates their price impact, must be incorporated explicitly to produce better estimates.

Using the same methodology, Andriamananjara et al. (2004) estimated NTM price wedges with log linear regression where the coefficients on the NTM dummy variables were transformed into percentage mark-ups in price by taking their anti-log and subtracting one. The percentage premia on products restricted by NTMs in Southeast Asia relative to the price of those products in countries without NTMs were 49 per cent for vegetable oils and fats and 67 per cent for paper products.

Kee, Nicita, and Olarreaga (2006) econometrically estimated the *ad valorem* equivalents (AVE) or the impact on the domestic price of imported goods of NTMs at the six-digit HS level for 117 countries. NTMs were of two broad types: the core, consisting of price and quantity control, technical, and monopolistic measures; and agricultural domestic support. The impact of NTMs on trade flows was first estimated by predicting imports using factor endowments and observing their deviations in the presence of NTMs. Gravity-type variables such as distance and an islands dummy were also introduced. The quantity impact was converted into price effects by moving along the import demand curve using previously estimated import demand elasticities. Data for three ASEAN countries show generally low AVEs in Indonesia ranging from 0.1 per cent to 7.4 per cent in the priority sectors, and much higher AVEs in Malaysia, ranging from 11.7 per cent to 58.5 per cent, and in the Philippines, ranging from 6.3 per cent to 60.5 per cent.

They also found that tariffs and NTMs reinforce rather than substitute for each other.

Ando and Fujii (2004) and Ando (2005) measured the economic impact of core and non-core NTMs in terms of tariff equivalents (TE). First, price differentials induced by tariffs and NTMs per commodity were calculated as the difference between the domestic producer price of domestic substitutes and the cost-insurance-freight (CIF) price of imports divided by the CIF price of imports. The tariff was subtracted from this to obtain the price differential due to NTMs. Next, this was decomposed into five types of NTMs, by regressing the TE against the frequency ratio for each NTM type for each commodity, to yield coefficients of the price distorting effect of each NTM type. Finally, TE by NTM type for twenty-one sectors at the four-digit level was obtained by multiplying the coefficients estimated from the regression by the frequency ratio per NTM type per commodity sector. NTM types were classified into core (price control measures and quantity control) and non-core (automatic licensing, monopolistic, and technical measures). They found that: (1) positive coefficients exist for all types of NTMs, implying price-distorting, import price-increasing, and domestic protection effects; (2) price control measures have the largest price-distorting effect; (3) quantity control measures show a much smaller price-distorting effect. In addition, countries participating in free trade agreements (FTAs) have high TEs of overall NTMs. Since they already apply lower preferential tariff rates within the group, they use such NTMs as technical measures to protect domestic industries.

Their estimates for four ASEAN countries show substantial overall tariff equivalents in the priority sectors. In Indonesia, TEs ranged from 27.5 per cent for food products to 92.6 per cent for vegetable products to 102.2 per cent for live animals and products, mostly due to technical regulations. Malaysia showed a 65.9 per cent TE for vegetable products and a 21 per cent TE for live animals, also because of standards. TEs for the same sectors in Singapore were much higher at 257.2 per cent and 150.3 per cent respectively, accounted for mainly by automatic licensing procedures. The other sectors in both Malaysia and Singapore had low TE estimates. The highest TEs were registered in Thailand, with 596.6 per cent in animal and vegetable oils and 132.4 per cent in food products mostly owing to automatic licensing; technical standards for live animals and vegetable products contributed to 79.6 per cent and 84.6 per cent respectively.

Fane and Condon (1996) collected price comparisons from different sources to estimate nominal rates of protection for individual commodities in Indonesia. Estimates ranged widely from –34 per cent to 146 per cent for agricultural products, –78 per cent to 1 per cent for wood, –71 per cent to

45 per cent for yarns, −57 per cent to 42 per cent for automotives. In Vietnam, the Center for International Economics (1999) computed a 289 per cent premium over the import price for motor cars, compared with a tariff of 210 per cent.

For the Philippines, de Dios (1987, 1993, 1997) calculated the ratio of domestic to border price of 180 commodities from 1985 to 1992 to examine the price effect of a comprehensive unilateral trade liberalization programme undertaken in the early 1980s. Domestic prices were based on wholesale domestic prices, while border prices were unit import values in Hong Kong and the Philippines for regulated and liberalized commodities, respectively. The varied patterns of price and quantity movements were explained by differentiating the goods according to those with net price ratios (i.e., Pd/Pb less 1) either below or above unity, and import levels below or in excess of US$100,000. The resulting typology was represented as four quadrants depending on the combination, to determine the common characteristics of goods whose prices and imports behaved similarly:

- Quadrant I (upper right): The combination of above-unity net price ratios and substantial imports characterized one-third of all restricted goods. Relative prices exceeded tariffs for most. Imports were considerable because of inadequate local production.
- Quadrant II (lower right): Relative net prices were below unity but imports were sizeable for tradeables with quality differences or imperfect substitutes.
- Quadrant III (lower left): Goods with net price ratios below unity and insubstantial or zero imports, were either non-tradeable or exportable so that prices were not directly affected by tariff or import policy changes but rather by demand patterns. Liberalization was redundant for this group.
- Quadrant IV (upper left): Goods whose domestic prices were greater than border prices and imports were negligible consisted of the majority of regulated commodities, and were non-tradeable, highly perishable, or had high weight-to-value ratios or high domestic landed costs, i.e., natural import substitutes. Price ratios exceeded tariffs for most. This included examples of long-protected goods, and imports were low for those that have been tightly restricted, eliminating the threat of imports.

Where tariffs exceeded price ratios, two explanations were suggested: (1) either quality differences were large and were reflected in low domestic prices, or (2) smuggling rendered the tariffs redundant, especially for regulated goods. Where imports were zero, the tariff was also redundant.

The assessment concluded that the level of relative prices and imports could be explained by the characteristics of the goods. However their movements after liberalization were not always in the expected direction. One reason offered was time lags depending on the goods. Or the tariffs that replaced the restrictions served to inhibit imports, enabling local producers to maintain the same price differences. Similarly, the price-disciplining effect of imports was not realized because of substantial quality differences. Another reason for some liberalized goods to appear in the upper right quadrant was that domestic costs were rendered high by extraneous factors rather than inefficient production methods, disabling producers from competing with imports. Unfavourable domestic conditions such as poor infrastructure deterred producers from responding positively to liberalization.

6. Implications of Multiple Trade Agreements

The recent proliferation of regional, bilateral, preferential or free trade agreements has become noticeable in view of their rapid increase, scope beyond tariffs or merchandise trade liberalization, overlap, cross-section of participants and regions, and depth of issue coverage. Regionalism or bilateralism now seems to be the preferred approach, in contrast to the unilateral trend that accounted for about 60 per cent of developing-country trade liberalization (World Bank, cited in Sally and Sen 2005). Currently there are 145 FTAs involving Asian and Pacific countries. Of this number, only 31 were notified to the WTO. Of the 114 that are not WTO-notified, 10 are under implementation, 25 have been signed, 31 are under negotiation while 40 are being proposed (www.aric.adb.org).

Southeast Asian countries have only one agreement, ASEAN, which is WTO-notified. As individual countries or as a group, Southeast Asia has twenty-six trade agreements with other Asian countries or groups, of which only four are WTO-notified, and twenty with non-Asian countries or groups, of which only one is WTO-notified. Most of these are under negotiation or at the proposal stage. There are seven trade agreements involving ASEAN as a group: two, the AFTA and the one with China, are under implementation; one, with Korea, has been signed; two, with India and Japan, have Framework Agreements; one, with Australia-New Zealand, is under negotiation; and one, with the EU, has been proposed and is under study. Singapore is the member that has the most trade agreements regardless of status as well as number under implementation, followed closely by Thailand in terms of total count.

Regionalism is a result of a combination of positive and negative influences. In Asia the emergence of bilateralism is attributed by Sally and Sen (2005) to the "perceived inability of the WTO to yield a multilateral consensus on major trade liberalization issues", as well as the "perception that bilateralism could be a building block towards global free trade". In their analysis, ASEAN cooperation at the WTO has practically collapsed compared to a decade ago. An enlarged and consequently unwieldy ASEAN, with wider inter-country gaps, have led to distinctly different national trade and economic policies and responses to crises. Yet non-tariff issues have remained even as the WTO work programme has challenged politically sensitive domestic regulations. Furthermore, WTO decision-making has become more politicized and polarized with expanded membership among less developed countries, making significant multilateral liberalization difficult and slow to achieve. These trends splintered ASEAN and made national differences more pronounced. Thus responses have been "go-it-alone" bilateral FTAs, or separate ways in the WTO (Sally and Sen 2005).

The provisions of seventeen FTAs governing NTMs show that only AFTA specified a time-frame for the elimination of NTMs while the ASEAN-Korea FTA prescribed the identification of NTMs for immediate elimination, and the Asia-Pacific Trade Agreement states that NTMs are to be relaxed gradually. The ASEAN-China FTA only generally mentions that NTMs shall come under negotiations. The rest adopt a stand not to introduce, adopt, institute, or maintain non-tariff measures or restrictions except in accordance with the WTO, to ensure that NTMs are transparent or that their application does not create unnecessary obstacles or minimizes possible distortions to trade.

6.1. General Implications

The profusion of trade agreements has given rise to analyses of their impact on pre-existing arrangements. At one end, a positive or complementary relationship exists between regionalism and the multilateral trading system because, as Mathews (2004) observes: (a) regional trade agreements (RTAs) strengthen the WTO by moving faster while sharing its goals; (b) smaller regional groups may tackle new areas and facilitate multilateral agreements more effectively; (c) despite fears of trade diversion, trade creation due to faster market access liberalization characterizes major RTAs; (d) RTAs facilitate the integration of developing countries into the world economy.

In Asia, Rajan and Sen (2004) observe that FTAs are increasingly regarded as effective means for trade liberalization among "like-minded" trading partners.

Such agreements extend past merchandise trade liberalization, are not restricted to the immediate neighbours, and have fewer members because of the depth of issues covered. They also ascribe the rush to form FTAs to: (i) "defensive" reasons, which can prevail over situations where the pace of integration is held back by the least willing member; (ii) political momentum for economies, regional alliances, and the WTO to hasten liberalization and integration; (iii) the demonstration effect; (iv) the need to exploit positions as "hubs of overlapping arrangements", and (v) key diplomatic and security needs.

They also note that the new regionalism involves multiple memberships and has been driven by the more open economies in Asia, exerting pressure on counterparts to follow suit. FTAs could actually complement the economic integration process in ASEAN (Sally and Sen 2005) by encouraging individual members to undertake domestic reforms to become more competitive, on the argument that economic diversity requires a concerted approach to integration.

At the opposite end, RTAs are a cause for concern for several reasons. (a) They fragment the multilateral trading system into a number of competing blocs, and the market power they acquire as they expand induces them to raise external barriers to influence terms of trade (Mathews 2004). They become a stumbling block if preferential access demotivates them to liberalize multilaterally (Rajan and Sen 2004). Being preferential, they discriminate against non-members and cause trade diversion. (b) Regionalism intensifies as non-members attempt to minimize the costs of trade diversion while both members and non-members seek the benefits of being secondary hubs by forming RTAs to maintain the value of their existing preferential access, resulting in disincentives for consolidating existing FTAs and overlapping complex agreements (Rajan and Sen 2004) that contradict the provisions of the WTO. A notable example is differing rules of origin (ROOs) that increase protectionism as a result (Mathews 2004). ROOs are meant to prevent trade deflection, but their complexity implies high compliance costs, a burden on origin-certifying institutions, and rent-seeking opportunities (Rajan and Sen 2004). (c) Discriminatory preferences and the time and money spent on negotiations and the implementation of these agreements distort markets and demand scarce administrative and negotiating resources and distract attention from multilateral negotiations (Sally and Sen 2005). The need to prove eligibility for preferences increases business costs instead. (d) Cross membership in multiple FTAs causes confusion about their rules, obligations and incentives, and contradictory commitments (Rajan and Sen 2004). Negotiations with similar partners can create inconsistencies and problems managing external trade relationships given the wide range of rules on exclusions for certain sectors and commodities (Sen 2004). (e) Domination of the initial set of

FTAs by middle- and high-income countries could worsen the development divide between rich and poor countries by diverting trade and investment from the latter (Rajan and Sen 2004).

6.2. Implications on ASEAN Liberalization Commitments

The impact of trade agreements on intra-regional trade depends on the degree of liberalization achieved that is in turn influenced by members' compliance with the terms of the agreements. In spite of measures towards greater economic integration in ASEAN, Sally and Sen (2005) noted that the share of intra-ASEAN trade has been stagnant over 1993–2003. The relative ineffectiveness of AFTA is attributed by Rajan and Sen (2004) to the number of exceptions from the Common Effective Preferential Tariff (CEPT) Scheme, i.e., temporary exclusion, sensitive agricultural and general exceptions, aside from backsliding by some members in their commitments. Manchin and Pelkmans-Balaoing (2006) confirm that the AFTA preferential scheme is of little consequence to intra-regional trade, and that margins in the low and high ranges have an adverse effect on trade instead: in the case of the former, administrative costs of obtaining preferences exceed their benefits, while for the latter high incidence of NTMs, negligible supply of the product within the region, or redundancy caused by other regional import substitution instruments cause low trade. They conclude that preferences stimulate trade only when preferential tariffs are at least 25 per cent lower than the MFN rates, implying a 10–25 per cent cost of requesting preferences within AFTA. Moreover, the zero margin between MFN and CEPT rates for most of intra-ASEAN products and continuous liberalization of MFN tariffs mean that low CEPT rates do not yield any significant advantage.

Yet regional and bilateral trade agreements have proliferated recently and negotiations are ongoing for more — in which ASEAN members are taking part — implying that these offer benefits that are not found elsewhere. Bilaterals allow greater control and lower transactions costs compared to multilaterals. Accordingly, ASEAN leaders implicitly endorsed the "2 plus X" approach, whereby any two members can choose to integrate certain sectors faster bilaterally. Thailand and Singapore, which has entered into numerous trade agreements despite being already liberal, are the two most enthusiastic liberalizers that are negotiating separate agreements because they perceive ASEAN negotiations to be slow (Rajan and Sen 2004). Indeed, the removal of NTMs by richer countries may have a stronger impact in the region, in view of the Kee, Nicita, and Olarreaga (2006) results that the average *ad valorem* equivalent of core NTMs increases with GDP per capita, making trade restrictiveness of NTMs in richer countries more visible.

Rajan and Sen (2004) consider ASEAN to be well placed to reap the benefits of being the de facto hub, as China, India, and Japan are due to fully implement FTAs with ASEAN by 2010, 2012, and 2011 respectively. Large-country counterparts in a trade agreement mean an expanded market for ASEAN products and more sources of cheap raw materials, but it also means more, and efficient, competitors in the region. The net impact of this configuration has yet to be seen. But to capitalize on this potential as a hub, they stress that ASEAN must maintain cohesion and deepen integration.

The impact of regionalism or bilateralism on commitments to liberalize within AFTA would nevertheless ultimately depend on the seriousness of ASEAN members in delivering on their obligations. Different factors influence the outcome in opposite directions. Successful liberalization within other RTAs is one likely positive influence on ASEAN if members perceive these successes to be worth replicating, that is, net national gains are certain. Membership in multiple RTAs with similar liberalization provisions and counterparts, however, implies the need to monitor the fulfilment of obligations by members under each agreement, contributing to higher transactions costs.

At the same time, the WTO neutrality rule disallows any tightening of restrictions against non-members and allows loosening among members, but does not disallow pre-existing restrictions. Hence restrictions that are in place at the time agreements are signed may be maintained by contracting parties, and this in fact characterizes the AFTA. Perhaps because NTMs may be used as a bargaining chip in negotiating the terms of other RTAs, there will be a tendency to hold on to them. Their non-transparency and discretionary application also make them difficult to monitor.

Increasing multilateral liberalization that further lowers MFN tariffs also puts pressure on newer preferential trade agreements to be more beneficial. Depending on which outpaces the other, liberalization could proceed because of this "competition". In a sea of RTAs, for instance, decisions would be based on an excess of the difference between MFN and RTA effective tariffs over the cost of proving eligibility for preferences.

A basic underlying factor influencing the delivery of commitments is the structure of the RTA (de Dios 2004). The experience of older RTAs indicates that objectives are achieved if the RTA is either self-enforcing, or "pools sovereignty" (i.e., the joint exercise of sovereignty, or a strong central authority) in which RTA rules are transposed into national law. In turn, these are affected by: (a) size of organization, because fewer members make benefit calculations and compliance monitoring or credible enforcement easier; (b) similarity in economic characteristics, which affects targets and commitments; homogeneous groups have similar needs but may also compete for the same markets; (c) nature and depth of commitments, because treaties may pool economic sovereignty with legally binding contracts specifying rules and consequences for non-compliance from the start, or compliance may be voluntary; (d) enforcement mechanisms; (e) prior strong intra-regional trade, since repeated transactions make self-enforcing agreements more likely owing to a desire to maintain good relations and the threat of retaliation. Intensive trade is due either to complementary production (given dissimilar factor endowments), or to trade in differentiated products owing to high incomes (given similar factor endowments).

Compliance enforcement mechanisms are therefore crucial: (i) where RTA rules take precedence over national law, compliance mechanisms are forceful; (ii) where agreements are limited to certain spheres and prescriptive, or decisions are taken only when a situation arises, or commitments are voluntary, compliance is likely to vary, and dispute settlement ineffective; (iii) formal mechanisms and arrangements are essential to institution-building as they improve on informal practices as well as instil a sense of obligation to the agreement by formally bringing countries under one jurisdiction. The effectiveness of enforcement in ASEAN is limited by the temptation to deviate from commitments, imperfect enforcement capacities, and a culture of non-confrontation where implicit or informal arrangements may take precedence over formal mechanisms (de Dios 2004).

Thus effective agreements counter the tendency for unilateral trade policy choices to be made, exert discipline credibly, and sustain membership. Obligations are honoured if incentives are compatible with the desired behaviour, or if net benefits are positive and clear. If net benefits are uncertain, not obvious, not immediate, or perceived to be negative or insubstantial, self-compliance and collective commitment are poor. This makes enforcement ineffective, ultimately affecting the attainment of objectives. Without external mechanisms, commitments need to be self-enforcing, and the best assurance of commitment is when parties view adherence to be in their mutual interest. If countries trade repeatedly, violations are deterred by a credible threat of subsequent retaliation.

7. Conclusion

In all countries, NTMs continue to exist in all sectors. The ASEAN NTM Database and UNCTAD TRAINS show a wide variety of NTMs in all nine priority sectors; in most cases regionally widespread NTMs of all types combined with intensive product coverage pervade the sector. In view of the estimation caveats, validating the notified NTMs would yield more definite estimates, but the absence of official objections to these database inventories seems to confirm their existence. There is also no evidence that the height and incidence of NTMs have dropped as deadlines for their elimination and reduction have been repeatedly missed.

NTMs are becoming significant restrictions to intra-ASEAN trade as tariff rates have fallen. A rough comparison between the maximum price impact estimates with maximum average most favoured nation (MFN) or CEPT rates in Table 5.1 demonstrates that NTMs could be binding and the

Table 5.1
MFN and CEPT Rates and NTM Impact Indicators
(In percentages)

Sector	Maximum average MFN tariff	Maximum average CEPT	Tariff Equivalent	Premia	Ad Valorem Equivalent
Fisheries	32.7	14.8			
Agro-based	26.8	7.5			
live animals & products			150.3	—	—
fruits & vegetables			—	205.0	—
vegetable oils			—	49.0	—
animal & vegetable oils			596.6	—	—
vegetable products			257.2	—	—
processed food			132.4	112.0	60.5
Wood-based	27.7	14.6			
wood products			6.7	9.18	50.6
Rubber-based	19.2	8.5			
rubber products			—	—	39.6
car tire				4.15	
Healthcare	11.3	4.7			
other chemical products			44.0	—	33.6
Textiles & apparel	37.4	11.4			
textiles			—	7.8	31.3
apparel			—	—	12.6
Automotive	39.9	9.8			
transport equipment			24.6	—	40.8
car, 1800, 4 cylinder CKD				5.3	
Electronics	18.8	10.2			
ICT	18.3	9.3			
electrical machinery			—	—	32.5
profl,scientific equipment			—	—	29.6
precision machinery			0.8	—	—

Sources: Oktaviani et al (2006); Ando and Fujii (2004), Kee, Nicita, and Olarreaga (2006), Dean et al. (2006), Andriamananjara et al. (2004).

excesses sizeable in particular sectors, negating CEPT objectives. Other studies observed that even when the margins between the MFN and CEPT are wide, trade is low due to the high incidence of NTMs.

Almost three decades have passed since commitments to NTM elimination were first enunciated by ASEAN, but action has not gone beyond numerous discussions on a work programme for their removal, illustrating a basic hesitation to act on commitments. An underlying factor found to influence the delivery of commitments is the structure of the organization (de Dios 2004). The experience of other RTAs indicates that objectives are achieved if the RTA is either self-enforcing, or "pools sovereignty" in which RTA rules are transposed into national law. In turn, these are affected by similarity in economic characteristics, nature and depth of commitments, enforcement mechanisms, and prior strong intra-regional trade. The effectiveness of enforcement in ASEAN is limited by the temptation to deviate from commitments, imperfect enforcement capacities, and a culture of non-confrontation where implicit or informal arrangements may take precedence over formal mechanisms.

ASEAN's disadvantage seems to be low incomes across the region and non-complementary production structures characteristic of similarly-endowed countries, which contribute to the cycle of weak intra-regional trade and poor compliance or self-enforcement. The lesson to be drawn from the experience of RTAs in which intra-regional trade expanded mainly due to income growth, is that ASEAN needs to make an extra effort to break out of this cycle. Focusing on particular products through a forceful drive to become low-cost producers is a step in the right direction, since the benefits of the RTA will depend on cost structures of members compared to those of non-members. The removal of trade barriers for these particular products is crucial, as this deepens integration and raises efficiencies that would give them a competitive edge. Gaining regional comparative advantage for specific "ASEAN products" would lead to larger extra-regional exports, bringing higher incomes that would advance intra-regional trade and help ASEAN extricate itself from the cycle. Unambiguous beneficial results of compliance would have a demonstration effect that would encourage replication in other sectors. The sectoral approach also makes the effort more manageable and acceptable to members, while results are more easily observed and quantified (de Dios 2004).

The need to meet regional trade objectives within ASEAN through full liberalization is assuming greater importance in the face of the proliferation of trade agreements — both those in which ASEAN is taking part and those outside ASEAN. Entering into other agreements seems to signal the capacity to deliver on commitments elsewhere, in view of the wide scope and depth of coverage of newer agreements. It also shows the desire to achieve results through other groups that are not possible or too slow under current arrangements. At the same time, since newer agreements must always be more liberal than pre-existing ones, there is pressure for current ones not to be left behind. Conversely, increasing multilateral liberalization induces newer preferential trade agreements to be more beneficial. But because restrictions that are in place at the time agreements are signed may be maintained by contracting parties, there may be a tendency to retain NTMs as a bargaining chip in negotiating the terms of other RTAs.

While the effectiveness of many newer agreements is not yet evident, successful liberalization within other RTAs is likely to positively influence ASEAN if members perceive those successes to be worth replicating and net national gains are certain. Undoubtedly, however, there is a cost to monitoring several overlapping arrangements and implementing obligations under each, particularly in proving compliance with rules of origin. Discriminatory preferences and transactions costs of negotiation and implementation may also distort markets. It is furthermore feared that bilateralism and preferential access discourage multilateral liberalization and the consolidation of existing FTAs instead, or creates inconsistencies.

The net impact of this configuration has yet to be seen. Whether ASEAN will bring itself to becoming a highly effective RTA will ultimately depend on the calculation by members of the relative net benefits of complying with commitments. After all, ASEAN was ahead of the regionalism trend and only needs to show results on commitments made decades ago. Notwithstanding the evidence of substantial adverse impacts of NTMs, individual ASEAN members must re-examine their intents against the direction they would like AFTA to take as a real free trade area in which goods flow unobstructed. This has serious implications for ASEAN economic integration.

APPENDIX

Table 5.A1
NTM Frequency in the Fisheries Sector using the ASEAN Database
(Percentage of 177 lines)

Code	NTM Type	Bru	Cam	Ind	Lao	Mal	Mya	Phi	Sin	Tha	Vie
										none	
2200	Additional taxes and charges			100							
2290	Additional charges, n.e.s.							100			
5100	Automatic licensing								76.8		
6100	Non-automatic licensing	76.8		20.9			100		76.8		
6240	Quotas linked with export performance						100				
6310	Total prohibition					3.4					
7100	Single channel for imports							100			
8100	Technical regulations	2.3	76.8	100	84.2			20.9			
8130	Labelling requirements			20.9				20.9			4.0
8140	Packaging requirements					76.8					
8150	Testing, inspection, quarantine reqs			97.7							91.5
8200	Pre-shipment inspection			20.9							

Source: Author's calculations.

Table 5.A2
NTM Frequency in the Agro-Based Sector using the ASEAN Database
(Percentage of 106 lines)

Code	NTM Type	Bru	Cam	Ind	Lao	Mal	Mya	Phi	Sin	Tha	Vie
1400	Tariff quota duties		none								2.8
2200	Additional taxes and charges			100							
2290	Additional charges n.e.s.							100			
5100	Automatic licensing			4.7							
6100	Non-automatic licensing	17.0		75.5		0.9	100	16.0	23.6	10.4	
6110	License with no specific ex-ante criteria								1.9		
6200	Quotas						0.9	2.8			
6240	Quotas linked with export performance						100				
7100	Single channel for imports							100			
8100	Technical regulations	68.9		98.1	12.3			70.8			
8130	Labelling requirements			29.2				29.2			
8150	Testing, inspection, quarantine reqs.			54.7							
8200	Pre-shipment inspection			29.2							39.6

Source: Author's calculations.

Table 5.A3
NTM Frequency in the Wood-Based Sector using the ASEAN Database
(Percentage of 165 lines)

Code	NTM Type	Bru	Cam	Ind	Lao	Mal	Mya	Phi	Sin	Tha	Vie
2200	Additional taxes and charges		none	100	none	none			none	none	none
2290	Additional charges n.e.s.							100			
6100	Non-automatic licensing	86.7					100				
6240	Quotas linked with export performance						100				
6270	Quotas for sensitive product categories	86.7									
7100	Single channel for imports							100			
8100	Technical regulations			7.3							

Source: Author's calculations.

Table 5.A4
NTM Frequency in the Rubber-Based Sector using the ASEAN Database
(Percentage of 270 lines)

Code	NTM Type	Bru	Cam	Ind	Lao	Mal	Mya	Phi	Sin	Tha	Vie
2200	Additional taxes and charges	none	none	100							
2290	Additional charges n.e.s.							100			
5100	Automatic licensing			16.3							
6100	Non-automatic licensing			20.7			100		0.4		
6170	Prior authorization for sensitive products					19.3					
6200	Quotas			1.5							
6240	Quotas linked with export performance						100				
6300	Prohibition			20.7						1.1	68.5
6710	Selective approval of importers			1.5							
7100	Single channel for imports							100			19.3
7120	Sole importing agency			19.3							
8100	Technical regulations			19.3	2.6			19.3		1.1	17.0
8130	Labeling requirements									4.1	
8140	Packaging requirements									4.1	
8150	Testing, inspection, quarantine reqs							33.3		4.1	
8200	Pre-shipment inspection			20.7							

Source: Author's calculations.

Table 5.A5
NTM Frequency in the Textiles and Apparel Sector using the ASEAN Database
(Percentage of 1,183 lines)

Code	NTM Type	Bru	Cam	Ind	Lao	Mal	Mya	Phi	Sin	Tha	Vie
1400	Tariff quota duties		none		none				none		11.2
2200	Additional taxes and charges			100							
2290	Additional charges n.e.s.							100			
5100	Automatic licensing			74.8							
6100	Non-automatic licensing	0.5					100			29.2	
6170	Prior authorization for sensitive products					0.1					
6240	Quotas linked with export performance						100				
6300	Prohibition			0.2							83.2
7100	Single channel for imports							100			

Source: Author's calculations.

Table 5.A6
NTM Frequency in the Healthcare Sector using the ASEAN Database
(Percentage of 245 lines)

Code	NTM Type	Bru	Cam	Ind	Lao	Mal	Mya	Phi	Sin	Tha	Vie
2200	Additional taxes and charges			100							
2290	Additional charges n.e.s.							100			2.4
3100	Administrative pricing										
5100	Automatic licensing	67.8		13.9					49.0		
6100	Non-automatic licensing	55.5	49.0	77.1		2.9		58.4	49.0	58.4	
6200	Quotas			0.4		2.9					
6240	Quotas linked with export performance						100				
6270	Quotas for sensitive products	51.8									
6300	Prohibition	49.0	49.0	1.6				49.0	63.7		78.0
6710	Selective approval of importers			3.3							
7100	Single channel for imports							100			
8100	Technical regulations	6.5		7.8	65.3			6.5		34.3	8.6
8110	Product characteristic requirements			1.2							
8120	Marking requirements			11.8							
8130	Labelling requirements			13.1				49.0	49.0		53.1
8140	Packaging requirements			11.8							
8150	Testing, inspection, quarantine reqs			1.2			49.0	11.8			49.4
8200	Pre-shipment inspection	0.4									

Source: Author's calculations.

Loreli C. de Dios

Table 5.A7
NTM Frequency in the Automotive Sector using the ASEAN Database
(Percentage of 1,103 lines)

Code	NTM Type	Bru	Cam	Ind	Lao	Mal	Mya	Phi	Sin	Tha	Vie
2200	Additional taxes and charges		none	100							
2290	Additional charges n.e.s.							100			
2300	Internal taxes and charges on imports								50.7		20.2
3100	Administrative pricing	78.3									
5100	Automatic licensing	55.9		2.3							
6100	Non-automatic licensing			96.5		78.3	100	78.3		6.7	
6170	Prior authorization for sensitive products					74.2					
6200	Quotas			14.5		78.3					
6240	Quotas linked with export performance						100				
6270	Quotas for sensitive products	78.3									
6300	Prohibition			18.2					78.3	0.9	87.9
6710	Selective approval of importers			92.8							
7100	Single channel for imports							100			21.1
7120	Sole importing agency			3.7							
8100	Technical regulations	55.5		59.3	77.8			4.6	50.7	4.9	54.4
8150	Testing, inspection, quarantine reqs							1.2			
8200	Pre-shipment inspection			18.8							15.2

Source: Author's calculations.

Table 5.A8
NTM Frequency in the Electronics Sector using the ASEAN Database
(Percentage of 1,077 lines)

Code	NTM Type	Bru	Cam	Ind	Lao	Mal	Mya	Phi	Sin	Tha	Vie
2200	Additional taxes and charges			100							
2290	Additional charges n.e.s.							100	0.6		
5100	Automatic licensing	9.0	0.2	53.9				2.7	0.2	0.8	
6100	Non-automatic licensing	11.5		77.3			100				2.2
6170	Prior authorization for sensitive products					22.5					
6200	Quotas			23.2							
6240	Quotas linked with export performance						100				
6270	Quotas for sensitive products	1.8						0.3	2.3	0.5	56.6
6300	Prohibitions			76.4							
6310	Total prohibition					3.2					
6710	Selective approval of importers			23.2							
7100	Single channel for imports							100			53.4
7120	Sole importing agency			53.2							
8100	Technical regulations			53.2	11.3			53.9	7.5	1.7	11.8
8130	Labelling requirements									0.1	
8140	Packaging requirements									0.1	
8150	Testing, inspection, quarantine reqs.							6.5	0.6	0.1	1.7
8200	Pre-shipment inspection			76.4							

Source: Author's calculations.

Table 5.A9
NTM Frequency in the ICT Sector using the ASEAN Database
(Percentage of 683 lines)

Code	NTM Type	Bru	Cam	Ind	Lao	Mal	Mya	Phi	Sin	Tha	Vie
2200	Additional taxes and charges		none	100							
2290	Additional charges n.e.s.							100			
3100	Administrative pricing										1.0
5100	Automatic licensing	13.8		40.7					0.9		
6100	Non-automatic licensing	14.9		87.0			100	2.8	0.1		2.8
6170	Prior authorization for sensitive products					30.6				0.3	
6200	Quotas			22.7							
6240	Quotas linked with export performance						100				
6270	Quotas for sensitive products	2.8									
6300	Prohibition			87.0					3.7		64.9
6310	Total prohibition					3.7					
6710	Selective approval of importers			22.7							
7100	Single channel for imports							100			64.3
7120	Sole importing agency			64.3							
8100	Technical regulations			64.3	13.3			64.3	2.8		13.8
8150	Testing, inspection, quarantine reqs.							9.2	1.0		2.3
8200	Pre-shipment inspection			87.0							

Source: Author's calculations.

NOTES

This chapter is a summarized version of the REPSPF Project Report 06/001a entitled "An Investigation into the Measures Affecting the Integration of ASEAN's Priority Sectors (Phase 2) Overview: Non-tariff Barriers to Trade in the ASEAN Priority Goods Sectors".

1. The term "non-tariff barrier" evolved from the historical precedence of measures meant directly to restrict import demand using non-tariff means. There is less agreement on what constitutes a non-tariff measure (NTM), mainly because they are imposed for various reasons, than there is consensus on their effects. In principle, an NTM exists if the wedge between domestic prices and foreign prices differs from that which is due to tariffs alone. While NTBs would not necessarily include measures that artificially promote exports or subsidize producers, the latter would be subsumed under the more general category of NTMs. (de Dios 2004)

2. Found in http://www.unctad.org. These definitions were adopted by the ASEAN 8th Interim Technical Working Group as it listed measures affected by Article 5.2 of the Common Effective Preferential Tariffs (CEPT) Agreement.

3. The Coordination Committee on the Implementation of CEPT Scheme for AFTA (CCCA) takes charge of the work program, although its role is confined to establishing which NTM is a trade barrier, since the task of addressing the measure falls on the relevant working groups.

4. The two other priority sectors, tourism and air travel, are services.

5. The list of commodities is available from the ASEAN Secretariat.

6. These are described in www.unctad.org.

7. Tabulations based on the UNCTAD TRAINS are available upon request.

8. Survey done by Coopers and Lybrand.

REFERENCES

Ando, Mitsuyo. "Estimating Tariff Equivalents of Non-Tariff Measures in APEC MemberEconomies". In *Quantitative Methods for Assessing the Effects of Non-Tariff Measures and Trade Facilitation*, edited by Philippa Dee and Michael Ferrantino. Singapore: World Scientific Publishing Co., 2005.

——— and Takamune Fujii. "The Costs of Trade Protection: Estimating Tariff Equivalents of Non-Tariff Measures in APEC Economies". Japanese Economic Association 2002 Fall Meeting, 13–14 October 2002, Hiroshima University, 2004.

Andriamananjara, Soamiely, Judith Dean, Robert Feinberg, Michael Ferrantino, Rodney Ludema, and Marinos Tsigas. "The Effects of Non-Tariff Measures on Prices, Trade, and Welfare: CGE Implementation of Policy-Based Price Comparisons". Office of Economics Working Paper No. 2004-04-A, U.S. International Trade Commission, 2004.

ASEAN Secretariat. *NTM Database* (as of 2006).

————. Progress Report on the Implementation of Horizontal Measures under the PIS presented during the 2nd Consultative Meeting for the PIS (COPS II) in June 2006.

Coopers and Lybrand. "Barriers to Trade and Movement of Goods in ASEAN". ASEAN Secretariat, 1998.

Center for International Economics. "Non-Tariff Barriers in Vietnam: A Framework for Developing a Phase Out Strategy". Prepared for the World Bank, 1999.

Crawford, Jo-Ann and Sam Laird. "Regional Trade Agreements and the WTO". CREDIT Research Paper No. 00/3 Centre for Research in Economic Development and International Trade, University of Nottingham, 2000.

de Dios, Loreli. *Non-Tariff Measures Affecting Philippine Imports*. Manila: Tariff Commission-Philippine Institute for Development Studies, 1986.

————. *Trade Impediments in the Philippines*. Tokyo: Institute of Developing Economies, 1987.

————. *A Review of the Remaining Import Restrictions*. Manila: Philippine Institute for Development Studies, 1993.

————. *Issues and Options for the Work Program to Eliminate NTBs in AFTA*. Jakarta: ASEAN Secretariat, 2004.

Dean, Judith M., Robert Feinberg, Jose E. Signoret, Michael Ferrantino, and Rodney Ludema. "Estimating the Price Effects of Non-Tariff Measures". United States International Trade Commission. Preliminary. 2006.

Fane, George, and Tim Condon. "Appendix to Trade Reform in Indonesia, 1987–1995". *Bulletin of Indonesian Economic Studies* 32, no. 3 (2006).

Kee, Hiau Looi, Alessandro Nicita, and Marcelo Olarreaga. "Estimating Trade Restrictiveness Indices". World Bank Policy Research Working Paper 3840, 2006.

Manchin, Miriam and Annette O. Pelkmans-Balaoing. "Rules of Origin and the Web of East Asian FTAs". Paper presented in the World Bank Policy Workshop on Rules of Origin and Standards, Hainan, China, 26–27 June 2006.

————. "Clothes without an Emperor: Analysis of the Preferential Tariffs in ASEAN". Tinbergen Institute Working Paper Series of 2006. Rotterdam, 2006.

Mathews, Alan. *Regional Integration and Food Security in Developing Countries*. Rome: Food and Agriculture Organization, 2003.

Oktaviani, Rina, Amzul Rifin and Henny Reinhardt. "An Investigation into the Measures Affecting the Integration of ASEAN's Priority Sectors (Phase 2): Review of Regional Trade and Available Tariff Rate Data", AADCP-REPSF Project 06/001a, 2006.

Rajan, Ramkishen S. and Rahul Sen. "The New Wave of FTAs in Asia: With Particular Reference to ASEAN, China and India". Unpublished manuscript, 2004.

Sally, Razeen and Rahul Sen. "Whither Trade Policies in Southeast Asia? The Wider Asian and Global Context". *ASEAN Economic Bulletin* 22, no. 1 (April 2005): 92–115.

Sen, Rahul. *Free Trade Agreements in Southeast Asia*. Southeast Asia Background Series No. 1. Singapore: Institute of Southeast Asian Studies, 2004.

UNCTAD Trade and Development Board. "Methodologies, Classification, Quantification and Development Impacts of Non-Tariff Barriers". Note by the UNCTAD Secretariat Geneva, 5–7 September 2005*a*.

————. "Report of the Expert Meeting on Methodologies, Classification, Quantification and Development Impacts of Non-Tariff Barriers". Geneva, 5–7 September. 2005*b*.

UNCTAD TRAINS (as of 2006).

http://www.aric.adb.org

http://www.unctad.org

6

An Assessment of ASEAN's Priority Sectors for Fast-track Integration

Christopher Findlay, David Parsons, and Herb Plunkett

1. Introduction

ASEAN integration offers significant gains to all members. It allows them to capture the gains from interactions with other countries both within ASEAN and with the rest of the world so as to facilitate faster economic growth and improve living standards. The gains include those from freer trade in goods and services, from more open capital flows and from transfers in technology.

Increasing economic integration with other ASEAN countries and with the world brings these benefits, but it also involves more competition and change. For example:

- Market shares are continually evolving, and new suppliers continue to emerge in the home market and in third-country markets. China and its impact on world markets is the most recent startling example, but the same processes are at work within ASEAN as well.
- Not only does competitiveness in traditional products change, but also new products emerge. The finer division of production processes, the

greater complexity in global supply chains and the growth of trade in components in the region are examples.

- There are new ways of organizing business and new forms of international business. The rise in significance of trade in services in its own right and as a complement to other forms of international business is an example.

- Foreign direct investment (FDI) has always been a critical part of the business-led integration of economies in East Asia. Businesses losing competitiveness in higher income countries have relocated offshore. Now new investors are emerging, and new partnership possibilities are developing. Examples are related to the growing flows of FDI from India and from China.

These changes are all sources of benefit, but the willingness of a community to open their economy demands a level of confidence about the ability to adjust to them. The importance of this confidence and its impact on the process of integration are key issues in capturing the gains from integration. We comment on the connections between community confidence, policy reform and economic integration below.

The specific goal of integration in ASEAN was laid out in Bali Concord II in 2003.[1]

> The ASEAN Economic Community shall establish ASEAN as a single market and production base, turning the diversity that characterises the region into opportunities for business complementation making the ASEAN a more dynamic and stronger segment of the global supply chain. ASEAN's strategy shall consist of the integration of ASEAN and enhancing ASEAN's economic competitiveness. In moving towards the ASEAN Economic Community, ASEAN shall, *inter alia*, institute new mechanisms and measures to strengthen the implementation of its existing economic initiatives including the ASEAN Free Trade Area (AFTA), ASEAN Framework Agreement on Services (AFAS) and ASEAN Investment Area (AIA); accelerate regional integration in the priority sectors; facilitate movement of business persons, skilled labour and talents; and strengthen the institutional mechanisms of ASEAN, including the improvement of the existing ASEAN Dispute Settlement Mechanism to ensure expeditious and legally binding resolution of any economic disputes (B3).

The creation of a single market would mean that the Law of One Price should hold in all goods and services markets (Lloyd and Smith, 2004 and Chapter 2 by Lloyd in this volume). Integration requires elimination of both border and beyond-the-border measures that discriminate against foreigners and the application of the principle of "national treatment" by which any item (good, factor, service provider) crossing a border should be treated the same as that from a domestic provider. In other words, all border measures that inhibit movement across borders should be removed, and once across a border a foreign provider should be treated the same as a domestic provider with respect to other policy measures, such as taxes and regulations.

Some regulatory processes apply to both domestic and foreign providers and also inhibit the integration of markets. These measures are not directly discriminatory but they limit transactions with foreign suppliers. Examples include systems of regulated standards applied to goods traded internationally and licensing systems applied to services.

The gains from integration are greatest in a global setting. Regional integration is a contributor to that goal, which is made explicit in the Bali Concord II text. While the specific target is integration within ASEAN, the goal has always had a global orientation, that is, regional integration is expected to support international competitiveness.

The ASEAN leaders at their Tenth Summit in Vientiane in 2004 signed the framework agreement for there to be further integration of their trade policies for eleven priority sectors. A twelfth sector, logistics, was added in 2006. For e-ASEAN and healthcare, both the goods and services components are included. The identified sectors were:

Goods:
• agro-based products
• automotive
• e-ASEAN (ICT)
• electronics
• fisheries
• healthcare products
• textiles and apparel
• wood-based products
• rubber-based products

Services:
• e-ASEAN (ICT)
• healthcare
• tourism
• air travel
• logistics

The aim of the work summarized in this chapter was to identify the existing barriers to further integration in those sectors. The research sought to identify barriers inhibiting trade in goods and services produced by and used in the identified sectors; and determine their relative importance.

The available regional trade and tariff rate data were reviewed and case studies of electronics, logistics, and textiles and apparel sectors were completed. Importantly, the research extended beyond the review of formal trade barriers to encompass the policies and other measures that prevent the free movement and provision of goods and services across national boundaries. In addition to the sector-specific research, an extensive business survey was undertaken in all ten countries to identify and assess the significance of the procedures, standards, regulations and laws of each country that make integration of markets within ASEAN difficult.[2]

Integration is not a one-off event, but a process, since as structural changes occur in all economies the adjustments required never stop. The removal of border barriers of the type examined in this project is a necessary condition for successful integration but it is not sufficient for success. The sectoral case study work in this project not only identified key border barriers demanding immediate attention, but also highlighted the value of taking a dynamic perspective to integration.

The work produced the following recommendations which are discussed in more detail in this chapter:

- Implement zero Common Effective Preferential Tariff (CEPT) rates in all priority sectors
- Adopt a programme of most-favoured nation (MFN) tariff rate cuts and a cap on the MFN rate of 10 per cent
- Accelerate implementation of the "single window" initiative in all member economies
- Ban all import licensing and quantitative measures, including tariff quotas
- Augment the list of priority non-tariff barriers for removal
- Commit to a transparency initiative in the services sector

Policies and their application vary between countries, suggesting that there may be value in particular countries following different reform paths. However, a key result from this project is the number of elements of a reform programme which countries will be tackling in common. This supports the scope for regional cooperation to contribute to successful reform.

Initiatives in some of these areas are already underway but the research reported here reinforces the value of that work. Variations in coverage of cooperative reform programmes and accelerated implementation are further implications. However, the apparent lack of confidence among the membership to conclude that work and for the initiatives to be fully implemented must be resolved.

In the following sections we review the key results on tariffs and non-tariff barriers (NTBs) for the priority goods sectors, and on impediments to trade and investment in the priority services sectors. We also review some of the results of the sectoral case studies.

2. Tariffs[3]

Average tariffs in the priority sectors are 3.71 per cent for the CEPT and 10.52 per cent for the MFN tariff. Despite these low averages:

- the range of tariff values within each sector is wide;
- a number of tariff peaks therefore remain;
- the margins of preference are significant; and
- significant exclusions from commitments are evident in automotive products and textiles/clothing.

Positive CEPT rates, even low ones, remain important impediments to ASEAN integration in the priority sectors. This is because the many identified barriers to trade act cumulatively in their effects on reducing competition and efficiency of priority sector development within ASEAN.

Many of the non-tariff measures (NTMs) that are barriers to intra-ASEAN trade in the priority sectors are associated with customs procedures related to the processing of shipments and collection of revenue. These issues are important in a dynamic context of continuing change and shifting competitiveness, the evolution of more complex production chains, and more trade in components.

With respect to strategy for regional economic integration, these points suggest the value of a trading arrangement that facilitates these adjustments, allows transitions in market shares, and allows the supply chain elements to relocate as competitiveness shifts. A couple of priorities for action are suggested by this perspective:

- The first is to continue to implement the agreed reduction of the CEPT for the goods of the priority sectors.
- The second is to accelerate the reduction in MFN rates.

In view of the tariff peaks in MFN and CEPT rates, margins of preference in the priority sectors, and the potential for trade diversion and smuggling, a continuing reduction in the margin of preference provided to ASEAN-sourced goods in the priority sectors is important. This could be done, for example, by adopting a goal of limiting MFN rates to a maximum of 10 percentage points above the CEPT rates.

An alternative approach is for each country to select, say, two or three key sectors in which to reduce peak tariffs. This will make some contribution to reducing the inefficiencies in the allocation of resources that are associated with diverse tariff rates. However, a move to cap MFN rates across the board will have more widespread effects, and a reduction in MFN rates at the same time, or a commitment to do so, will also limit the distorting effects of the margin of preference. This is consistent with the goal of using integration within ASEAN to support the development of international competitiveness in the priority sectors.

Finally, it is important to note that there are important connections between tariff reform and reforms designed to deal with issues related to the application of non-tariff measures. For example, as noted below, the most significant non-tariff issues limiting integration are currently related to customs procedures. Lower tariffs affect the incentives which are at the heart of many of those issues. Also relevant in the context of rapidly changing supply chains and finer divisions in the structure of production is the operation of duty (tariff and tax) refund schemes for items re-exported. The administrative issues around these schemes are also less significant in a low tariff environment.

3. Non-tariff Measures[4]

It has long been recognized that to facilitate ASEAN economic integration, members need to "ensure transparency on non-tariff measures and eliminate those that are barriers to trade". Accordingly, the Roadmap for Integration of ASEAN specified that NTBs are to be eliminated by 2010 for the ASEAN-5, 2012 for the Philippines, and by 2015/2018 by Cambodia, Laos PDR, Myanmar, and Vietnam. However, progress in eliminating "unjustified and unnecessary" NTMs has been disappointing in the past, notwithstanding the recognition of their adverse effect on ASEAN integration and their cost to members. For identification, NTMs were classified into four groups, namely:

1. technical barriers to trade;
2. sanitary and phytosanitary measures;
3. security and environment measures; and
4. import licensing procedures and/or other administrative measures.

Subsidies, anti-dumping and countervailing duties were excluded.

Criteria endorsed by the Nineteenth AFTA Council in 2005 for eliminating "unjustifiable and unnecessary" NTMs were:

1. NTMs that are non-transparent, discriminatory in application, without scientific basis, and where an alternative less restrictive measure is available, would require immediate elimination (red box);
2. NTMs that are transparent, non-discriminatory in application which nullify or impair some benefits or obligations of the country, that affect highly traded products in the region or products under the nine priority sectors, that cannot be clearly justified or identified as a barrier, would be subject to negotiation (amber box); and
3. NTMs that are transparent, non-discriminatory in application, have no alternative measure, have scientific basis, are imposed for public health and safety or religious or national security reasons, are WTO-consistent and reasonable such as sanitary and phytosanitary and environment regulations, are justified and could be maintained (green box).

A review of existing research was undertaken for the nine priority goods sectors. The data reveal that NTMs are prevalent and extensive. There is some variation between sectors but measures commonly identified were non-automatic licensing and technical regulations were pervasive, as well as imposed testing and inspection.

The available empirical studies of the effects of NTMs consistently show that they have significant adverse effects. Typically, the studies show that the protective and taxing effect, or the *ad valorem* tariff equivalent, of NTMs is substantially higher than the formal tariffs that apply to the trade, and often many times the MFN rate.

The business survey conducted as part of the research identified a number of impediments in common across sectors. Most of these were related to the manner of implementation of current measures, mostly associated with customs regulations and procedures. Furthermore, full utilization of CEPT is inhibited by difficulties, delays, or costs of securing the certificate of origin (Form D), aside from unclear administrative procedures.

These impediments are significant but also business people and officials both have incentives to find a way around them. This is evident in the survey responses that identify "unofficial expediency fees" as an issue. These fees are related to the other problems of delay or uncertainty in customs procedures. The fees are paid to accelerate the movement of goods or reduce aspects of uncertainty. Those problems arise in the first place because of the complexity of the administrative process. Actions to solve those problems will also help resolve the issue of the expediency fees.

The business survey reinforced the value of attention to a variety of measures already included in the ASEAN inventory. Impediments commonly referred to by survey respondents were licensing and technical measures. There is a variety of measures not included in the ASEAN inventory which are also identified by business as significant impediments. At the sector level, these are restrictive official foreign exchange allocation, quotas, restricted government-sanctioned insurance and shipping companies for imports, some technical regulations, internal taxes and charges on imports. At the country level, the barriers are additional charges on imports, restrictive foreign exchange allocation, minimum payment settlement period for imports, administrative price fixing, internal taxes and charges, requirement to ship directly, quotas, and regulations on the use of credit to finance imports.

These results demonstrate the value of:

• commitments already made to implement reductions in tariffs; and
• commitments already made to work towards the ASEAN Single Window.

To this list of commitments might be added another which reduces the scope for bureaucratic discretion. This is to commit to the removal of (all) licensing whether apparently automatic or not. Further, all quantitative restrictions on trade are not consistent with a single market, and should also be banned. This includes, for example, tariff quotas.

There is a risk, however, in reform of NTMs. Removal of tariffs or existing NTMs is sometimes followed by the construction of substitute measures. There is some evidence in electronics of the excessive application of regulation related to standards conformance and testing, for example. Anticipating new areas of concerns and developing cooperative mechanisms to avoid relocation of NTM issues will be important.

While some NTMs are specific to particular sectors, many of the most significant NTMs are common across countries. Adopting common goals in reform programmes to remove NTMs creates the opportunity for deeper regional cooperation to support that work.

4. Services[5]

Overall, the assessment reveals that the extent of liberalization in the priority sectors under ASEAN Framework Agreement on Services (AFAS) has been extremely low. This applies to both conditions of market access (generally measures applying to all potential entrants) and to National Treatment (measures which discriminate against foreign suppliers), with no great difference in the extent of commitment to them.

In some of the priority sectors, but with exception of e-ASEAN, the shares of the sub-sectors that are scheduled are low. In particular, with respect to healthcare services, few ASEAN countries have committed to liberalization. Most of the logistic-related industries have not been scheduled to be liberalized. Similarly, the degree of commitment to liberalize services related to tourism is quite low in most countries.

A relatively larger number of commitments have been made for telecommunication services (e-ASEAN). Although severe limitations are often attached, almost half of the related industries are scheduled to be liberalized under AFAS.

For the air travel sector, three related (non-air traffic rights) activities to which the GATS provisions apply are treated as a separate category (sector) under AFAS and included in the list for liberalization by many ASEAN members. However, many limitations are attached to the commitments.

In general, relatively few commitments have been made for services trade through the movement of people.

The analysis indicates that the price-raising effects of the service restrictions are higher than those due to trade barriers. This implies that removal of the various restrictive measures would facilitate market competition that would lead to a decline in prices. In turn, the decline in prices would increase the demand for the services and induce an expansion of intra-regional trade in services. And because the priority service sectors have close linkages with many goods-producing industries through their effects on the cost of acquiring inputs and delivering goods, the economy-wide effects would be favourable and significant.

For services, the most restrictive measures according to the business survey results relate to regulatory and business licensing procedures. These are followed by measures governing commercial ownership and commercial presence, and other measures such as no procedures or cumbersome procedures for the duty-free admission of service-related imports. Of the individual measures identified, businesses considered the most severe across all sectors were limitations on the total number of operations or the quantity of output. A common theme from business is concern about the lack of transparency of the rules and regulations applying to the service industries.

This result makes the case for a new transparency initiative in ASEAN. Reaching higher degrees of transparency helps respond to business concerns. Transparency requires the documentation and codification of services policy. The exercise has greater value if policy can be documented in a way that facilitates benchmarking across countries. This work also supports the specification of commitments in AFTA or in the WTO and, therefore, increases the capacity for effective negotiation. Finally, transparency also makes an important contribution to the dynamics of domestic reform, as the nature of policy measures and their impacts become more widely understood.

Given the range of instruments applied and the complexity of their interaction, this process is not easy or simple to complete. It provides great scope for regional cooperation as a result.

Access to services at world prices and of world class supports international competitiveness and, therefore, domestic adjustment. The supply chain perspective focuses attention on the services that facilitate the transactions, for example, services transport systems, infrastructure, and logistics. Results for the logistics sector show the value of reform in measures affecting establishment and operations in that sector. Linking back to the NTM programme, the performance of the logistics sector also depends on the progress of customs reform. Noting the earlier points about the links between tariff reform and success in customs reform, the mention of the link to logistics means that the three reform agendas have a triangular connection and progress in each supports work on the other two.

5. Sectoral Studies

5.1. Textiles and apparel[6]

Given its importance to many ASEAN economies, a special study was made of the NTMs restricting ASEAN trade in the textiles and apparel sector. It covered the seven major suppliers in ASEAN, namely Cambodia, Indonesia, Lao PDR, Malaysia, Philippines, Thailand, and Vietnam.

ASEAN has considerable production capability in textiles and apparel. In the seven countries studied, the apparel sub-sector is export-oriented and nearly all of those exports are to third-country markets, principally the United States and the European Union. Most of the fabric used in exports is sourced from outside the ASEAN region, notwithstanding the strong production capabilities in textile yarns and fabrics in Indonesia, Malaysia, and Thailand.

Since many global quotas were phased out and the Agreement on Textiles and Clothing (ATC) came into effect, there has been considerable consolidation of the textile and apparel sector in member countries. This consolidation and the development of strong and integrated production within the sector in ASEAN have been hindered, not only by formal border measures (such as tariffs and trade agreements), but also by many NTMs.

Information was sought from companies, industry associations and government officials covering the full value supply chain on the occurrence of

NTMs and their impact on trade and regional integration. The NTMs included elements of customs administration, technical barriers to trade, trade remedies, subsidies, political economy/institutional arrangements, exchange rate restrictions, quality controls, taxes and tariffs, investment restrictions, other restrictions such as on labour, and outward processing arrangements. It included firms involved in: yarn-fabric-garment production; design, wholesale and retail marketing; accessory suppliers and suppliers of staple fibre for yarn production; and freight forwarders.

Many interviewees regarded the structural problem and institutional weaknesses within the sector in ASEAN as more serious than NTMs, notwithstanding their widespread occurrence and restrictiveness. While measures associated with customs administration were the most cited NTM, outward processing arrangements were considered to be the most consistently encountered and, by far, the most restrictive. NTMs associated with technical barriers to trade, taxes and tariffs, and with investment were frequently cited. Consistently encountered were NTMs associated with taxes and tariffs, investment and subsidies, and these were also considered to be the next most restrictive.

While the situation in individual countries varies, further reform within the ASEAN region to develop a more efficient and integrated textiles and apparel sector needs to be directed at reforms to set a zero CEPT rate on all textiles, clothing and related imports. Also, improvements need to be made in customs procedures and documentation requirements.

The textile and apparel sector study confirms the high occurrence of customs-related NTMs. Inspections were cited the most often, followed by documentation. For producers of textile fabric, sampling and testing is a major technical barrier. For apparel suppliers, this is less so because it is handled by buyers who presumably pass costs on to customers. Tax and tariff issues had the third-highest occurrence and very significant averages in consistency and restrictiveness.

Restrictions on Outward Processing Arrangements (OPA) were the most cited and had the highest consistency and restrictiveness. The main obstacle is tax treatment: goods are taxed each time they cross borders, thus discouraging intra-industry trade. For intermediate products that are re-exported, the issue is VAT on imports. Re-exports are eligible for VAT rebates but this takes up to twelve months and do not fully compensate companies. The VAT problem is more serious for firms that are not entirely exporters, since they are exempt from VAT and tariffs only if they prove to have re-exported the goods.

The study shows that enabling small firms oriented to the domestic market to participate in the production of apparel for export will require better tax administration procedures and transparent documentation.

5.2. Electronics[7]

A review of non-tariff measures in the electronics sector reveals a generally positive but sometimes mixed scorecard for ASEAN.

NTMs in the electronics sector are generally less prevalent than in some other sectors and for the components sector, which comprises nearly half of trade and production, trade-distorting NTMs are rare.

The majority of the more prohibitive NTMs, used across all countries, are imposed for non-economic purposes. For example, prohibition and licensing are used to: control equipment and products that can be used for example in counterfeiting and mass duplication of DVDs, CDs and video for piracy or for pornography; inspect tapes, disks and videos; or restrict and control specialized radio and telephone equipment for security and a range of machines for gambling and amusement. However, for some products, particularly consumer products and in some countries, NTMs are used to impede or block the flow of imports to protect domestic industry. Technical measures are widely used to control safety standards but in some cases these may be used to impede imports. The ASEAN MRA on Electronics and Electrical Products is still in its early stages and testing of safety standards can be cumbersome and expensive.

Among the key recommendations are therefore on customs procedures and other NTMs:

a. Customs Procedures
    *   Continue to place the highest priority on the development of an ASEAN Single Window to streamline customs administration through implementation of world class National Single Windows.
    *   Ensure that the National Single Windows not only result in efficient paperless procedures but also have a real impact on the predictability and certainty of handling times, and produce clear and formal-only payments systems.
    *   Develop capacity-building measures to fast track National Single Windows in the less developed ASEAN countries before the end date of 2012 to avoid an increasing gap in the standard of customs procedures within ASEAN.

b. Non-Tariff Measures
  *   In the process of phasing out NTMs, focus on cutting processing time and on eliminating informal payments. Electronic licensing is being implemented in some countries to address this issue.
  *   Continue to place a high priority on expanding the number of products included in the ASEAN MRA on Electronics and Electrical Products and on increasing the number of countries that recognize these product standards.

5.3. Logistics[8]

A special study was made of logistics because of the importance of the services provided to the goods sectors through its influence on the cost of acquiring inputs and cost of delivering goods to users and consumers. Some thirty-five firms were selected for semi-structured interviews on the basis of their knowledge and representing various players in the logistics supply chain in ASEAN. The focus of the study was on identifying the existence and significance of unnecessary impediments to the supply of logistics services and on the quality of services provided.

In brief, the study found that inefficient customs procedures and inspections are the greatest barrier to logistic service in ASEAN. Of the customs procedures and inspections found to be critically significant as unnecessarily burdensome were:

  *   time consuming documentation;
  *   burdensome inspection requirements; and
  *   the different classification of goods in different countries.

Identified as very significant barriers to the provision of logistic services were the land transport regulations relating to the limitation of fleet size, equipment usage, and on hours of operation, and foreign firms being prohibited from operating fleets with less number of vehicles per district. Customs procedures and inspections that also rated as very significant were the lack of border crossing coordination and inefficient inbound clearance processes.

Barriers rated as moderately significant were: for foreign investment, the regulations relating to ownership and the discriminatory licensing of foreign firms; for aviation, the cabotage regulations; and for customs procedures and inspections, the arbitrary independent rulings, volatility in border traffic, multiple uncoordinated offices and improper penalties.

As indicated above, developing efficient logistic services would have a pervasive and favourable effect on the ASEAN economies because of their usage in the priority sectors and more generally throughout the economies.

6. Conclusion: The Challenges of Implementation

The results highlight the significance of commitments already made by ASEAN members to reduce tariffs and to remove NTMs. The work also leads to suggestions of additional items, for example, the extension of the ASEAN NTM inventory and new work on transparency in services. It leads to suggestions of accelerations of parts of the work programme, particularly of the ASEAN single window programme but also to faster tariff cuts (both CEPT and MFN) and removing all licensing and quantitative measures. Implementing even this extended ASEAN agenda is, however, only the first step towards integration.

The second step is to build the environment within which business has the confidence to respond. This depends on government actions on a range of institutional, administrative and structural issues, alongside the reform of border measures.

Business concerns will be that the reductions of border barriers will simply raise the share of local markets to offshore suppliers without the confidence that at the same time the resources released will find employment in competitive locations in new export activities or new import competing activities. Business will also remain concerned about its ability to identify its capacity to reorient production in the export sectors in which its country could be competitive.

These concerns arise because, to meet the competition, business will have to upgrade products, to innovate in delivery, and to meet changing expectations of customers with respect to delivery. Success depends on the capacity to find sufficient skills in the labour force and the supporting infrastructure, including technology policy, competition policy, infrastructure policy, education policy, as well as matters of government administration, at the ports for example. Whether these policies and administrative capacities are in place is the question.

Without assurance on this question, commitments to reform are more likely to be resisted or delays are more likely to be sought. Reforms might also be undermined by lobbying for new measures. If so, there is a lack of results despite the commitments announced, which in turn challenges the credibility of the ASEAN-led reform process. Closing the credibility gap depends on:

(a) taking the second step alongside the first; and (b) elaborating the scope of the ASEAN border reform agenda in the directions suggested above. But even this may not be sufficient. The impact of this two-step strategy (as evident, for example, in investment flows, production growth and trade flows) must also be sufficient to shift business expectations.

The second step of building the domestic business environment is, unfortunately, never ending because international competitiveness is always shifting. For instance, while the priority sectors are good places to start this work, they are the vanguard, and as work proceeds in those sectors new priorities will emerge. Furthermore, the appropriate elements of the second step will vary country to country, according to history and to stage of development.

The focus on the second step builds but also redirects the scope of regional cooperation. The second step agenda includes matters that are determined by policy "behind the border": they contribute to the rate at which an economy can adjust to and take advantage of integration. The opportunities are greater if these adjustments can be made, but there are significant challenges in accepting that route. Building the confidence to accept that route has always been a key rationale for regional cooperation but the focus now includes sharing of experience of domestic reforms.

Of value to the whole membership, therefore, is a common appreciation of the linkages between the progress to a single market and the impact of domestic reform, and the appreciation of the scope for cooperation to work not only on the border issues but to contribute to progress "behind the border" as well. This work would help close any ASEAN "credibility gap" with business: it depends on governments not only *undoing* the policy impediments to integration but also *doing* the institutional development that supports structural change.

NOTES

This chapter is based on a series of studies conducted under REPSF 06/001 entitled "An Investigation into the Measures Affecting the Integration of ASEAN's Priority Sectors (Phase 2)". Thanks to Lim Chze Cheen, Peter Lloyd, Philippa Dee, and Loreli de Dios for comments on summary report on which this chapter is based. All errors are those of the authors.

1.   See http://www.aseansec.org/15159.htm.
2.   ACNielsen, an independent research company, interviewed a total of 931 companies across twelve priority sectors.
3.   Tariff rates in the priority sectors are discussed in more detail in Chapter 4 by Oktaviani, Rifin, and Reinhardt in this volume.

4. The significance of non-tariff measures is discussed in more detail in Chapter 5 by de Dios in this volume. See also Dee and Ferrantino (2005) for a review of studies of the impact of NTMs and de Dios (2004) for earlier work on NTMs in ASEAN.
5. The review of impediments to trade and investment in the priority services sectors was prepared by Ryo Ochiai. Dee (2005) reviews the methodology for assessment of the impact of barriers to trade and investment in services. See also the papers in Sidorenko and Findlay (2003).
6. The Case Study of Textiles and Apparel was prepared by William E. James, Peter J. Minor, and Kakada Dourng of Nathan Associates Inc.
7. The Case Study of Electronics was prepared by a team from the Indonesian Chamber of Commerce and Industry led by David Parsons of Waitpinga Associates.
8. The Case Study of Logistics was prepared by Robert de Souza, Mark Goh, Sumeet Gupta and Luo Lei (The Logistics Institute – Asia Pacific).

REFERENCES

De Dios, Loreli C. "Issues and Options for the Work Program to Eliminate Non-Tariff Barriers in AFTA". ASEAN–EU Programme for Regional Integration Support Project 04/07, 2004.

Dee, Philippa. "A Compendium of Barriers to Services Trade". Prepared for the World Bank, 2005.

———— and Michael Ferrantino, eds. *Quantitative Methods for Assessing the Effects of Non-Tariff Measures and Trade Facilitation.* Singapore: World Scientific, 2005.

Lloyd, Peter and Penny Smith. "Global Economic Challenges to ASEAN Integration and Competitiveness: A Prospective Look". REPSF Project 03/006a, 2004.

Sidorenko, A. and C. Findlay. *Regulation and Market Access.* Canberra: Asia Pacific Press, 2003.

7

ASEAN Tax Regimes: Impediment or Pathway to Greater Integration

Ian Farrow and Sunita Jogarajan

1. Introduction

Taxation has the potential to either impede or become one of the pathways to greater integration and economic growth within ASEAN. Taxation is only one of many considerations made by businesses in making investment decisions; other factors such as transparency, supply chains, labour force, and markets are clearly important to investment decisions, but taxation is clearly a key factor that must be considered.

ASEAN aims to become a more integrated economic entity, in many ways similar to the multi-nation model of the European Union. This economic community objective, with a specific focus on designated priority sectors, was detailed in the Vientiane Action Plan agreed by ASEAN in late 2004. While there has been considerable progress across a wide range of policy areas to enhance integration, taxation is a policy area in which progress has to date been more protracted.

2. Double Tax Agreements between ASEAN Member Countries

Double Taxation Agreements (DTAs), as the term suggests, are treaties between states that aim to avoid double taxation and prevent fiscal evasion. DTAs seek to resolve conflicts between states with respect to the income tax liability of taxpayers operating across jurisdictions. DTAs also provide mechanisms for cooperative action to prevent fiscal evasion.

The DTA issue for ASEAN is that while many ASEAN member countries (AMCs) have bilateral tax treaty arrangements, both within ASEAN and with non-ASEAN economies, none have comprehensive tax treaty coverage across all the other AMCs. The typical DTA coverage by each AMC is often limited to just over half the other AMCs. Some AMCs also have very limited treaty networks, specifically Brunei Darussalam, Cambodia, Lao PDR, and Myanmar.

A limited DTA network within ASEAN is an impediment to regional economic integration and development because it increases business tax costs, imposes administrative burdens, creates transaction uncertainties, and provides a general disincentive to regional investment and profit repatriation.

The "age" of the ASEAN DTA network is also a salient issue. The average ASEAN DTA is between ten and fifteen years old. This may also be considered an impediment to cross-border investment because AMC fiscal and regulatory reform has overtaken DTA terms — making many DTAs de facto obsolete. In addition, economic and technological changes over the last decade have created "new income" unable to be readily characterized under some DTAs. This potentially increases the complexity and costs associated with transactions in selected value-adding service industries, such as R&D services. It may also lead to revenue losses for AMC governments.

Recent DTA negotiations have also trended towards lower withholding tax rates. Older DTAs typically impose relatively high withholding tax rates. As a result of this, AMCs may miss investment opportunities based on the imposition of high headline withholding tax rates and lack of relief. Older DTAs may also force AMCs to take unilateral action to provide relief for inbound and outbound investors. Such a tax environment does little to foster regional economic integration.

ASEAN best practice in DTAs, demonstrated by Indonesia, Singapore, and Vietnam, is to have an extensive, modern bilateral treaty network with other AMCs. The lack of comprehensive coverage and a guaranteed minimum standard of double tax relief within ASEAN results in additional costs and risks to investment into those non-treaty countries. The absence of a treaty can also create uncertainty; fail to provide "tie-breaker" rules to establish the tax jurisdiction and leads to inconsistent and often inadequate approaches to taxation and tax relief.

3. Treatment to Non-ASEAN Member Countries

The treatment of income and capital flows between AMCs (intra-ASEAN) is also often not as favourable as the treatment between AMCs and non-ASEAN countries. This is based on the proposition that the imposition of "high" withholding taxes will be a disincentive to income and capital flows. The impact of this inconsistent treatment is to make income and capital flows between AMCs and countries outside ASEAN more advantageous than intra-ASEAN ones, acting as a disincentive to greater regional investment and economic integration. This situation discourages investment into, and the repatriation of profits from AMCs to other AMCs.

Different AMCs are in different DTA bargaining positions, especially on withholding tax rates. However, in order to facilitate the goal of economic integration, it would be logical to suggest that AMCs should allow cross-border income and capital flows to be as free as possible within ASEAN. In addition, the region as a whole may appear to be less attractive to foreign investment because of the additional tax costs and administrative burdens associated with intra-ASEAN trade.

Best practice within ASEAN is offered by those countries that have implemented unilateral measures to reduce or eliminate double taxation, including the foreign-source income exemptions offered by Brunei Darussalam, Malaysia, and Singapore. This is an approach that is consistent with global best practice.

The next best practice has been through the negotiation of bilateral treaties between AMCs that have delivered a similar outcome to the unilateral one, but subject to the reciprocity that is entailed in the treaty negotiated position.

4. Double Taxation of Income

Subject to limited exceptions with respect to some dividend flows, AMCs often impose secondary additional taxation on earnings from business profits in the form of dividends, interest and royalties and in some cases capital gains. Note that Brunei Darussalam, Malaysia, and Singapore do not impose withholding taxes on dividends in addition to taxes levied on the profits and income of companies, regardless of whether the recipient is a resident or non-resident.

Withholding tax is usually imposed in addition to the underlying tax that was paid or payable on the actual earnings, profits or gains. When withholding tax is imposed it represents a second or double layer of taxation in the source country of the earnings. When profits are repatriated to the home or resident jurisdiction — depending on the type of relief mechanism they employ — the income and gains may be subject to another layer of tax, against which the underlying and/or withholding tax may be creditable. If it is not creditable, a possible third layer of taxation may be payable.

The effect of these multiple or cascading layers of taxation — double taxation — is to penalize the repatriation of profits and, therefore, act as a disincentive to investment. No ASEAN country imposes a similar form of double taxation on its domestic income and hence many jurisdictions create a discriminatory treatment of regional income compared with domestic income, in contrast to the stated objective of ASEAN to create a single integrated economic market. This may reduce the attractiveness of both intra-ASEAN investment and external investment into ASEAN.

5. Other Intra-ASEAN Tax Issues

Each AMC imposes conditions on access to, and eligibility for, tax relief provided through foreign tax credits or exemption relief. The various conditions can often mean that the relief is unavailable.

In some cases, the policy objective of double tax relief is present but the administrative mechanisms to provide the relief are neither efficient nor certain. The net effect of such administrative difficulties is to create transaction uncertainty and potentially increased business tax costs.

Accessing refunds of withholding taxes can often be difficult, as can be proving eligibility for lower withholding tax rates in a DTA or accessing an entitlement to foreign tax credits.

For income classes, such as dividends and interest, DTA definitions and concepts are generally consistent across jurisdictions. Where two countries do not share a common definition then access to double tax relief may not be possible at all, especially where the DTA is silent on the matter or one is absent, thereby raising the prospect of double taxation without any relief being permitted.

One area where domestic approaches can differ widely is with respect to the imposition of withholding taxes on services of varying kinds. The most common services subject to withholding tax are contractor fees.

Variances in this area present practical problems for individuals and firms undertaking cross-border work, as well as for revenue authorities in attempting to tax such transactions.

6. Incentives for ASEAN Priority Sectors

ASEAN's Vientiane Action Plan agreed in November 2004 identified eleven priority sectors for full integration by 2010 as part of an ASEAN Economic Community. These eleven priority sectors include agro-based products, automotive products, electronics products, fisheries products, rubber-based products, textiles and apparels products, wood-based products, air travel services, e-ASEAN products, healthcare products, and tourism and travel-related services.

Most AMCs provide incentives for the development of specific sectors of their economies. Some of these incentives are directed to the ASEAN priority sectors while other incentives have been instituted to foster specific sectors of national economies where growth is desired. AMCs are clearly not unique in providing such incentives, which are a characteristic of many taxation systems.

Tax incentives provided by AMCs are closely aligned with the structures of their respective economies. Singapore, for example, is unlikely to provide significant incentives for sectors which are either non-existent or not desired in its economy such as agro-products, automotive, fisheries and wood-based products.

Incentives offered by AMC tax regimes vary considerably. In several cases, there is a generic tax incentive that may be approved by a government agency such as a Board of Investment that will entitle particular projects to certain tax benefits. Even in circumstances where the incentives are provided for a particular sector, there are often conditions such as investment thresholds below which the incentives will not be available, incentives may be subject to the projects taking place in specific regions or incentives may require certain levels of local participation (either employment or ownership).

7. Impediments for ASEAN Priority Sectors

Impediments for the priority sectors arising from the taxation systems of AMCs are largely indirect in the form of incentives directed by AMCs to other sectors of their economies. These indirect impediments represent a diversion of incentives and, therefore, encourage investment away from priority sectors to other economic sectors. In the case of a tax regime that is strictly neutral with respect to the priority sectors and other sectors of the economy, it can also be argued that it does not specifically encourage the priority sectors. In most AMCs there are a range of incentives applying to the priority sectors to varying degrees, but they typically also provide a range of incentives to non-priority sectors.

Analysis did not identify specific tax impediments to the priority sectors in respect of the international tax regimes of AMCs. The impediments are essentially generic tax impediments as described above, in matters such as withholding taxes, lack of full relief from double taxation, inconsistent definitions and administrative issues. The impediments to the priority sectors identified within the tax regimes of AMCs are, therefore, largely indirect and arguably less important than the generic tax and other institutional impediments to integration.

Impediments to integration of the ASEAN priority sectors can come in other forms other than direct taxation, such as indirect taxes, customs duties, and restrictions on enterprise ownership. There is also preference given in the tax and incentive programmes of many AMCs to national, rather than broader ASEAN, individuals and firms or economic activities, such as incentives specifically restricted to locally made products, rather than products from the wider ASEAN community.

The key conclusion is that the direct tax-related impediments to the integration of the ASEAN priority sectors are generic in nature rather than specific to the priority sectors.

8. Greater Integration and Tax Avoidance

Greater economic integration brings with it a multitude of benefits associated with the likely increased investment into the region. However, economic integration also increases opportunities for tax avoidance as taxpayers have an increased ability to structure their transactions to take advantage of differing tax systems. With the current pace of globalization and tax competition between countries to attract investment, this problem is increasingly difficult to manage. Countries have traditionally dealt with the threat by introducing sophisticated tax avoidance rules. Increasingly, however, countries are taking a coordinated bilateral or multilateral approach to the issue.

Tax harmonization would probably represent the ultimate mechanism for combating tax avoidance. Taxpayers would not be able to engage in cross-border tax avoidance behaviour if all tax systems were identical with a unified tax rate and/or tax base. However, tax harmonization remains an ideal that is unlikely to be achieved as long as taxing rights remain the sovereign right of each individual country. Indeed, the European Union tried and failed to achieve consensus in its attempts to introduce a harmonized corporate tax rate.

Countries can still act in concert to prevent tax avoidance through coordination and cooperation by tax authorities. By working together to address common tax administration issues, tax authorities can secure increased revenue collection for all countries. Coordination and cooperation can be achieved at a bilateral level through the inclusion of mutual cooperation and exchange of information provisions in bilateral tax treaties or at a multilateral level.

In an increasingly globalized economy, it is inevitable that some taxpayers will engage in cross-border behaviour that is designed to minimize their tax liability. This is likely to be of increased significance to ASEAN as it achieves greater economic integration. ASEAN can respond to the issue by leaving it to be dealt with by individual member countries, through bilateral cooperation between member countries, or through a multilateral approach instituted by ASEAN.

9. The European Union Model

The experience of other economic unions is useful in order to analyse approaches which may be applicable for ASEAN in the elimination of tax related impediments to economic integration generically and across the priority sectors.

There is no other economic union which has practised anything comparable to the level of economic integration practised by the European Union (EU). The EU has considerable experience in mitigating or eliminating tax-related impediments to economic integration across a regional economic organization.

The EU originally tried to harmonize taxation across all member states but was unable to gain agreement for the proposal. The convergence approach eventually adopted by the EU is one that might be considered by ASEAN as an appropriate mechanism for the AMC tax regimes. As with the current EU model, this approach would not seek to eliminate legitimate tax competition between AMCs, but rather allow each AMC to continue to operate their own taxation arrangements, consistent with their revenue requirements and economies. A convergence approach would, however, establish baseline standards for taxation including matters such as common revenue base definitions and consistent standards. A convergence approach would provide a high degree of predictability on tax issues for investment attraction, both from within ASEAN and external to ASEAN. Consistent standards among AMCs would also remove the opportunity for arbitrage between tax systems because of differing definitions.

Institutional issues that would need to be addressed would be the mechanisms for implementing a convergent tax regime across ASEAN. In this respect, it might comprise a standing committee or panel of the AMC revenue agencies, possibly under the aegis of the ASEAN Secretariat.

A multilateral ASEAN tax treaty between AMCs, similar to the EU, would be the optimum solution. Such a tax treaty arrangement would remove the need for each AMC to negotiate separate bilateral tax treaties with each of the nine other AMCs. A treaty would provide for consistency within ASEAN that would enhance the attractiveness of the region as a foreign direct investment destination. A multilateral tax treaty would also benefit Cambodia, Lao PDR, Myanmar, and Vietnam, since they would not need to resource the often lengthy separate treaty negotiation processes. A multilateral tax treaty would also provide a tax treaty accession process similar to the EU for new applicants for ASEAN membership (such as Timor Leste). The difficulty in establishing a multilateral tax treaty within ASEAN would be the lengthy and complex process to achieve consensus between AMCs that have very different economies.

10. Agreed Positions as a Way Forward

An alternative to a comprehensive ASEAN tax treaty would be for AMCs to adopt common "Agreed Positions". This would be a less intensive process than a tax treaty negotiation process and could be implemented in progressive steps enacted rather than as a final treaty outcome.

Agreed Positions on taxation within ASEAN could be adopted by consensus between ASEAN Finance Ministers that would be similar to, but less stringent than, the Directives process applied by the EU. Similar to the EU Directives process, ASEAN Agreed Positions on taxation would establish some minimum taxation standards and act as a mechanism for cooperation between revenue agencies to address issues such as fiscal evasion.

Agreed Positions could focus on what might be described as "the easier issues" first, such as income source recognition, transfer pricing allocation issues between AMCs and information sharing protocols between AMC revenue agencies.

Agreed Positions would be determined by agreement between the AMC revenue agencies. Similar to the EU process, the Agreed Positions would be made by unanimous decision and would establish minimum taxation standards and address issues such as common tax definitions and tax base definitions. The Agreed Positions would include timetables for their adoption by all AMCs. Similar to the EU, adoption of the Agreed Positions on taxation would be part of the criteria for the accession of any new member states to ASEAN. This process would be one through which minimum standards could be established and also act as a mechanism for cooperation between revenue agencies to address issues such as tax evasion.

11. No Less Favourable Tax Treatment

One mechanism for the promotion of greater integration within ASEAN would be the adoption of a non-discrimination principle for AMC resident corporations and individuals operating in other AMCs. This would emulate the "no less favourable" tax treatment arrangements operating in the EU. Key features of this approach might include the tax treatment of (individual and corporate) nationals of other AMCs no less favourably than the nationals of the AMC and also allowing nationals of other AMCs to be able to access various taxation and investment incentives on at least equal terms to the nationals of each AMC.

Non-discrimination between AMC nationals would be likely to encourage integration of AMC economies, including the priority sectors where incentives are available. Several options would need to be considered by ASEAN with the introduction of a "no less favourable tax treatment" principle. These would include: whether the principle should apply universally within ASEAN, whether the principle should be limited to the designated priority sectors, and whether there should be a phase-in to enable adjustment by some AMCs, particularly Cambodia, Lao PDR, Myanmar, and Vietnam.

12. Withholding Taxes

ASEAN should consider a maximum withholding tax rates regime between AMCs. A key issue is that AMCs often have more favourable arrangements with non-ASEAN countries than they do with other AMCs with respect to withholding taxes applied to dividends, interest and royalties. ASEAN should address this anomaly and disincentive to ASEAN integration by adopting an Agreed Position for maximum withholding tax rates between AMCs. Consideration could also be given to a timetable for phased reductions for withholding taxes between AMCs, possibly leading to their eventual abolition.

13. Treaty Negotiation Flow-through

ASEAN should also consider adopting a treaty flow-through process. AMCs typically have a range of DTAs with non-ASEAN countries. Singapore, for example, has negotiated some fifty-eight such treaties. The concept behind the flow-through provisions would be to allow other AMCs to accede to treaties negotiated with non-ASEAN countries. As a means to advance a collective bargaining position and manage the effort required, the treaty negotiations could be led by one or two AMCs on behalf of ASEAN. The treaty negotiated would then be available but not mandatory for accession by other AMCs.

14. Most Favoured Nation Arrangements

ASEAN should consider adopting most-favoured nation arrangements internally. Under these arrangements, AMCs would be obliged to offer all other AMCs the same treaty terms as any negotiated with any non-ASEAN countries. Similar to the Agreed Position proposed for withholding taxes on dividends, interest, and royalties, such an arrangement would mean that AMCs would have treaty arrangements with other AMCs that were at least as favourable as treaty arrangements with non-ASEAN countries.

15. Dispute Resolution and Information-sharing Panel

ASEAN should consider establishing a formal dispute resolution mechanism for AMC revenue agencies on taxation issues. The necessity for such a mechanism will increase with further ASEAN integration.

A preferred model would probably be a Panel process rather than a Court system. A Panel comprising the revenue agencies of the AMCs could also act as a means of enhanced information-sharing to address tax avoidance issues.

A convergence model for ASEAN tax regimes would necessarily require a mechanism for dispute resolution between AMCs on taxation issues. It is not recommended that the European Court of Justice model be adopted, since this would necessarily result in a diminution of national sovereignty. In cases where there are issues between revenue agencies and taxpayers, these should be resolved within the jurisdiction of the relevant AMC.

Disputes between AMCs on taxation issues could be considered by a Panel representing the AMC revenue agencies. The ASEAN Secretariat could potentially have a key role in facilitating this process. An alternative, perhaps secondary method of dispute resolution might be referral to the Permanent Court of Arbitration, to which five AMCs are already members.

16. Future Developments

ASEAN should monitor taxation developments in the European Union. Because of the advanced state of its economic integration and convergence on taxation issues, the EU is likely to continue to be the source of concepts and practices that are designed to assist economic integration. Recent EU initiatives such as "home state taxation" for the small and medium business sector and the "common consolidated corporate tax base" for larger businesses are concepts that ASEAN may wish to consider in the future.

17. The Challenge for ASEAN

Addressing the twin issues of relief from double taxation and the prevention of fiscal evasion between AMCs is something that ASEAN will need to undertake if it is to progress the development of an ASEAN economic community, as envisaged in the Vientiane Action Plan. While it is difficult to quantify the extent of intra-ASEAN or extra-ASEAN cross-border tax avoidance, based upon other economies it is reasonable to assume that cross-border tax avoidance is occurring and that increasing integration and globalization means that the situation is likely to deteriorate over time.

A Working Paper on financial integration in Asia released by the International Monetary Fund opined:

> The differences in tax regimes across the region, and differences in treatment of residents versus non-residents hinder the development of regional capital markets as they prevent free movement of capital across the region. These problems are fairly universal, and typically dealt with bilateral tax treaties (as with the G-7 countries) that try to balance the revenue and capital market development considerations. A more pro-active regional approach to identifying tax-related problems, and policies toward a more harmonized approach to capital markets taxation would be advantageous.[1]

The importance of these issues will increase as AMC economies grow and as ASEAN economies become both more integrated and more globalized. Economic integration will increase the potential for taxpayers to structure transactions to maximize any advantage from the different ASEAN tax arrangements. Globalization and competition for foreign direct investment are likely to make these issues progressively more difficult to manage.

Importantly, ASEAN has begun to act on these issues with the Joint Ministerial Statement of the 11th ASEAN Finance Ministers' Meeting (Chiang Mai, Thailand, 5 April 2007) declaring:

Cooperation in Taxation
13. We agreed to strengthen cooperation on taxation under the AFMM to accelerate the completion of bilateral agreements on avoidance of double taxation and cooperation in other tax matters. We agreed to establish a

forum on ASEAN Cooperation in Taxation to be represented by Heads of ASEAN Tax Administration Units.

The issue therefore becomes when and how, rather than whether these issues will be addressed by ASEAN.

NOTES

This article is based upon "ASEAN Tax Regimes and the Integration of Priority Sectors: Issues and Options", project (05/005) co-authored with Sunita Jogarajan of KPMG under the auspices of the AusAID-funded REPSF of the ASEAN-Australia Development Cooperation Program (AADCP).

1. D. Cowen, R. Salgado, H. Shah, L. Teo and A. Zanello. *Financial Integration in Asia: Recent Developments and Next Steps* (Washington, D.C.: International Monetary Fund, 2006).

8

An Overview of the Foreign Direct Investment Jurisprudence

M. Sornarajah and Rajenthran Arumugam

1. Outline of the Historical and Theoretical Perspectives

Foreign direct investment (FDI) activity in the strict sense, of consequence to international law, began in the mid-nineteenth century, essentially dominated by the capital exporting countries in Europe and surged dramatically after Second World War, but this time predominately led by the U.S. multinational corporations (MNCs). Traditionally, the recurring underlying reasons for MNCs to venture abroad include: to strategically capture world market, secure raw materials, minimize transaction costs and reap economies of scale, among others.

It follows that MNCs in the nineteenth and early twentieth centuries and still at present are pervasive power-wielding organizations: they can unleash political, social, and economic upheavals in the host countries. Not surprisingly, MNCs together with their home states have exerted demands to be treated to an external international law standard. Accordingly, for these reasons MNCs can be subjected to the regulatory controls of the host countries. Moreover, the popular Calvo doctrine squarely places MNCs treatment in par with national treatment, neither more nor less.[1]

In the immediate post-colonial period, MNCs were still to a large extent, treated with suspicion by most of the independent states. Thus, these states were determined to pursue their right to "economic self-determination" without substantial foreign linkages.

There was, however, a complete paradigm shift in some developing countries' economic policy strategies in the 1980s — FDI was embraced as part of their overall development strategy. Muchinski (1995, p. 11) explains:

> In the process a number of generalisations about MNEs have been put to doubt. First, it is clear that the MNE has not overwhelmed the nation state as a unit of power. States have responded to the issue of foreign direct investment and have used political power to coordinate economic power where necessary ... Secondly, while early accounts of the MNE concentrated on its tendency towards monopoly, more recently awareness has arisen of the highly competitive nature of the international economy in which MNEs operate... Thirdly, the assumption can be discarded that the MNE is a uniform type of business entity whose behaviour can be predicted through logical deduction form its characteristics.

In general, the policy towards FDI is premised on either the classical or dependency theory. The former views FDI as economic stimulant and catalyst for socioeconomic development. In stark contrast, the latter connotes FDI contributing to wastage of limited resources and wholly self-serving the MNCs and their respective home states. Arguably, the dependency theory can be faulted in the light of empirical evidence clearly showing that in the past two decades, FDI-export driven developing countries have indeed registered unprecedented economic growth (World Investment Report 2000).

On balance, FDI is certainly crucial to developing countries, namely, to access foreign technology transfer, to understand entrepreneurial know-how, in creating employment, and as a formidable capital earner. Not surprisingly, since the 1980s, the rules of the game for FDI have changed dramatically. Asian countries like Japan, South Korea, Taiwan and Hong Kong (PRC), Malaysia and Singapore, and to some extent Thailand have matured as capital-exporting states. Conversely, the erstwhile home states such as the United States, the United Kingdom and Germany are now playing host to inward FDI. Also, the former Soviet Union nations, Republic of China, and the Indochina countries have to a large extent abandoned the central command economic system, and instead adopted free-market policies.

Understandably, given a range of actors in the FDI scene, competing interests would tend to manifest, and this routinely increases the potential for conflicts. Therefore, the political economy of FDI is inherently pervasive, let alone its central domination in policy debates. It is little wonder that short of a multilateral binding rule-based agreement, FDI imprints are seen in international arenas such as the United Nations (UN), World Trade Organization (WTO), the World Bank, and the Organization of Economic Co-operation and Development (OECD).[2] With the ongoing internationalization of business activity, an international legal framework for FDI is verily wanting. As Sornarajah (2004) put it:

> The need for compromise and the consequent emergence of an order within which foreign investments relations could be pursued is an urgent one… the fact that the law is presently mired in conflict does not show an absence of law. In each situation, a set of principles will have to prevail on the basis of the finding of a confluence or convergence of the basic rules of the two contending systems. If the strands of the rules contributing to this confluence can be isolated, then meaningful foundation for settled rules of law for the future can be established.

2. Role of Law and Legal Institutions in Economic Development

Legal theories abound. Broadly speaking, legal jurisprudence is based on or is a combination of the natural law and positivist law theories.[3] The former propounds that law naturally flows through the facility of reason. In normative terms it is characterization of fair, just, and equitable thinking. The latter argues that the status of law attaches to anything that has been laid down (posited) as law in accordance with the requirement of the legal system in question.

Hence, law has a highly functional dynamics and at a very fundamental level maintains social harmony and order. It also follows that ultimately the legal culture of a nation is carved out by its history, cultural norms and values, religious belief, political ideology, and social thinking.

Today, the doctrine or ideology of rule of law, which superimposes good governance, is apparently an all-encompassing notion, among others, is applicable to a nation's both substantive as well as procedural laws, judiciary bureaucracy, and political set-up. Some jurists argue that the advent of globalization has indeed made its influence even stronger. Several international economic organizations (IEOs) have become its greatest proponents.[4] The World Bank identifies the following as fundamental components of rule of law:[5]

- There is a set of rules that are known in advance.
- Such rules are actually in force.

- Mechanisms exist to ensure the proper application of the rules and to allow for departure from them as needed according to established procedures.
- Conflicts in the application of rules can be resolved through binding decisions of an independent judicial or arbitral body.
- There are known procedures for amending the rules when they no longer serve their purpose.

Is there a correlation between the law and economic development? On balance, the answer seems affirmative. Available data suggests a strong connection between the role of law and intermediate growth factors (Pistor and Wellons 1999, p. 29). This notwithstanding, it should be borne in mind that other variables also contribute to the sustainability of economic development.[6]

Max Weber attributed the success of capitalist economy in Europe during the nineteenth century, among others, to the availability of "formal rational law" which produced an environment of high calculability or certainty of laws and strict observation of the principle of separation of powers. This theory seems to be based on ideological predispositions. Not surprisingly, it is often criticised as being "ethnocentric". Coase (1988) on the other hand, adopting a nuanced approach, theorized that coherent laws and institution primarily help to reduce economic transactions costs. The perspective of Coase tends to be more workable and readily acceptable, particularly by developing countries.[7]

Systematic research surrounding law and economic development paradigm is rare, or at best, is rather thin and sketchy (Pistor and Wellons 1999, p. 20). This is in part due to the acute divergence of research methodologies and perspectives — popularly dubbed as "scholars in self estrangement".

La Porta et al. (1999, pp. 5–13) have shown that laws and their strict enforcement have substantial effect on boosting investment confidence. In detailed studies of six Asian economies in connection to law, Pistor and Wellons (1999, p. 21) observed that for the most part, market-allocated laws and rule-based procedures tend to engender economic growth.

Seidman, Seidman, and Walde (1999, pp. 285–87) argue that law and legal institutions if utilized in a pragmatic and responsive manner would induce economic as well as political and social development. Without exaggeration it can be said that in the light of the Asian crisis and the ongoing globalization and democratization process, the law and economic development paradigm thinking has become more acute in the region. Arguably, the Asian crisis revealed, if not reaffirmed, two patterns. First, high-performing Asian economies (HPAEs), namely South Korea, Taiwan and Hong Kong (PRC), and Singapore possessed fairly sound legal systems and, more importantly, bureaucratic and political credibility. Second, HPAEs like Indonesia and Thailand, however, did not embrace proper rule of law and, consequently, bore considerably a lesser degree of bureaucratic and political credibility, which culminated to a greater willingness of business, bureaucratic and political elite to engage in rent-seeking and predatory behaviour.

At a conceptual level, the legal infrastructure creates an ascertainable "structure of expectations". At a practical level, the law does not eradicate all uncertainties, but it does substantially reduce commercial risk. First, the law conceptualizes and underpins the rights, obligations, and liabilities of all business parties. Second, the existence of law allows business parties to purse their commercial transactions with a reasonable degree of certainty and predictability. Third, the law provides legal recourse and due process. Fourth, and most importantly, it promotes and sustains business confidence. Taken together the law provides the incentives for economic allocative efficiency as well as risk allocation. Correspondingly, the law deters opportunistic or free rider behaviour that spawns negative externalities leading to market failures.

To this end, investment laws from an economic perspective engender an orderly framework by which prospective investors are encouraged to undertake projects that are consistent with a country's economic goals (De Soto 1990).[8] However, law is not a mere abstract notion existing in a vacuum. To be successful, studies show that the law has to work in tandem with a credible political set-up and prudent economic policies, among others.

Corollary to the law and development thinking is the practical reality of the politics of law reform. Amidst both national and international pressure many developing countries are reforming their laws through importation of model laws, essentially from the developed countries. Regrettably, many such transplants have shown visible signs of rejection (Seidman, Seidman, and Walde 1999). In sum, such receiving nations, because of acute differences in political ideology, cultural and social norms, were unable to absorb the imported laws in its entirety.

It is important that legal reform is undertaken in a holistic manner. Apart from the need to have responsive economic laws, it is equally or perhaps even more important to have a judiciary as well as a bureaucracy that is professional, independent, and unbiased.

3. Outline of Areas within Investment Treaties

Despite the inherent difficulties in deriving an international legal ordering for FDI, there are sources that provide legal principles and thinking. These include customary law, treaties (bilateral and regional), general principles of law, judicial decisions, non-binding soft laws, multilateral instruments like the Trade Related Investment Measures (TRIMs), Trade Related Intellectual Property Measures (TRIPs), and General Agreement on Trade in Services (GATS).

The international law on the protection of the assets of foreign investors was a highly contentious area prior to the advent of investment treaties. Much of the law was made in the context of the relations between the United States and the states of Latin America. In the rest of the world, investments flowed in the colonial context where disputes were settled in the courts of the imperial system. The foreign investor, being a citizen of the metropolitan state, would be satisfied with the decisions of these courts. Where investments were made in an area not subject to colonial control, issues would normally be settled through the exercise of military power. What was called "gunboat diplomacy" took care of such minor irritants. The link between power and the law was easy to see in these times. The law often disguised power.

Uncertainty came to be introduced into international law by the developing countries' claims to a New International Economic Order, a pillar of which was that the local economy, particularly natural resources, should be controlled entirely by national laws and disputes with foreign investors should be settled by local courts. Great uncertainty was introduced into the law as a result, because a significant number of states espoused the New International Economic Order. Given the vigour of the non-aligned movement in the 1970s, these ideas maintained support.

Given this schism, different developed states sought to solve the problem of certain rules relating to the protection of foreign investment through entering into bilateral investment treaties (BITs). This is the historical and the legal context for the prominence of such treaties.

Investment treaties are usually made to give protection to foreign investments from expropriation and ensure certain standards of treatment to them while they function in the host state. The assumption is made that the existence of such investment treaties promotes the flow of investments into the host state. There is no empirical evidence to support this assumption. The research on the subject comes to inconsistent conclusions.

Attitudes to them vary in the literature. Some praise them as providing the necessary confidence to ensure flows of foreign investments into the developing state, particularly one without sufficient legal safeguards in its own national system for the protection of assets and property rights. They see in these treaties the imposition of external standards to which states have to measure up to and enabling them to explain decisions on the basis of standards deemed desirable. In the globalizing world, where there is competition to attract foreign investment, the treaties are seen as necessary to create the framework for attracting such investments. The international financial institutions, like the World Bank and the International Monetary Fund, also promote them.

Investment treaties attract negative appreciation as well. They are seen as mere photo opportunities for visiting dignitaries, the most innocuous treaty to sign being an investment treaty. But, their negative impacts are felt much later.

There are pluses and minuses in investment treaties. They are here to stay. Apart from the making of bilateral investment treaties, there are now several regional treaties. ASEAN was a pioneer in the field, making such a treaty in 1987, long before the more famous Chapter Eleven of the North American Free Trade Agreement (NAFTA), which contains provisions on investment protection. Following NAFTA, other free trade agreements have chapters on investment. Most of the investment chapters in FTAs track the models of investment treaties made by the large state within the bloc that makes the FTA. Thus, the NAFTA provisions are nothing more than the U.S. Model BIT cobbled into the main treaty. Bilateral FTAs also have investment provisions in them. The effort to make a global investment treaty through the OECD and later the WTO resulted in failure. This, in itself, may accelerate the trend towards bilateral and regional investment treaties. But, it may also indicate caution, because with experience, some negative effects of these treaties are beginning to be clear.

The negotiator of these treaties in the Asian region must adopt a global perspective to these treaties. She must know the benefits and the pitfalls in these treaties so that she could shape the policy of her state towards these treaties. For this, she must have an awareness of contents of the treaties, the variance in the formulation of the provisions in them, the existing interpretations of the various provisions and the use to which they have so far been put. It is to give some understanding of such matters that this short guide is written. It highlights the principal areas in an investment treaty and indicates the different formulations used in existing treaties. Where possible, it also discusses the analysis of the provisions in the growing case law on the treaties.

3.1. The Preamble

All investment treaties, like other treaties, start with prefatory clauses or a preamble indicating the purposes that are to be achieved by the treaty. It is usual to state this purpose as being the promotion of reciprocal flows of foreign investment. The view or belief that such flows are beneficial to the economic development is also stated. This provision does not create an obligation on either party to stimulate the flow of foreign investment into the other state. Prefatory clauses of the treaty do not create any binding obligations in law but merely state the aims and objectives of the treaty.

3.2. Admission of Investments

There are two types of investment treaties. Some provide for the right of entry and establishment. These treaties create an obligation to permit the foreign investor of the other member states to enter the host state and establish businesses there. Their basis is to be found in the notion that foreign investment flows should be liberalized. Regional treaties such as the investment chapter of the NAFTA and the ASEAN Investment Agreement provide models of such liberalization treaties. If such treaties are entered into, the host state loses the right to screen the entry of investments individually as now happens in many states of the Asian region. However, it would be possible to exclude sectors of the economy from the scope of the rights of entry and establishment. Such liberalization treaties are made by the United States, Canada, Japan, and South Korea. They are seldom seen in the ASEAN region.

The traditional pattern of treaties is to stress only the aspects of treatment and protection of the foreign investment after the multinational corporation has made entry. Most European states make treaties that deal only with these two aspects. Asian states too have preferred such treaties as they retain many devices for screening the entry of investments in their national laws.

Many developing states have foreign investment laws that give screening authorities the power to determine whether the foreign investments mesh in with their economic development objectives. Such screening is also done to assess the impact of the investment on the environment and on the balance of payment situation. Feasibility studies have been made in many states as to the impact of the foreign investment on the host state economy and the environment by the foreign investor as a condition to entry. The screening authority will then determine on its own whether the admission of the foreign investment should be permitted or not. States which contain such foreign investment laws and regulations will be averse to making treaties permitting free flows of foreign investments.[9]

3.3. The Preservation of National Laws

The same effect can be achieved more comprehensively through the preservation of the host state's laws and regulations in the foreign investment treaty. Thus, the Model Bilateral Investment Treaty of the People's Republic of China gives the protection of the treaty only to investments that are made in accordance with the laws of China. This would mean that where the laws are violated by the foreign investor, the investment would move outside the protection of the treaty. There are similar formulations in other Asian treaties.[10]

As indicated, many states still maintain measures in their laws that are designed to ensure that foreign investors who enter operated their investments in such a manner so as to enhance the host state's economic policy objectives. They have instituted regulatory controls, which are designed to achieve these objectives. Whether these economic policies are misguided or not is beside the point. The fact is that they exist and are imposed on the basis of the sovereignty of the states. The BITs that are made preserve the regulatory laws imposing restrictions and active performance requirements on foreign investors. Most of the formulations that are contained in the BITs, which preserve the rights of the host states' laws, are formulated in such a manner as to ensure that future changes to the law are also preserved despite the provisions of the BITs. BITs then reflect an uneasy balance between the idea that there should be restraints on the sovereignty of the host state to deal with foreign investment as it pleases and the idea that foreign investment is a process which takes place entirely within the territory of the host state and is subject to the sovereign dictates of the host state's economic objectives.

3.4. The Definition of Investment

There are two principal methods used in defining investments used in investment treaties. The first is the enterprise-based method, which defines the enterprise that is to be protected as itself an investment and then defines the assets of the enterprise as included in the definition of the investment. As investments are made by enterprises, this is seen as a logical technique. The U.S. Model BIT largely adopts this technique. The other technique is to itemize each of the type of assets that a foreign investment may take into the country and list them as protected investments. So, these would range from physical assets such as machinery and equipment to intangible assets such as patents, know-how, the range of intellectual property rights as well as licences and permits necessary to carry out the investment. This is referred to as the assets-based definition and is the usual one that is employed in treaties made by most Asian states. Usually, however, what results is a combination of both types of definitions.

One controversial issue as to definition of investment is whether portfolio investment is to be included in the definition of investment. The ASEAN Investment Agreement has taken a definite stance on this indicating that portfolio investments are not to be considered as investments for the purpose of the Agreement. The aversion to the inclusion of portfolio investments may be due to a succession of economic crises caused by sudden withdrawals of portfolio investments. There may also be the fact that portfolio instruments circulate around the globe, and it may not be possible to know whom an obligation of protection is due. Asian states are not alone in excluding portfolio investments from the scope of their investment treaties.

3.5 Definition of the Investor

Foreign investments can be made by natural persons or by MNCs. There is no difficulty regarding the definition of a natural person. Usually, protection is confined to citizens though permanent residents are sometimes included. The treaties of Malaysia and Singapore often include permanent residents. Problems arise only in the case of double nationality.

Foreign investments are usually made by MNCs. Difficulties are presented by the concept of corporate nationality. In common law countries (Singapore, Malaysia) corporate nationality is based on the theory of incorporation so that any company that is incorporated in the country assumes its nationality. In civil law systems, the theory of nationality is based on where the effective management of the company is located. The latter theory is used by the non-common law states of Asia. The consequences of using these different theories need to be explored.

They are largely discussed in the context of three situations. The first situation is where a small state makes a treaty in the hope of becoming a platform for exporting foreign investment to a large state with a growing economy. The Mauritius–India treaty is a good example. The difficulty here is that a U.S. company (like Enron) could establish itself in Mauritius and then move into India to construct the Dhabol project. The termination of that project by the State of Maharashtra has involved India in much litigation based on the Mauritius treaty, jurisdiction being based on the fact that Enron is a Mauritian company as it had incorporated a subsidiary in Mauritius and moved into India through that subsidiary.

The second problem is round tripping. This is where nationals of the state move money into another state, which has a treaty with their home state, and then move it back into their home state as foreign investment.

Treaty protection could be invoked, as a company would have been incorporated in the state.

A third problem associated with corporations is the multiplicity of suits and the possibility of inconsistent awards. *Lauder v. Czech Republic* (2002) provides an example. Lauder (son of Estee of perfume fame) had dominance through his company of the television industry in the Czech Republic. There was state interference. The Lauder Company was a subsidiary of a Dutch company. Lauder himself was an American citizen. Here, two actions were brought, one on the basis that the Czech company was a subsidiary of a Dutch company, under the Netherlands-Czech treaty and another by Lauder as a shareholder in the Czech company under the U.S.-Czech treaty. Inconsistent awards were made. One was won by the Czechs. In the other, Lauder was awarded a large sum as damages. The facts were exactly the same. This situation has caused a lot of anxiety in circles which study investment treaties as well as among arbitration lawyers.

There are many ways attempted to get over these situations. The approach of the U.S. Model BIT is instructive: A party may deny the benefits of this treaty to an investor of the other party that is an enterprise of such other party and to investments of that investor if the enterprise has no substantial business activities in the territory of the other party and persons of a non-party, or of the denying party, own or control the enterprise.

3.6. Standard of Treatment

There are three standards that are used in treaties.

National standard of treatment implies that the foreign investor should be treated on terms of equality with the local citizens. This treatment is a much-prized standard of liberalization of foreign investment, as it requires equality between the domestic investor and the foreign investor. Perfect liberalization would require such a standard of treatment both at the pre-entry and the post-entry phases of foreign investment. Apart from NAFTA and the American and Canadian bilateral investment treaties that provide for pre-entry national treatment, those investment treaties that provide national treatment confine such treatment to the post-entry phase alone, leaving sufficient discretion in the state to decide whether or not to permit entry to the foreign investor.[11]

Most-favoured nation (MFN) treatment means that privileges that are created in other future treaties for nationals of states parties to these new treaties will flow through automatically for nationals of the states which are party to the treaty. MFN clauses are usually in trade treaties, and there is greater experience as to the interpretation of these treaties in the area of international trade.[12]

Fair and equitable standard is an amorphous standard which usually means that certain rights and privileges usually regarded as having been accepted in customary international law should be accorded the foreign investor. There is a strong view that this standard is higher than what the developed states have held out to be the customary international law standard in international law. But, after the urging of this standard in some NAFTA cases and their success, the NAFTA Commission has issued an interpretative note indicating that fair and equitable standard is not higher than the international minimum standard.[13]

Whereas in the past, the focus of litigation was on expropriation, treatment standards have now become the basis of litigation in many recent cases. There does seem to be a tendency to expand the meaning of the phrases such as "fair and equitable" standard or "minimum" standard, which are nebulous terms with no fixed content. Their use would result in the building up of precedent to give meaning and content to the formulae.

3.7. Repatriation of Profits and Other Proceeds

Repatriation of profits accruing from the investment is vital to the foreign investor. The *raison d'être* of the whole investment is that profits can be taken home so that shareholders could benefit from the investment or that it could be utilized for the expansion of the MNC. Home states of foreign investors would, therefore, insist on guarantees in treaties that assure the ready repatriation of profits as well as the proceeds of the assets realized upon liquidation or compensation paid in the event of the expropriation of the investment in freely convertible currency at the prevailing exchange rate. But, such repatriation may affect the balance of payment situation of the host state, particularly in times of foreign exchange crisis. Besides, the host state may prefer that at least part of the capital gains is reinvested in the host state. Strong repatriation provisions may therefore be resisted by states which anticipate balance of payment problems.[14]

Sudden flight of capital precipitated the Asian crisis and, as a result, hindered economic development. Relocation of FDI could have similar effects. An inflexible provision on repatriation will permit liquidation and relocation speedily. Such a result is avoided by some provisions.[15]

On a larger plane, the issue arises as to whether there could really be limitations placed by treaties on the right of the state to institute controls over its internal wealth. The treaties do not prevent devaluation of the currency.

The taxation of profits, which is a way of diminishing the extent of the profits, is not dealt with. So, there are indirect ways of dealing with the situation of repatriation of excessive profits. Where direct methods such as exchange controls are imposed, the question arises as to whether the fact that general international law permits such controls and the IMF Agreement allows it, would make the provisions permitting repatriation nugatory. The issue has not been raised in connection with the exchange controls in Malaysia. Some of the Malaysian BITs contain clear provisions on repatriation. But, the exchange control laws of Malaysia have not been challenged by any of the parties to the treaties. This may be because of a belief that these provisions do not override the right of a state to impose such measures in times of economic strife. One may argue that there is a fundamental right in a state to take such a course of action, which overrides its treaty commitments.

3.8. Expropriation

Expropriation of property by the host state poses the greatest risk to foreign investment. Host states have traditionally sought to fashion guarantees against the risk of such expropriation. The limitations on the right of expropriation that such expropriation should be for a public purpose and be non-discriminatory continue to be stated but the effect of such limitations in modern law are limited. It is as to the requirement of compensation that there is much dispute. The hallowed formula used by the developed states has been to require the payment of prompt, adequate, and effective compensation. The United States, which generated the Hull standard, has been consistent in its practice of including the formula in all its investment treaties. The OECD's draft multilateral investment agreement contains the Hull formula. Some investment treaties state the standard in terms of the requirement to pay full market value. The shifting of the emphasis to the valuation of the property does not affect the requirement that there must be payment of full compensation.

The payment of full compensation was seen as a hindrance to the institution of economic reform programmes by many developing states. They did not deny the requirement of compensation but sought a standard that would enable them to pay compensation having regard to the fact that the foreign investor may have made adequate profits from his investment in the course of his presence within the state. They sought to replace the Hull formula with the alternative formula of "appropriate compensation". The standard of appropriate compensation is a flexible standard which the developing states sought to introduce through a series of General Assembly resolutions. There is considerable authority to suggest that this alternative, flexible standard has had an impact on international law.[16]

The large number of treaties made in recent times with the ongoing trend towards liberalization favours the Hull formula. Most Asian treaties now use this formula. The removal of the most significant risk to foreign investment by the promise of full compensation is seen as leading to increased flows of foreign investment. Yet, other states see this as a significant restraint on their right to rearrange their economies by nationalizing foreign investment they perceive as not beneficial. They feel that flexibility is provided by the alternative formula of appropriate compensation, which enables the state to take account of the making of past profits or the unfairness of the expropriation to the foreign investor in assessing the amount of compensation. This may mean less than full compensation or it may mean more than full compensation, particularly in a situation where the foreign investor had been attracted into the country and his investment expropriated before it could produce profits. The alternative formula would also enable consideration of benefits brought to the state like the superior technology transferred or the infrastructure upgrading as well as harm caused to the host state through environmental depletion.[17]

The compensation debate, which animated the law to a large extent in the past due to differences in attitudes to the question between the developed and developing countries, is now a dormant issue. What has become significant is the issue as to what constitutes a taking. There are two types of takings, direct and indirect, and both are stated in the investment treaties. But, the use of the additional phrase "or anything tantamount to a taking" has given rise to the view that there is a third type of taking.

The wide view is that the clause covers regulatory takings, such as takings to protect the environment or the health interests of the host state. This has caused considerable concern, particularly to non-government organizations (NGOs) interested in the areas of environmental protection and human rights. Much of the hostility to investment treaties comes from these quarters. The need to assuage these sentiments is visible in the new versions of the American and Canadian Model BITs.

The issue of whether a state's regulatory powers over foreign investment will be curtailed by the expropriation provisions of investment treaties has caused acute concerns. The case law seems to indicate that it would. It is in that context that modern investment treaties have addressed the issue by carving out provisions that would ensure that the protection of the environment or other interests of the state should not be construed as amounting to expropriation.

3.9. Performance Requirements

The liberalization treaties require that there be no performance requirements imposed on foreign investment. This may cause problems in view of the provisions of the existing foreign investment laws of many Asian states. Save Singapore, other ASEAN member countries do exercise some form of performance requirements, perhaps not those that are disallowed under the TRIMs.

Developing countries tend to maintain such requirements that enhance the value of the foreign investment. But, developed countries refute the argument on the account that performance requirements distort international trade. To some extent, the TRIMs, an instrument of the WTO, is based on the prohibition of performance requirements on the basis of this argument. Though studies concentrate on the trade-distortive effects of such requirements, there are studies which show that the use of performance requirements has ensured the harnessing of foreign investment to the economic objectives of the host state.

3.10. Dispute Resolution

It is the dispute resolution provisions that have caused much anxiety in recent times as they have generated a large number of disputes submitted to arbitration, particularly to the World Bank sponsored International Centre for the Settlement of Investment Disputes (ICSID). ICSID was created in 1965 by the Convention for the Settlement of Disputes between States and Nationals of Other States. As its name implies, this World Bank sponsored convention created ICSID as a specialist centre for the settlement of investment disputes.[18]

If the assumption that investment treaties bring benefits to economic development be the basis of the treaties, some states believe that the amount of litigation they have to face may offset these benefits.[19] There is a current of disquiet arising from the amount of litigation that has arisen. Such litigation is costly. Developing countries, especially, do not have the expertise to deal with such disputes. They have to seek expertise from foreign lawyers to deal with such issues. The imbalance in the investment treaties is starkly evident here.

It would be good to explore strategies that would avoid the invocation of the dispute resolution provision. It has now become usual for treaties to require that negotiation of the dispute should be attempted for a specific period, at least for six months. Another technique that is employed is to require that there should be an attempt at seeking remedies through the local courts for at least a period of time. The Malaysia–Sri Lanka treaty, for example, contains a provision that requires that remedies through the local courts be attempted for at least one year. This would enable the matter to be settled within the host state itself. It will also enable the dispute to be identified and some legal settlement offered. The requirement that the investment should be approved for purposes of the protection of the treaty is also a useful device.

3.12. Safeguard Provisions and Exceptions

Investment treaties usually contain safeguards and exceptions to the standards of protection and standards of treatment that they offer foreign investors. The existence and variety of these safeguards and exceptions themselves defeat any claims as to the possibility of customary international law developing from these treaties. The nature of these safeguards and exceptions in relation to the treaty as a whole and in relation to specific provisions must be carefully scrutinized in order to determine the precise balance that has been struck in each treaty.

Safeguard provisions are intended to conserve at least a degree of regulatory space. But such space is preserved more effectively by provisions which are attached to the definition of the investment that is protected. A more effective way to preserve regulatory space is to confine the protection of the treaty only to those investments that conform to the regulatory regime of the host state. Such a limitation also achieves the objectives of economic development as the regulatory framework exists to promote such development. The extent of the regulatory space that can be preserved depends on the ability and bargaining strength of each state.

4. Recent Experience of ASEAN Member Countries with Investment Arbitration

The recent experience that ASEAN member countries have had with arbitration as well as the experience of other states outside the region will promote certain reluctance at least in some member countries. It is necessary to recount this recent experience. Some states have not had any reported arbitrations and are missed out.

4.1. Indonesia

Indonesia has not had any treaty-based arbitration but has had long-running investment arbitrations. In *Amco v. Indonesia* (1984) 23 *ILM* 351, (1988) 27

ILM 1281, a long-running ICSID arbitration, Indonesia went through an annulment process of the ICSID system in order to assert its right to take over a building project after the cancellation of an investment permit by its administrative agency for the non-satisfaction of a condition that capital must be brought for the project from abroad. The fact that the army had taken over the building complicated the matters. But, eventually, the right of the cancellation of the permit was recognized but what was condemned was the manner of its cancellation without due process. The view taken in *Amco v. Indonesia* has had supporters as well as detractors. There is a case for the view that the cancellation of the permit was justified on objective grounds.

The more recent arbitrations have come about as a result of contracts largely in the power sector signed by PERTAMINA, the state oil monopoly, and PLN, the state electricity corporation, with foreign firms to construct power plants. The contracts were on terms disproportionately disadvantageous to Indonesia in comparison to power projects in the region. When the Asian economic crisis broke out in 1997, there were cash-flow problems attending the projects. A series of Presidential Decrees suspended all the major projects. Three of the foreign investment companies went to arbitration. The arbitrations turned out to be acrimonious. The Indonesian courts issued injunctions against the holding of the arbitrations.

Two of the arbitrations, notwithstanding the injunctions, were held and resulted in awards against Indonesia. The Himpurna Arbitration (Paulsson, de Fina, and Piyartna) involved the alleged kidnapping of an arbitrator and led to bitter discussions of the episode. The Karaha Bodas Arbitration (Bernadini, El-Kosheri, and Derains) resulted in an award of over US$120 million against PERTAMINA. The third arbitration, the Paiton Energy Arbitration (Schwebel, Sornarajah, and Cardenas) was stopped when President Wahid intervened to order a settlement of the dispute. The dispute still remains unsettled. PERTAMINA has contested the enforcement of the Karaha Bodas Award before the courts in the United States, Hong Kong, and Singapore. The cases in the United States and Hong Kong have gone against PERTAMINA but appeals are pending.

This short survey indicates that Indonesian experience with investment arbitration has been an unhappy one. The awards in Himpurna and Karaha Bodas are by no means clean awards in that they arise from contracts heavily tainted with allegations of bribery. The procedures adopted and the law applied in both arbitrations are shaky. The enforcement of the awards will most likely be resisted all the way by PERTAMINA. There have been no treaty-based investment arbitrations against Indonesia. This may be because the investments protected under Indonesian treaties are only those investments "made in accordance with laws and regulations from time to time in existence" in Indonesia. The narrow definition of protected investment under the Indonesian treaties makes the invocation of the dispute settlement provisions of Indonesian treaties difficult, a fact indicated by the only Malaysian case discussed in the next sub-section.

4.2. Malaysia

Malaysia has had just one case involving foreign investment. But, it is relevant to point out that Malaysian investors in other states are beginning to institute arbitrations against their host states. Here, the dual role of an ASEAN state becomes evident. It is at once the recipient and the exporter of capital. As a recipient it is a target of arbitrations and has to use the shield. As an exporter, its investors hold the sword. This ambivalence will shape attitudes each of the ASEAN member states will have to the problems posed by investment arbitration. Malaysia will seek to become adept at playing the game as it has potential benefit for it, and it has acquired the legal sophistication to deal with this dual role. The more industrialized states of ASEAN such as Singapore and Thailand are in a similar position. As their capacity to operate in the international sphere as equals increases, they will be more willing to accept commitments in investment treaties that they see as enabling their investors to take investments abroad under conditions of protection.

The only arbitration that arose against Malaysia was *Grueslin v. Malaysia* (2000) 5 *ICSID Rpts* 483,225, which was a treaty-based arbitration. It arose out of exchange control legislation that Malaysia had imposed. The theory was that there was an expropriation involved in the exchange control laws as profits could not be repatriated and the assets had probably diminished in value as a result of the currency peg. But, to get to the point of arguing this, it had to be shown that the arbitration tribunal had jurisdiction. As under Malaysian treaties only approved investments received protection, Malaysia argued successfully that the claimant's investment was not protected by the treaty as it did not have such approval. Here, the contrast with the Argentinean situation is instructive. Argentina has been inundated with arbitration actions following its economic crisis. But, Malaysia escaped such arbitration through the simple devise of ensuring that not all investments automatically obtain the protection of the treaties. It is a lesson that must be kept in mind.

4.3. Philippines

The Philippines has also been hit with arbitrations, both treaty-based and contract-based. It had a spectacular arbitration, the Westinghouse Arbitration, following the unseating of Marcos. Westinghouse had built nuclear power plants, allegedly upon islands that contained dormant volcanoes. The incoming Aquino government accused that the contracts were obtained by bribery and refused to pay. Westinghouse went to arbitration and won an award. The nuclear plants remain unused to this day. More recently, the Pitaco Case involved the building of a new airport near Manila. Again, disputes arose. The airport remains unopened, and the dispute has moved through litigation before the courts and is now being arbitrated. The airport, meanwhile, remains unused. The politics of these projects attracts considerable attention among the public. The vast sums involved in vain in a poor country in non-usable projects do cause concern.

But, the dispute that has caused most concern is *SGS v. Philippines* (ICSID Case No. ARB/02/6, 29 January 2004). This case involved the employment of services of SGS, a Swiss company that specializes in providing customs services. SGS was to provide customs clearances for shipments to Philippines at the ports of origin of goods. Technically, the provision of services outside Philippines did not amount to foreign investment. But, a small component of the contract was that the customs operations in the Philippines would be computerized by the SGS. SGS argued that this small component of the agreement made the whole agreement a foreign investment contract, which fell within the protection of the Swiss–Philippines treaty. The tribunal accepted this argument. Controversially, it held that the general "umbrella clause" in the treaty, which stated that all commitments made to the foreign investor must be honoured, protected the investment. This conclusion was opposite to the conclusion arrived at in *SGS v. Pakistan* (ICSID Case No. ARB/01/13, 6 August 2003). The award again has caused much concern among Philippine lawyers.

4.4. Myanmar

Myanmar has had one arbitration. It was the first arbitration brought under the ASEAN investment treaties and is, therefore, analysed below. Briefly, the tribunal ruled that the jurisdictional requirements of the ASEAN treaties on investment had not been satisfied.

ASEAN member countries have not been hit with the same number of arbitrations as countries like Argentina in recent times. As explained, this is largely because of the fact that the ASEAN states have defined the investments protected by their treaties restrictively. Whether this is a good thing or not is a matter that must be considered. From the point of view of attraction of foreign investment, this may, at first glance, be thought of as a minus point.

But, experience shows that none of the investments that have entered ASEAN member countries have sought the type of approval that is necessary for treaty protection. This may give rise to the conclusion that treaty protection did not influence their choice of location.

5. The First ASEAN Investment Treaty Award

There has been, to date, only one arbitration brought under the ASEAN Investment Treaty and the ASEAN Framework Agreement on Investment. It must be remembered that the ASEAN Framework Agreement does not create a cause of action or avenue for dispute settlement. Its importance will appear when the case is described. The case is *Yaung Chi Oo Ltd v. Republic of Myanmar* (2003) 42 *ILM*. The case involved, as claimant, a Singapore company, which was formed by two sisters, who were both nationals of Myanmar but had permanent residence in Singapore. The facts stated are as alleged by the claimant, the company had purchased a decrepit beer factory that had been in existence from colonial times and turned it around into a successful venture with high sales. The claimant alleged that the beer factory was taken over through the intervention of the military. Myanmar claimed that there were good and sufficient reasons for the intervention by the state as there were improprieties relating to tax and other matters for the governmental interference.

The arbitration mechanism was invoked through the default mechanism in the Investment Agreement which enabled the claimant to approach the President of the International Court of Justice to appoint the tribunal if a party delays or refuses to nominate an arbitrator. Myanmar appeared before the tribunal that was appointed by the President and objected to the jurisdiction of the tribunal. The principal objection was that the investment was not approved by the Myanmar government for purposes of the protection of the investment. There were other objections such as that the investment was not a Singapore investment and that it was not managed from Singapore as the sister who was effectively in control was not in Singapore but was mostly resident in Myanmar. The argument was that there was no effective management of the company from Singapore as was required by the treaty. Myanmar also raised the issue of "round tripping". The argument was that it was not Singapore funds that were invested but funds that were really Myanmarese that were first brought into Singapore and then channelled back into Myanmar and that it could not have been the intention of the treaty to regard such funds as Singapore funds and offer it protection. The tribunal considered these objections, which would have future relevance to any disputes under the existing ASEAN investment treaties if they remain unchanged. It is best to deal with the minor issues first and deal with the argument, which was upheld by the tribunal last.

5.1. Corporate Nationality

The argument that was presented was that the mere incorporation of the company in Singapore was insufficient under the 1987 ASEAN Investment Treaty to characterize the investment as a Singapore investment as the treaty required it to be effectively managed in Singapore. Myanmar argued that this was not possible as the sister who was the principal figure in the company was continuously present in Myanmar and managed her Singapore company from Myanmar. As such, the effective management of the company could not have been located in Singapore. The claimant sought to meet this argument by relying on the fact that Singapore law treated every corporation that was incorporated in Singapore as a Singapore company and that as long as the requirements of the Singapore company law such as submission of annual accounts to the Registrar of Companies was satisfied the company must be considered as effectively managed in Singapore. The tribunal was prepared to hold for the claimant, pointing out that most transnational business in ASEAN was family-run and that it would be difficult for the principal figure in the business to be always located in the place of incorporation. Here, the tribunal was conscious of regional business patterns and was prepared to interpret the treaty in accordance with such business patterns.

Nevertheless, the manner in which corporate personality is defined will cause problems in the future ASEAN disputes and efforts at drafting future investment treaties. As much as the tribunal was prepared to take a bold view of business patterns in the region, the issue arises as to whether similar latitude would be shown to an entirely foreign business enterprise which merely incorporates in an ASEAN state and ventures into other states of the region. All ASEAN member countries do not follow an incorporation theory of corporate personality. Many, following the civil law system, would require effective management also to be located in the state that offers the protection. It is to accommodate these states that the 1987 Treaty required effective management to be shown. This matter requires further review and the Tribunal had not spoken the last word on this difficult subject.

5.2. Round Tripping

Myanmar also alleged that the funds were not brought into Myanmar from Singapore but were really Myanmarese funds that were taken from Myanmar into Singapore and then funnelled back into Myanmar through Singapore so as to give the impression that this was a foreign investment that was entitled to treaty protection. This is a common allegation made in the context of Asian investment. Thus, it is often suggested that some of the investment in China is really made through assets that are originally Chinese but routed through Hong Kong for a variety of reasons. It is possible for nationals of a state to obtain treaty protection through this device of "round tripping". It is a matter that has caused much anxiety in other arbitral disputes in other parts of the world. The tribunal was prepared to hold with the claimant on this and dismissed the argument that there was indeed round tripping involved.

5.3. Absence of Approval

In common with many investment treaties in the region, the ASEAN Investment Treaty also requires that the investment be specifically approved in writing for the purposes of the investment treaty. Myanmar, not being one of the original ASEAN states which made the 1987 treaty, was a later adherent to the treaty, and the approval had to be given after the date it became a member of the ASEAN. The claimant was conscious of the fact that this would prove a hurdle in its way to presenting the claim to the tribunal. The claimant sought to overcome this hurdle, first by arguing that the licence it had obtained from the Myanmar Investment Board was the only approval that could have been secured under Myanmar law and that this was sufficient for the purpose of the requirement of approval. The second argument was based on the ASEAN Framework Agreement. The argument was that the ASEAN Framework agreement had created the concept of an "ASEAN Investor", creating a right in such an entity to roam freely and make investments in the whole of the ASEAN region. The argument was that the intention of the ASEAN member states was to provide an enforcement mechanism for the concept through the existing 1987 treaty, which provided for dispute settlement. The Framework Agreement did not have a dispute settlement provision. This was an attractive argument based on the principles of the Vienna Convention on the Law of Treaties that when there is a later treaty on the same subject between the same treaties, the two treaties should be read together, as complementary treaties seeking to supplement defects and strengthen propositions. However, this attractive argument, which may well have been the intention of the states, was given short shrift by the tribunal, which refused to accept it. It rather held that the Framework Agreement was a "programmatic" treaty. It meant that it was aspirational and that the ASEAN Investor may have rights to roam about the region but has no protection. The tribunal was not robust enough to read the treaties as creating an effective framework of investment protection with effective mechanisms of protection, which are a necessary facet of investment treaties. It rather saw the Framework Agreement as a hollow exercise.

In this context, the law of ASEAN on investment, as read by the tribunal in *Yaung Chi Oo v. Myanmar*, is defective. The two ASEAN treaties are balanced instruments on investment unlike investment treaties in other parts of the world. It excludes portfolio investments. It enables disputes to be brought by the host state against the foreign investor, an absolutely novel proposition not found in any other investment treaty. The first treaty ensured regulatory space by requiring approval. The two treaties provided adequate safeguards for the interests of the host state as well as the investor. They could have been the basis of the building up of an effective law, except for the fact that the tribunal has interpreted the Framework Agreement as merely aspirational, thus robbing it of any content. To that extent the tribunal's refusal of jurisdiction is a disappointment in the ASEAN context and requires further examination.

6. Concluding Remarks

As indicated earlier, ASEAN already has an investment treaty that includes liberalization as well as protection of foreign investment. One would expect that picture to continue. Any investment treaty negotiated with non-member states of the region should capture the essential features of the existing treaties with some cautious measures built into it to ensure that the regulatory controls each state seeks to exercise in the context of its own stage of development are carefully provided for. Though the existing treaties may serve as models, it must be remembered that they were negotiated in the context of commitments that ASEAN states had made to each other and, hence, contain stronger principles than would be afforded to states outside the grouping. On the other hand, there may be a need to ensure that the benefits of greater flows of foreign investment are captured; assuming that such flows would take place consequent upon the making of such treaties.

There is no doubt in the minds of investors that the states of the region welcome investments. This is already indicated in the investment laws of the different member countries of ASEAN. The investment provision of a regional FTA will not have any signalling function to perform. The policy that the region as a whole is welcoming to investment is an existing policy as is the policy of retaining different degrees of regulatory control over investments. The two policies should not be seen as mutually incompatible.

They exist in any investment policy of any region, both developed and developing.

The existing instruments on investment in the ASEAN Framework Agreement on the ASEAN Investment Area (1998) and the Agreement for the Promotion and Protection of Investments (1987) reflect the trends, policies, and laws that existed in the region at the time of their making. Any new investment provision negotiated in the context of an FTA with a regional partner or a partner from another region will have to take into account newer policy goals and changes that have come about within the ASEAN region. Among them are the fact that there is a greater flexibility shown towards foreign investment and a greater confidence in dealing with foreign multinational corporations. As indicated in the studies above, the foreign investment laws of the region have undergone changes which indicate more favourable attitudes towards foreign investment.

But, on the negative side, there is the fact that litigation of disputes has increased and in most of them, the claim to jurisdiction has been based on the dispute settlement provision in the treaties. Some of the claims made against the states have involved large sums and the claims have often been made at awkward times such as when the state is facing an economic crisis. In these situations, states may become wary of entering into treaties. They may feel that their sovereignty is compromised as they are constrained from making decisions, which may be considered necessary in the context of the situation. It is therefore necessary to ensure that there are sufficient safeguard measures in the treaties that enable a state leeway to take action when faced with situations that require the taking of action in the event of economic necessities justifying interference with foreign investment. Such action may involve prevention of repatriation of profits or even the suspension of the operation of the investment in times of such urgency.

But, once such a principle is accepted, as indeed it is coming to be accepted even in the context of investments made between developed states, the issue is whether the investment treaty would become of little use. The maintenance of such regulatory space for control may emasculate the need for the treaty or the investment chapter, which are predicated on protection of the investment. If subjective appreciations of necessity are to provide a defence for the conduct of the state, the need for the treaty provisions become otiose. If objective considerations are to dictate the nature of the regulations, they would be met with the criticism that the sovereign right of a state to decide what is in its best interests are being subjected to external control and that sovereignty is thereby lost. Since what has been contemplated in the treaties is settlement of disputes by arbitration, difficult issues arise as to the democratic legitimacy of the foreign arbitration tribunal to settle disputes, which implicate the economic life of a state and call for such a predicament being balanced against the conflicting interests of a multinational corporation.

The model that is provided by the existing ASEAN investment treaties may not reflect the current thinking of many states of the ASEAN. They have made more sophisticated investment treaties and chapters on investment within FTAs. There will be other competing models that will have to be looked at. There have been many treaties made that are based on liberalization in recent times by the different ASEAN states. These include treaties made by Singapore and Malaysia, which are states that have reached a more advanced stage of development than the other member states of ASEAN. Singapore has made FTAs with the United States and India, both of which contain investment chapters based on liberalization notions. Malaysia has made such a treaty with Japan. More importantly, a state that is not at the same level of development as Singapore or Malaysia, Vietnam has made a treaty with Japan. So, the idea of liberalization may seem to cut across stages of development but all these treaties also provide for wide reservations. It is difficult, therefore, to determine the extent to which these newer treaties could provide a model for the negotiation of ASEAN investment treaties with non-member states.

Within the geographical region, there are other examples that are to be had. One such example is the FTA made between Australia and the United States. An important feature of the investment chapter is that it does not provide for an investor to state dispute settlement mechanism, leaving dispute settlement to inter-state procedures as existed during the times prior to the coming of investment treaties. There are various explanations for this situation. One is that this was a treaty between developed states and that they would be content with the remedies provided by the domestic courts of either state. But, this does not seem to be a reasonable explanation. It would be an explanation that would not be easy to give a state like Singapore, which believes that it has an effective system for the resolution of commercial disputes, and as advanced a system of commercial laws as any developed state. The better explanation appears to be that the burgeoning extent of litigation under NAFTA has scared states off investor to state provisions in investment treaties. The return to the old rules on diplomatic protection will not assuage the anxieties of foreign investors.

The solutions that have been adopted in the investment chapter of the Singapore–U.S. FTA are worthy of study, even though perhaps not worthy of repetition in the exact form. The investment chapter in that FTA contains safeguard provisions that ensures a relative amount of regulatory space for the host state over foreign investment. Provisions are made separately for measures taken for the protection of the environment, for safeguard measures taken in the interests of public health, safety and morals, and issues relating to taxation are separately provided for. The provision on expropriation was subject to an exchange of letters which provided that regulatory takings are to be exempted from the scope of the rule in the article on expropriation that required full compensation. There is, one would argue, adequate balancing of the regulatory space for the host state with the interest of foreign investment in liberalization and protection. But, eventually such a balancing is not to be effected by the states that are parties to the treaty but by the tribunal that is called upon to decide a dispute that arises. The extent to which the tribunal could tilt the balance has caused concern in recent times. Some have argued that the balance is tilted towards the interests of the foreign investor against the interests of host states. This may have been another reason for the anxiety with the dispute settlement mechanism in the investment treaties. But, absent a meaningful dispute settlement mechanism, the treaty itself would be looked upon as meaningless. The ultimate problem is balancing the interests of foreign investment which include the need for protection of the investment, transparency of the host state laws and liberalization of investment flows with the interests of the state in the regulation of the investment having its own economic objectives in mind. The search for this balance has been elusive.

The balance will become even more difficult to strike when one has to consider a regional association between states with widely disparate stages of development. One indication of a solution was provided by the earlier ASEAN Agreement on Investment, which sought to liberalize flows of investment within the region. It staggered the commitments of the less developed states as regards entry into certain sectors of the economy. Such a strategy is mandated by the existing laws of the member states in any case. A way of balancing should be to preserve the right of each state to decide on the extent to which it seeks to liberalize. This would also be consistent with the approach in several of the instruments in trade like the General Agreement on Trade in Services. A similar approach could be made in the case of investments when it comes to a regionwide investment treaty.

The vulnerability of the less developed member states has to be taken care of in the treaties that are to be made. Foreign investment may promote development but it does have the capacity to undermine it too. It is likely that less developed economies that lack sophisticated bureaucracies to deal with foreign investment may not be able to adequately harness the economic benefits that foreign investment brings. Such situations must be remedied through institutional support. There should ideally be provision for such support in the treaty that is made, enabling the regional institution to interfere and provide assistance to the state in need of such assistance. In situations such as an economic crisis, there should be mechanism for institutional or regional assistance to an ailing member state to cope with economic problems accentuated by the presence of foreign investment.

It may be possible to make a common template that could be used by ASEAN for the negotiation of investment chapters in FTAs or investment treaties. But, this would be a very difficult task to accomplish. Ultimately, the solution may be for each ASEAN state to negotiate its own investment treaty or investment chapter in an FTA having regard to its own economic circumstances and ideological disposition towards foreign investment. A great degree of coincidence is necessary in these matters for a common ASEAN-wide approach to be adopted. At the present stage, it is difficult to envisage the existence of such a coincidence of interests among the states. Nevertheless, it may emerge if discussions among the member states make progress and common agreement emerges.

NOTES

This is a summarized version of Chapter 2 of the REPSPF Project Report 04/10 entitled "AIA-Plus: Beyond Free Trade Agreements".

1. Essentially, this Calvo doctrine originated in the Latin American states, but other developing countries have taken much inspiration from it. The doctrine strictly disallows foreign investors to claim diplomatic protection as a means of settling an investment dispute with the host states, but to rely on local remedies.
2. The various FDI instruments promulgated by these international organizations are at best, model law/guidelines, as such do not serve as an instructive conceptual framework for FDI-related national legislation. These include: the OECD Guidelines on Multinational Enterprises, the UN Code of Conduct on Transnational Corporation and the World Bank's Guidelines on the Treatment of Foreign Direct Investment, among others.
3. The proponents of natural theory, among others, Kelsen H., Robert S. Summers, Fuller L.L. and Finnis J.M., advocate requirements of practical reasonableness, namely a coherent plan of life, no arbitrary preferences among values, no arbitrary preferences among persons, efficiency within reason, respect for basic value in every act, the requirements of the common good and following one's conscience. Well-known positivist theory proponents include Austin J., Hart H.L.A. and Jeremy Bentham.
4. Both IEOs (e.g., Asian Development Bank, World Bank) and bilateral donors have begun to regard law reform issues in the 1990s as part of their adjustment programmes — lending for law reform increased in the 1990s when good governance became part of the development agenda.

5. The doctrine of rule of law originally has a constitutional law flavour, but is increasingly used in a very wide context. Although a general definitional consensus of the doctrine seems to exist, however, its working methodology may differ among sovereign nations.

6. The other variables include political credibility, human capacity, economic factors such as availability of natural resources, markets, and macroeconomics consideration.

7. Coase (1988, p. 114) explains: "In order to carry out a market transaction, it is necessary to discover who it is that one wishes to deal with, to inform people that one wishes to deal and on what terms, to conduct negotiations leading up to a bargain, to draw up the contract, to undertake the inspection needed to make sure that the terms of the contract are being observed, so on. These operations are often extremely costly, sufficiently costly at any rate to prevent many transactions that would be carried out in a world in which the pricing system without cost."

8. De Soto, in his research with respect to Peru, found overwhelming evidence that an inefficient legal system reduced investment, led to stagnation of growth of big and efficient enterprises; limited usage of properties as collateral, and led to stagnation resulting from the lack of a system transferring and organizing property rights, among others.

9. In these circumstances, these states will adopt strategies that ensure their control over the access of foreign investment is not destroyed by the treaty. Thus, many treaties state that protection of the treaty will be given only to "approved investments". This would require the assessment of the potential effects of the foreign investment by the relevant administrative authorities before the protection of the treaty is engaged. Such provisions are used in BITs and multilateral instruments made by Southeast Asian states.

10. The Myanmar–Philippines Treaty (1998) protects investments made "in accordance with the Constitution, laws and regulation" of the parties. The Canada–Thailand Treaty (1997) protects investments that have been approved by the competent authority of Thailand under its investment laws. The schedule contains the investment statute of Thailand. Protection is contingent on the foreign investor conforming with the laws and regulations of the host state. Through such means the state ensures that its economic and other values, including the environment, are protected from abuse by the foreign investor. Thus, every investment treaty is a carefully calibrated compromise between the local states regulatory needs and the need to attract foreign investment by guaranteeing treatment and protection standards.

11. National treatment standards have been the bases for the litigation in *SD Myers v. Canada* (2001) 4 *ILM* 1408 and the *UPS v. Canada* (2003) litigation. A constitutional challenge to NAFTA has been mounted in the context of that latter litigation, alleging that the NAFTA provisions give greater rights to foreign

investors than to nationals. (NAFTA awards can be found in several websites, e.g. www.naftaclaims.com.)

12. An example of the combination of the MFN and national treatment and providing for the better of the two standards is in the Model BIT of the United States: "Each party shall permit and treat investment, and activities associated therewith, on a basis no less favourable that that accorded in like situations to investment or associated activities of its own national or companies or of nationals or companies of any third country, whichever is the most favourable..."

13. International Minimum Standard is derived from customary international law, as conceived by the developed states. It is a concept created in the practice of developed states which requires the treatment of an alien (also foreign investor) in accordance with an external standard which would normally be higher than the national standard. This standard is particularly relevant in disputes involving compensation for expropriation.

14. Some BITs provide for the situation of such problems by phasing out the time period in which repatriation should take place in situations where there is a foreign exchange crisis. They provided for the repatriation of a certain percentage of the profits where there is such a crisis and the repatriation of the rest of the profits after the situation has passed.

15. The Chile–Norway BIT states that "equity capital can only be transferred one year after it has entered the territory of the Contracting Party unless its legislation provides for a more favorable treatment". Chilean BITs generally contain this provision.

16. The World Bank Guidelines seeks to marry the two formulae by requiring appropriate compensation but suggesting that the payment of full compensation is the appropriate solution in the usual situation of expropriation of foreign property.

17. The formula of appropriate compensation continues to be used despite the amorphous nature of the standard involved in the formulation. There seem to be an accumulation of treaties incorporating the Hull formula in recent times. But, the continued affirmation of the standard of appropriate compensation in other treaties and the statement of some tribunals that the inclusion of the Hull standard is not conclusive but is only the starting point for the assessment of compensation keeps the alternative standard alive.

18. The Centre had few cases to settle until 1991 when *AAPL v. Sri Lanka* (1991) 30 *ILM* 577 was decided. For the first time, the possibility of invoking jurisdiction on the basis of a provision in the investment treaty was attempted successfully in that case. Since then the number of cases before ICSID has catapulted. The types of litigation theories attempted have also been rather startling and the whole area of investment arbitration has become a "wilderness of single instances". With the increase in the number of investment treaties in the 1990s, the scope

for such arbitration became expanded, resulting in rather difficult results with which many states are dissatisfied.

19. In 2003, Pakistan faced several arbitration cases in which the total sum claimed exceeded US$1 billion, a sum in excess of its national reserve. Argentina, a new entrant to states that make investment treaties, currently faces twenty-six different cases, all arising from its financial crisis and the exchange controls imposed as a result. The Argentinean President has promised to look into the issue of withdrawing from the investment treaties. The Lauder cases against the Czech Republic resulted in inconsistent awards on the same facts, resulting again in the response of the government that it would rethink its commitments under investment treaties.

REFERENCES

ASEAN Secretariat. *Investing in ASEAN: A Guide for Foreign Investors*. Jakarta: ASEAN Secretariat, 1999.

Cambell, D. and A. Wolff. *Legal Aspects of Business Transactions and Investment in the Far East*. The Netherlands: Kluwer Law and Taxation Publishers, 1989.

Coase, R. H. *The Firm, the Market and the Law*. Chicago: University of Chicago Press, 1988.

De Soto, Hernando. *The Other Path: The Invisible Revolution in the Third World*. New York: Harper and Row, 1990.

Ganesan, A. V. "Strategic Options Available to Developing Countries with Regard to a Multilateral Agreement on Investment". UNCTAD Discussion Paper No. 134, Geneva, 1998.

Hallward Dreimeier, M. "Do Bilateral Investment Treaties Attract Foreign Direct Investment? Only a Bit ... and They Could Bite". Working Paper No. 3121, World Bank, 2003.

La Porta, R., F. Lopez-de-Silanes, A. Shleifer, and R. Vishny. "Investor Protection: Origins, Consequences, Reform". Working Paper 7428. *NBER Working Paper Series*, Cambridge, MA, 1999.

Muchlinski, P. *Multinational Enterprises and the Law*. Oxford, U.K. and Cambridge, MA: Blackwell Publishers, 1995.

Pistor, K and P. Wellons. *The Role of Law and Legal Institutions in Asian Economic Development*. Hong Kong: Oxford University Press, 1999.

Salacuse, J. and N. Sullivan. "Do Bilateral Investment Treaties Really Work: An Evaluation of Bilateral Investment Treaties and their Grand Bargain". *Harvard Journal International Law* 46 (2005).

Seidman, A., Robert B. Seidman, and Thomas Walde. "The Way Forward". In *Making Development Work: Legislative Reform for Institutional Transformation and Good Governance*, edited by Ann Seidman, Robert B. Seidman and Thomas W. Walde, pp. 285–87. Kluwer Law International, 1999.

Soon, L. Y., ed. *Foreign Direct Investment in ASEAN*. Malaysia: University of Malaya, 1990.

Sornarajah, M. "The New International Economic Order, Investment Treaties and Foreign Investment in ASEAN". *Malaya Law Review* 27 (1985): 440.

———. *The International Law on Foreign Investment*. Cambridge: Cambridge University Press, 2004.

Tumman, J. P. and C. F. Emmert. "The Political Economy of U.S. Foreign Direct Investment in Latin America: A Reappraisal". *Latin American Research Review* 39 (2004).

United Nations on Trade and Investment. World Investment Report 2000: Cross Boarder Mergers and Acquisitions and Development, New York: UNCTAD, 2000.

9

ASEAN's FTA Negotiations with Dialogue Partners: Identifying Strengths and Weaknesses in Business Opportunities

Rahul Sen and Sanchita Basu Das

1. Introduction

The past decade has seen a rapid proliferation of regionalism among the Asian economies, which was initiated with the formation of the ASEAN Free Trade Area (AFTA) in 1992 and was essentially a free trade agreement (FTA) in goods. Thereafter, in the aftermath of the 1997–98 financial crisis and the inability of the WTO to further the multilateral trade liberalization agenda, highly trade-dependent countries in ASEAN, viz., Singapore, embarked on a new wave of regionalism as a means of enhancing the free trade agenda. More recently, other ASEAN countries such as Thailand (and later Malaysia), as well as other Asian economies, viz., Korea, Japan, China and India, have been actively pursuing this strategy to enhance economic and strategic cooperation among "like-minded" trading partners. It is in this context that ASEAN's FTA negotiations with its five major dialogue partners (DPs) — Australia and

New Zealand (CER), China, India, Japan, and Republic of Korea (ROK) — assumes importance.

Since FTAs in the current context implies liberalization of not only goods, but also services and investment, it is imperative that in order to complete successful negotiations of ASEAN's proposed FTAs with its five major DPs, ASEAN will need to enter into investment negotiations with these countries. However, these countries are significantly different in terms of their economic structures and extent of economic linkages vis-à-vis ASEAN. Thus, a successful investment negotiation that can drive a two-way investment flows would require an understanding of the underlying potentials and risks of these five FTA partners with ASEAN. In this regard, the main objective of this chapter is to study the strengths and weaknesses of the five DPs vis-à-vis ASEAN, and hence carve out the possible areas of competition/complementarities of the same in the global market.

2. ASEAN as an Investment Destination: Strengths and Weaknesses

2.1. Internal Strengths

ASEAN is a growing market of 567 million people with a combined gross domestic product (GDP) of US$1.07 trillion. Economic growth in the region is primarily driven by investment in productive sectors, reflecting international investors' confidence in ASEAN's economic prospects. The countries strengths range from natural resource-based production to highly capital-intensive industries (electronics, textiles, automotive sector). Collectively, the region is a highly competitive production base, stemming from good infrastructure and productive skilled labour. Investors also benefit from ASEAN's geographic location between India (South Asia) and China and Japan (East Asia). In addition, ASEAN has a well-developed financial market and it is a hub for cost-effective sea and air transport.

Consistently strong emphasis on education over the years has put ASEAN ahead of many emerging markets in meeting the needs of international businesses. Progressive liberalization policies contribute to maintaining ASEAN's global competitiveness, which makes ASEAN a natural place of business for international firms. Following AFTA, tariffs are down to 0–5 per cent for over 96 per cent of the goods traded; ASEAN is now moving towards establishing an ASEAN Economic Community (AEC) by 2020 (this has been brought forward to 2015). This promotes ASEAN not only as an integrated market but also as a single investment destination.

2.2. Internal Weaknesses

ASEAN has no legal entity of its own. This can lead to some legal problems if some party wants to challenge the legality of an ASEAN policy decision. It cannot obtain any tax-exemption status, and this may deter big MNCs from contributing funding support to ASEAN projects. The expansion of ASEAN to ten members has made it harder for the organization to maintain focus and reach consensus as the preferred ASEAN way allows maximum flexibility and takes into account changing domestic circumstances. The socio-economic disparities within and among countries in the region is striking. According to UNDP's 2004 Human Development Report, based on US$1 a day poverty threshold, while Malaysia and Thailand recorded less than 2 per cent poverty incidence, Cambodia and Laos suffers with poverty incidence of 34 per cent and 27 per cent respectively. Further, sporadic internal disputes continue to dampen bilateral ties among ASEAN members and the spirit of closer cooperation. For example, Thailand's relations with its neighbours to the west and east — Myanmar, Laos, and Cambodia — have at times gone beyond verbal sparring.

The region also suffers from uneven focus on key areas (such as trade, investment, technology, and security) and is not able to address issues like human rights, treatment of ethnic minorities, political and civil rights due to sensitive political nature of one or some member government(s). All these eventually lead to a slow response during crisis periods and hence weaken the process of economic integration. Efforts are currently ongoing to frame an ASEAN Charter that can provide a legal entity and perhaps a strong foundation to create legal institutions for economic integration.

Lastly, having recovered from the impact of the Asian financial crisis, the reforms in the banking sector have been slow, causing the region to remain vulnerable to any softening of external demand. Both the currency and stock market still remain unpredictable. There are also concerns about the rate of growth of household borrowing and the acceleration of asset prices.

2.3. External Opportunities

ASEAN is registering rapid growth in services and knowledge-intensive industries such as tourism and hospitality industry. Given the rapidly rising healthcare costs in many ASEAN countries due to ageing population and sexually transmitted diseases, opportunities exist for mutually beneficial cooperation in healthcare activities and in generic and other drugs. The rising affluence of the workforce has strong implications for demand for lifestyle consumer goods and financial products. Already, the consumer market of US$320 billion is larger than India's and close to that of coastal China.

ASEAN economic structure is varied due to the wide economic diversity among its member nations, ASEAN offers a wide variety of sectors for investments. Countries such as Malaysia, Singapore, and Thailand are more poised to take on high-end manufacturing as well as services, whereas countries like Indonesia, which has of a pool of unskilled labour and abundant natural resources, might be more suited for low-end manufacturing.

Regional economic integration in ASEAN is gathering strong momentum. ASEAN is now reaching out to establish FTAs with China, Japan, Republic of Korea, and CER, re-emphasizing its position as a major production base in the world market. Besides, ASEAN is also committed to deepen its intra-regional economic integration with participation from the private sector.

2.4. External Threats

Despite the existence of AFTA, ASEAN trades more with other countries (80 per cent) than among its member countries, leading to more concerns about currency stability against major international currencies like the U.S. dollar. The export competition posed by Chinese goods in the important markets of the United States and Japan is a major concern of regional policy-makers. The region also faces limited competition from India in the sphere of business process outsourcing, as both countries are popular destinations for lower-skilled jobs. Problems in East Timor and Southern Thailand increase the risk for the whole region from time to time. Bird flu, which can be deadlier than the SARS outbreak, is endemic to Southeast Asia and poses the biggest risk to public health in the region.

Nevertheless, in ASEAN, the prospect of increasing threats will impel the member countries to shore up their strengths and fix up their weaknesses. The growing competition from China and, to a lesser extent and in a more limited scope, from India will push ASEAN into hastening the integration of the regional market.

In the light of the above, the next sub-sections analyse the respective strengths and weaknesses of each DP vis-à-vis the same for ASEAN.

3. ASEAN–CER

Since the late 1960s, CER has worked closely with ASEAN economies lowering trade barriers both internally and externally. While in the late 1960s only 5 per cent of Australian exports went to ASEAN, this has now grown more than threefold, thus making it one of Australia's main export markets. Imports from ASEAN have followed a similar path, increasing rapidly over the last decade. This can also be seen from Table 9.1, where all the trade intensity indices are greater than 1, suggesting trade flows are larger than expected given the neighbouring groupings' importance in world trade.

The CER-ASEAN linkage mimics the above description, and it is increasingly becoming a two-way linkage. Hence in 1993, it was formally proposed that the scope for cooperation between AFTA and the CER be examined, and in 2002 a broad-gauged Closer Economic Partnership between the two groups were signed. Finally, in 2005, this has moved to FTA negotiation stage in 2005, which is expected to be completed in the next two years with complete implementation within ten years.

3.1. Internal Strengths

The CER economies have been growing impressively in recent years, averaging around 4 per cent during 1993–2003. While both ASEAN and CER have some strength that is similar (like economic dynamism), they differ in terms of resource endowments. Apart from being well endowed in natural resources, other relevant CER strengths are open economy, stable governments, and capital markets. It also offers high skills and income, strong services sector and better environmental standards. Both ASEAN and CER have supportive external relations, especially with the EU and the United States.

3.2. Internal Weaknesses

ASEAN and CER differ in their sectoral, socio-economic and political make-ups. CER suffers from relatively low total factor productivity, small and ageing populations, low savings rate, high debt, and too much dependency on resources.

Table 9.1
Merchandise Trade Intensities of ASEAN-6 with CER

	ASEAN-6–CER		
	1993	*1998*	*2003*
Trade Intensity Index	1.36	1.99	2.29
Bilateral Trade Intensity Index for Total Trade	1.72	2.04	2.05
Export Intensity Index	1.38	2.00	2.08
Import Intensity Index	2.06	2.08	1.98

Source: UN Comtrade, authors' calculations.

3.3. External Opportunities

The merchandise export similarity index of ASEAN and CER in the world market support the fact that there is not much of similarity between the exports of the two groupings, more so with respect to the U.S. trade (Table 9.2). With the broad categories of services exports, the export similarity index of ASEAN and CER in the world market shows greater similarity with the order of the categories being travel, transport, communications, and financial services a distant fourth (Table 9.3).

Similarly, the Revealed Comparative Advantage (RCA) Index, which is used to assess a country's export potential (Balassa and Noland 1989), depicts that CER has a greater share of highly competitive products while ASEAN has a greater share of lowly competitive products (Table 9.4).

Looking at the analysis in Table 9.4, it can be said that both CER and ASEAN offer immense opportunities to each other. Firstly, the groupings would benefit from a growing regional economic bloc through greater regional integration, including investment. Opportunities will come up from having opened up economies and integrated production base/networks, especially in services like travel and tourism. There are a number of strong economic complementarities between CER and ASEAN. Some of the opportunities are already reflected in the type of bilateral investments that have taken place in the past, for example, ASEAN investment in energy, agri-business, real estate,

Table 9.2
Export Similarity Indices for Merchandise Trade of ASEAN-6 and CER

	1993	1998	2003
Exports to the World	27.17	30.11	28.88
Exports to the U.S.	60.77	30.62	40.43

Source: UN Comtrade, authors' calculations.

Table 9.3
Export Similarity Indices for Services Trade of ASEAN-6 and CER to the World Market

Services Sector	1993	1998	2002
Computer, communications and other services	15.7	19.2	19.7
Insurance and financial services	0.8	0.7	1.6
Transport services	15.9	24.6	23.9
Travel services	43.1	32.2	38.2

Source: UN Comtrade, authors' calculations.

Table 9.4
RCA Indices for Merchandise Exports of ASEAN-6 and CER

Number of Products (% Share in total exports)

Categories	Range	1993 ASEAN-6 Pdt	Share %	1993 CER Pdt	Share %	1998 ASEAN-6 Pdt	Share %	1998 CER Pdt	Share %	2003 ASEAN-6 Pdt	Share %	2003 CER Pdt	Share %
Non-competitive	Less than 0	781	20.4	825	24.5	817	24.7	797	24.4	799	29.6	800	22.8
Low-competitive	0.0 – 0.49	173	43.6	110	11.5	157	30.5	123	13.8	172	33.2	116	20.5
Mid-competitive	0.50 – 0.69	43	16.3	30	7.5	35	37.2	37	6.1	36	24.1	30	3.9
High-competitive	0.70 – 1.00	28	19.8	53	56.4	17	7.6	56	55.7	18	13.1	59	52.7
Total		1,025	100	1,018	100	1,026	100	1,013	100	1,025	100	1,005	100

Source: UN Comtrade, authors' calculations.

and tourism services, and CER investment in ASEAN as a regional logistics hub (air transport). Moreover, ASEAN is uniquely positioned to facilitate intra-regional and inter-regional cooperation across a wide range of fields, including economics and security. The increasing interaction within the Southeast Asian region due to globalization, technology changes and common interests in responding to numerous challenges (for example, financial contagion, SARS, transnational crime, and migration) facilitate a greater need for intra-regional policy coordination.

3.4. External Threats

Even though there are opportunities, threats also exist. However, some of the differences in weaknesses between CER and ASEAN may encourage FDI flows on the basis of risk management. For example, a narrow dependence of one group can be overcome by diversifying new investment opportunities in the other group. There are other risks, too — bird flu or slow progress in ASEAN integration — but these could be minimized through diversification and stronger linkages through FTA. The opportunities just discussed could also become threats and vice versa. For example, a lack of international trade liberalization or an energy crisis magnifying isolation could threaten the opportunities from opening economies, but greater regional integration diminishes these by forming larger "domestic" markets and offering the opportunity to form a "building block" towards multi-lateral trade liberalization. Similarly the threat of terrorism to international integration is countered by cooperative approaches that have already been applied between ASEAN and Australia.

Therefore, the above analysis suggests that with ASEAN–CER FTA, there are opportunities for gains from trade and investment through specialization (in components) and technology transfer. Currently, each partner is underinvesting in the other and competing on the international stage for investment funds. This can be seen in Table 9.5, where the FDI intensity index declined over time to less than one, suggesting the bilateral investment is less than expected given the partner's importance. Hence, an FTA would bring in more gains from greater integration.

Table 9.5
FDI Intensity of ASEAN with CER

	1995	1998	2003
FDI Intensity Index	4.00	−10.46	0.75

Source: Authors' calculations, UNCTAD.

The services sector would appear to offer more opportunities for mutually beneficial economic cooperation where the impediments are less obvious than tariffs. Relevant sectors include tourism, education, health, transport, telecommunications, and financial services. These include priority sectors in tourism, health, e-ASEAN, and aviation (which are being negotiated separately).

However, often the negotiated outcome is not the preferred outcome suggested from straight analysis because of political economy aspects. These points to the importance of the strategies being based on an economy-wide perspective and not on any special interests. The same principle applies to good domestic policies, which go a long way in building trade, and investment flows, not only between ASEAN and CER countries but involving the rest of the world.

4. ASEAN–China

The bilateral relation between China and ASEAN started to develop in 1991 when China expressed its interest to cooperate with ASEAN in the field of science and technology. The relationship was further strengthened with economic and trade cooperation in 1993 and with an agreement to exchange ideas among senior officials on political and security issues. In July 1996, China became a full dialogue partner of ASEAN, and by early 1997 they already finished five parallel frameworks of dialogue. This increased the bilateral trade between ASEAN and China, which jumped more than sixfold to US$55 billion during 1993–2003. The upward trend of all the indices, shown in Table 9.6, further strengthens the fact that both ASEAN-6 and China are becoming increasingly important trade partners to each another. Throughout the decade, while China was seen as a cheap source of food products and basic manufacturing goods for ASEAN, ASEAN was seen as a source of raw material for the rapidly growing industrial sector of China.

Table 9.6
Merchandise Trade Intensities of ASEAN-6 with China

	ASEAN-6–China			China–ASEAN-6		
	1993	*1998*	*2003*	*1993*	*1998*	*2003*
Trade Intensity Index	0.83	1.16	1.12	0.97	1.15	1.29
Export Intensity Index	0.82	1.19	1.14	0.96	1.16	1.32
Import Intensity Index	0.97	1.14	1.29	0.83	1.16	1.12

Source: UN Comtrade, authors' calculations.

Finally, in August 2001, China made a strong push, proposing tariff reduction and other measures to be phased over 2003–2009. At the ASEAN–China summit in November 2001, Chinese Premier Zhu Rongji formally made the proposal for the formation of a China–ASEAN FTA to be carried out within a span of ten years (Sheng 2003).

4.1. Internal Strengths

China boasts of a pool of cheap unskilled and skilled labour, which translates to the fact that it has the necessary human resources to undertake both low-end and high-end manufacturing and services products. The Chinese government has shown a strong commitment to market reforms and economic growth (average real GDP growth more than 9 per cent for the last ten years) and has taken strong measures to combat corruption.

4.2. Internal Weaknesses

On the economic front, China runs the risk of an overheating economy. Its banking and financial systems are poor and hence inefficient at channeling investment funds. While there have been efforts to fight corruption, it remains a major issue for China. The infrastructure sector is not yet developed, and its transportation cost is high. Furthermore, due to strong rivalry among provinces in terms of attracting more foreign investments and other resources from the central government, in many cases their policies have turned out to be uncoordinated, thus making it difficult for the entire country to move in one direction.

4.3. External Opportunities

The economic analysis (Table 9.7) shows that there is limited complementarity between China and ASEAN. Although more than 40 per cent of Chinese goods are in the mid- to high-competitive range, the composition of goods changed overtime from primary produce to manufacturing products. Hence, one can say that ASEAN-6 and China are not cut-throat competitors where merchandise exports are concerned.

For services, Table 9.8 indicates that there are greater potential in the financial and transport services sectors. As China continues to expand and move towards a more developed economy, the demand for these services will also increase exponentially.

That said, there is considerable scope for cooperation between ASEAN and China in specific areas. China–ASEAN's combined population of over

Table 9.7
RCA Indices for Merchandise Exports of ASEAN-6 and China

Categories	Range	Number of Products (% share in total exports)					
		1993		1998		2003	
		ASEAN-6	China	ASEAN-6	China	ASEAN-6	China
Non-Competitive	less than 0	781 (20.4)	673 (19.1)	817 (24.7)	661 (19.9)	799 (29.6)	656 (16.7)
Low-Competitive	0.0 – 0.49	171 (37.8)	168 (22.5)	157 (30.5)	195 (32.5)	172 (33.2)	230 (42.7)
Mid-Competitive	0.5 – 0.69	45 (22.1)	83 (21.7)	35 (37.2)	91 (23.6)	36 (24.1)	96 (31.1)
High-Competitive	0.7 – 1.00	28 (19.8)	86 (36.7)	17 (7.6)	66 (24.1)	18 (13.1)	28 (9.5)

Source: UN Comtrade, authors' calculations.

Table 9.8
RCA indices for Commercial Services Exports of ASEAN-5 and China[a]

Series Name	ASEAN-5			China		
	1993	1998	2002	1993	1998	2002
Computer, communications and other services	0.07	0.06	−0.10	0.01	−0.03	−0.09
Insurance and financial services	—	—	0.01	—	—	−0.41
Transport services	−0.22	0.03	0.11	−0.17	−0.41	−0.21
Travel services	0.12	0.00	0.11	0.12	0.25	0.26

Note: a. Data on Brunei are not available and hence is not included. Data on ASEAN-5 are
not available for 2003.
Source: Authors' calculations.

2 billion offers an attractive market for each other. As discussed, there is immense opportunity in China's market for services, as the country's growing living standards would demand more services from financial and tourism sectors. Moreover, China's huge population with limited agricultural resources implies enormous opportunities for ASEAN countries in the primary sector. Going ahead, China is expected to show further expansion as the Economist Intelligence Unit (EIU) predicts that its per capita GDP will rise from US$1,230 in 2004 to US$1,790 in 2009. As Chinese citizens become wealthier, their demand for goods and services will increase, which will eventually translate into many business opportunities for ASEAN.

As China is trying to upgrade its infrastructure and fight back corruption, there are more foreign banks entering the Chinese market. These measures, if implemented successfully, can streamline FDI inflows into China, and bring in more business opportunities for foreign businessmen interested in wooing the Chinese market.

From China's perspective ASEAN offers a consumer base of 500 million. The EIU forecasts that per capita GDP in ASEAN-7[1] will rise from US$1,460 in 2004 to US$2,160 in 2009, thus a richer ASEAN will lead to an increased demand for goods and services. Furthermore, ASEAN countries are sources of FDI, and with greater liberalization in China it can become a more attractive destination for ASEAN foreign investments. Singapore and other ASEAN countries have already poured substantial investments into China.

4.4. External Threats

From ASEAN's perspective, China's increasing capacity to produce high-valued manufacturing goods could present a threat. For example, in the area of electronics China's growing capacity could lead to more competition between China and ASEAN in a third country. From Table 9.9, we can say that both ASEAN-6 and China are competitors in the manufacturing sector, more so with respect to the U.S. market. Competition from China in the area of labour-intensive manufactures is already posing a threat to ASEAN countries. This could intensify as China continues its process of economic integration.

On the other hand, under services trade, ASEAN-5 and China are less competitive (see Table 9.10). However, the export similarity index has been rising since 1998. This could be due to the rising importance of the tourism sector, which accounted for more than 50 per cent of China's total services exports since 1998. Yet, in other services sectors, China is lagging behind ASEAN-5 in terms of trade shares. Hence these could be the areas in which ASEAN-5 can maintain a strong foothold over China.

Apart from the export similarity, the current Taiwan–China tensions also act as a threat for the region as this could have adverse implications for intra-Asian trade and investments. China's inability to comply with its WTO commitments could also have a devastating effect for ASEAN countries' trade and economic prospects.

China is currently facing an environmental crisis, with air quality in major cities deteriorating rapidly, or reaching hazardous levels. The country suffers from widening income gap that could lead to possible social unrest.

Table 9.9
Export Similarity Indices for Merchandise Exports of ASEAN-6 and China

Year	Exports to the U.S. market	Exports to the world market
1993	33.40	41.07
1998	37.49	43.18
2003	46.96	47.17

Source: Authors' calculations.

Table 9.10
Export Similarity Indices for Services Trade of ASEAN-6 and China

Sector	1993	1998	2002
Computer, communications and other services	35.7	35.9	32.3
Insurance and financial services	0.8	0.7	0.7
Transport services	15.9	9.6	14.5
Travel services	42.6	32.2	38.2
Overall	95.0	78.4	85.7

Source: Authors' calculations.

Other issues that could pose a threat for ASEAN–China trade relations are competition from Japan in manufacturing and from India in services (particularly information technology), rising protectionism in developed countries against China's labour-intensive exports (such as garments), the current territorial disputes with China, and the perception that China's economic and military rise will threaten the economic and political security of the countries in the region.

Given the analysis, it can be deduced that although ASEAN and China might get increasingly competitive in the manufacturing sector, they are not stiff competitors with respect to specific products. On the other hand, ASEAN should move up the value chain, thus taking advantage of intra-industry trade (IIT) between ASEAN and China. This is shown in Table 9.11, where the aggregate Grubel Lloyd (G-L) index increased almost twofold and IIT level has increased by more than five times.

ASEAN countries can reduce their cost disadvantage vis-à-vis China as there are other aspects in the production and distribution processes where the ASEAN grouping can improve. For example, in case of textiles and clothing, as material costs account for a substantial portion of the total cost of production, there is considerable scope for cost reduction from greater economic cooperation within ASEAN. Indonesia and Thailand can supply yarns and other ASEAN producers can set up supply chain as a means of lessening competition among themselves. Improvements in transport, delivery and bureaucracy may also compensate for the relatively high wage costs in ASEAN.

Thus, to secure an advantage over China, ASEAN should focus on improving product and service quality, efficiency and reliability. They should try to move up the value chain and develop their own niches. The grouping should also focus on specific product areas where they have significant advantage over China including mineral and petroleum products, technology-intensive products (semi-conductors and high-valued electronic components), natural resource-based products (timber and paper products), food and food products, textiles, metal and metal products, leather and leather products,

Table 9.11
IIT Estimates for ASEAN-6 Trade with China

	1993	*1998*	*2003*
G-L aggregate index	24.2	38.6	43.0
IIT level (US$ million)	9,592.9	19,619.2	52,281.9

Source: Authors' calculations.

chemicals, plastics and services. It is vital that these advantages are enhanced by investing further in education and by making use of ASEAN's natural resources on sustainable and efficient basis.

Apart from focusing on new areas, ASEAN countries should look for ways to complement China. They should focus on agricultural products, intermediate capital goods, and mineral products and should get a preferential entry under the ASEAN–China FTA. However, the ASEAN countries must "set their house in order" to respond to the preferential access-induced economic opportunities in the Chinese market.[2]

ASEAN and China are less in competition with each other in services area compared with manufacturing. Hence, ASEAN should take advantage of financial services (including insurance) and transport sector.

In terms of ASEAN–China investment linkages, ASEAN is a heavier investor in China than vice versa. According to Table 9.12, China's FDI into ASEAN-6 countries has been lesser in magnitude relative to world FDI to ASEAN-6, and this value has been declining over time. On the other hand, ASEAN prefers to invest more intensively in China relative to investing in the rest of the world. This could be due to the fact that Singapore is one of China's largest investors.

Hence, in order to attract more FDI from China, ASEAN should increase its attractiveness as an investment destination by providing more security and convenience to prospective investors. This can be done by achieving harmonization of customs procedures and minimization of customs requirements and making ASEAN standards consistent with international standards. Establishing institutional and legal frameworks to support regional cooperation and dispute settlement will also be helpful.[3]

On the whole, ASEAN–China economic relations look promising. However, given China's rapid rate of economic development, ASEAN's strategy to stay ahead of China has to be executed quickly. Moreover, the increasing attractiveness of Chinese economy should also compel ASEAN to cooperate and execute sound economic strategies with China.

Table 9.12
FDI Intensity Index of ASEAN-6 with China

	ASEAN-6–China		China–ASEAN-6
	1998	*2003*	*2003*
FDI Intensity Index	0.22	0.01	1.7

Source: Authors' calculations.

5. ASEAN–India

Since the inception of India's Look East Policy in 1991, the scope and density of relations between India and ASEAN has been steadily rising (Kumar, Sen, and Asher 2006). India became a sectoral dialogue partner of ASEAN in 1992. The sectors were trade, investment, tourism, and science and technology. This led to a discernible upward trend in bilateral merchandise trade between the two countries. More specifically, trade between ASEAN-6 and India more than tripled during the period 1993–2003. Looking at the trade intensity index over the decade (Table 9.13), ASEAN-6 has regarded India as a more important trading partner compared with what India regards ASEAN-6, in relation to their trade with the rest of the world.

Hence, mutual interest in wider engagement led ASEAN to invite India to become a full dialogue partner of ASEAN during the Fifth ASEAN Summit in Bangkok in December 1995 (ASEAN Secretariat 1995) and a member of the ASEAN Regional Forum (ARF) in July 1996. An important milestone was achieved with the hosting of the first ASEAN–India Summit in Phnom Penh, Cambodia in November 2002. Finally, a Framework Agreement on establishing an FTA between ASEAN and India was signed by the Indian Prime Minister during the Second ASEAN–India Summit in Bali in October 2003. The ASEAN–India FTA is expected to encompass a strategic and political partnership, thus going well beyond a traditional FTA agreement (Bhattacharya and Ariff 2002). It is, however, important not to underestimate the challenges that lie ahead in achieving the ASEAN–India FTA as much will depend on how ASEAN as a grouping evolves in the future, and its capacity to effectively sustain and enforce any ASEAN-wide agreements.

Table 9.13
Merchandise Trade Intensity Index of ASEAN-6 with India

	ASEAN-6–India			India–ASEAN-6		
	1993	*1998*	*2003*	*1993*	*1998*	*2003*
Trade Intensity Index	1.37	2.65	2.45	1.36	0.97	1.80
Bilateral Trade Intensity Index for Total Trade	1.43	1.97	2.00	1.06	1.45	1.92
Export Intensity Index	1.21	2.13	2.59	1.17	0.88	1.67
Import Intensity Index	1.44	1.13	1.24	0.66	1.57	1.95

Source: Authors' calculations.

5.1. Internal Strengths

India's trillion dollar economy is widely expected to continue to grow at about 12 per cent in nominal terms and between 7–8 per cent in real terms due to favourable demographics, high saving–investment ratios (above 30 per cent of GDP), relatively efficient financial and capital markets, and a private corporate sector from which global companies are beginning to emerge. A recent report by McKinsey Global Institute (2007) projects that India will become the world's fifth largest consumer market by 2025, and discretionary spending will account for 70 per cent of all spending. Thus, it is not just the rapid growth of the Indian economy and the consumer market, but the sheer size of the Indian economy which makes it an attractive economic partner. While India's economic growth is driven more by domestic demand than is the case for many East Asian economies, its total trade in goods and services in 2006 was US$437 billion, approaching 50 per cent of GDP. India's share in global trade is expected to increase from 1.5 per cent in 2006 to 2 per cent before the end of this decade. The size as well as the growth of India's global trade should be attractive to ASEAN countries.

India has a remarkably young population, and English-speaking skilled manpower and professional managers are available at a competitive cost. A study reports that by 2020 while the average Chinese will be about 37 years old and Japanese 48 years old, Indians will be only 29 years old. Hence India's favourable demographics and the nature of its pension reforms based on individual savings are likely to sustain high savings and investment rates in future.

India has a rich base of mineral and agricultural resources. It has one of the largest manufacturing sectors in the world, spanning almost all areas of manufacturing activities. The financial sector is highly developed. The country has about 10,000 listed companies (about 2 per cent of all registered companies) and twenty-three registered stock exchanges in various cities. India's market capitalization is approaching US$1 trillion; and its capital markets are intermediating between savings and investments in a relatively efficient manner. The Indian economy is largely driven by the private sector enterprises and has the second highest number of entrepreneurs per capita after Thailand. For investors, the country also offers well-balanced fiscal incentives and a sophisticated legal and accounting structure.

5.2. Internal Weaknesses

Despite its strengths, ASEAN investors may see India as a difficult or challenging market. The country is facing a deteriorating fiscal position and is hampered by low productivity of its state sector, limited levels of FDI, and weak infrastructure. India suffered political instability for the last few years due to the failure of any single party to win an absolute majority in Parliament. However, political instability has not changed India's economic course altogether. It has albeit delayed certain decisions relating to the economy. Another much inherent problem of Indian economy is the slow pace of economic reforms. One important issue that needs to be addressed soon is increasing the flexibility in deployment of labour and capital. This means changing labour laws that currently make it almost impossible to retrench workers.

The rapid economic growth of the last few years has put heavy stress on India's infrastructural facilities. A positive economic outlook could further snap the already strained lines of power and transportation unless massive programmes of expansion and modernization are put in place. Although Indian courts provide adequate safeguards for the enforcement of property and contractual rights, case backlogs frequently lead to long procedural delays. Finally, many ASEAN firms have identified corruption as an obstacle to FDI flows. According to a report, corruption is considered to be the third worst problem faced by foreign investors in India after bureaucratic red tape and power shortages. Transparency provisions are therefore likely to be important in the context of a potential bilateral investment agreement.

5.3. External Opportunities

India is cautiously negotiating foreign forays into its economy. It is liberalizing the sectors to garner benefits from greater capital flows, specially the FDI. The large and the growing middle class are driving the consumer product growth at over 12 per cent per annum. The country offers a whole range of investment opportunities from agriculture to services sector. Within the agricultural sector excellent opportunities exist in areas of food processing and agri-infrastructure development. FDI is allowed in almost all segments of the financial sector — venture capital (up to 100 per cent), insurance (up to 26 per cent), banking (up to 49 per cent), and mutual funds (up to 100 per cent). Abundant investment opportunities exist in communication infrastructure, wireless, software development, and IT-enabled services. Market openings have emerged across four business sectors — IT services, software products, IT-enabled services, and e-business.

The Indian government has announced significant policy initiatives to attract foreign investment in oil and gas fields. Opportunity exists in LNG production, regional gas trade, development of non-conventional sources, refineries and pipeline network. To boost infrastructure development, the government continues to simplify FDI rules in several sectors. The government is actively seeking investment in infrastructure — ports, roads, railways, power and telecommunications — that require an estimated US$276 billion funding in the next five years. Malaysian Airports Berhad is already involved in a joint consortium involving India's GMR Infrastructure Group and others for developing the Delhi and Hyderabad Airports in India.

Among the key aspects of India's calibrated globalization have been unilateral liberalization and deregulation measures, particularly relating to the external sector. The average tariff rates in manufacturing sector in 2006 were about 10 per cent, comparable to other APEC members. India's exchange rate policies are market-based; and it has substantially liberalized capital flows in both directions, including for resident Indians. As in other areas, it is pursuing gradual and prudent path towards full convertibility. The current uncertain international economic environment, given large macroeconomic imbalances in the world has made Indian policy-makers more cautious.

5.4. External Threats

India has a long-standing territorial dispute with Pakistan over the ownership of Kashmir, which led to a tense relationship between the two countries. India's relations with Pakistan have direct relevance to the energy sector in India, as it complicates plans for regional natural gas and/or oil pipelines (from Central Asia). Separatist movements also exist in some northeastern states, which if exacerbated could have a negative impact on the country's economic development. With globalization of education, India also faces some limited threats in terms of more Indian students looking abroad for higher education. This may not only affect the quality of Indian universities but also may divert the best skills away from the country.

Today, though India is the pre-eminent destination for offshore IT services, China and the Philippines has the fundamentals to emerge as credible offshore IT services destinations in the medium to longer term. Both these countries have a sizeable, low-cost talent pool, which could meet global IT-enabled services (ITES) manpower needs, and the Governments are taking significant steps to improve their attractiveness for the ITES industry. Compared with earlier days, India is now more integrated with the world economy. Thus, shocks like oil price hike and sluggish global demand could have a more pronounced impact on India's overall growth outlook.

That said, there exist significant complementarities between ASEAN and India with respect to their economic structures and trading partners, suggesting that a potential FTA between the two is likely to be mutually beneficial. ASEAN's major manufactured exports have been electronics while India's major competitiveness lies in ready-made garments. As shown in Table 9.14, the overall export similarity index for ASEAN and India merchandise exports to the world has increased marginally during 1993–2003, and has remained at 27.5 in 2003, indicating that about three-quarter of products exported by both countries are completely dissimilar in pattern. It appears that the overall similarity between exports of ASEAN-6 and India is thus very low, particularly due to their divergence in composition of export baskets. The index is also found to be lower in case of India's and ASEAN'S exports to the United States, which is the major trading partner for both countries. The level of similarity is as low as 20 per cent, which further confirms the large complementarities between ASEAN's and India's exports. This points out to the fact that removal of tariff barriers and trade promotion measures by both ASEAN-6 and India in a potential FTA will bring about significant mutual gains for both countries.

Table 9.15 presents a summary estimate of export similarity index for ASEAN-6 and India in their global services exports. The overall index during 1993–2002 is between 60 and 90 and has been declining overtime. It is observed that although the similarity between service exports of ASEAN-6

Table 9.14
Export Similarity Indices for Merchandise Exports of ASEAN-6 and India

	1993	1998	2003
Exports to the World	26.4	24.7	27.5
Exports to the U.S.	20.0	19.3	21.0

Source: Authors' calculations.

Table 9.15
Export Similarity Indices for Commercial Services Exports of ASEAN-6 and India to the World Market

Sector	1993	1998	2002
Computer, communications and other services	29.6	42.5	32.3
Insurance and financial services	0.8	0.7	1.5
Transport services	15.9	16.0	10.3
Travel services	42.9	26.6	12.3
Overall	89.1	85.9	56.4

Source: Authors' calculations.

and India is low for most categories, it is higher than that for merchandise exports. This is particularly true for ICT and professional services, including outsourcing. In other categories, there is virtually no or very limited degree of export similarity, indicating complementarities yet again.

Looking at the relative measure of RCA (Table 9.16) in merchandise trade both for ASEAN-6 and India, in 2003, while 60 per cent of India's merchandise exports lay within the mid- to high-competitive range (the products under this category are generally textiles and textile yarns, clothing and clothing accessories), that for ASEAN was only about 37 per cent (products under this category comprised of mineral oil, telecom equipments and parts and components of electronic products), with the bulk of its exports being in the low-competitive range.

As for the services, it is observed that in 2002, India attended global comparative advantage in exports of communication, computer-related services (ICT and professional business services including outsourcing), while ASEAN had comparative advantage in travel and transport services. In insurance and financial services, both countries are not observed to be globally competitive (Table 9.17).

As mentioned earlier, the possibility of export competition of ASEAN-6 and India in the manufacturing sector is limited, suggesting greater complementarities that should be exploited for mutual gains, through an FTA in goods. The services sector is also going to provide large mutually beneficial gains to both ASEAN and India. While India's technological competence in the ICT sector is widely accepted, ASEAN can draw benefits from India's expertise. Tourism is another sector where large expansion possibilities exist. This sector can also provide scope for substantial tourism-related investments, such as infrastructure. Education, both professional and liberal, is another area where India can provide expertise. Health services, at site as well as in India, are another major area where both trade and investment opportunities exist. Bilateral services trade expansion will be significantly aided by liberalization of temporary movement of skilled professionals in these sectors.

Therefore, a potential ASEAN–India FTA is likely to yield significant mutual gains for both parties since there exists a high degree of complementarity in their export structures to the global market, especially in merchandise exports. Liberalization and trade promotion in goods as well as trade facilitation would create significant market opportunities for both countries to explore the synergies of each other for mutual benefits. There is a modest degree of overlap in the commercial services exports of the ASEAN-5 and India to the world, but liberalization of services through an ASEAN–India FTA would

Table 9.16
RCA Indices for Merchandise Exports of ASEAN-6 and India

Categories	Range	Number of Products (% share in total exports)					
		1993		1998		2003	
		ASEAN-6	India	ASEAN-6	India	ASEAN-6	India
Non-competitive	less than 0	781 (20.4)	695 (14.3)	817 (24.7)	725 (14.3)	799 (29.6)	697 (21.4)
Low-competitive	0.00 – 0.49	173 (43.6)	118 (16.0)	157 (30.5)	121 (16.4)	172 (33.2)	159 (16.0)
Mid-competitive	0.50 – 0.69	43 (16.3)	51 (12.5)	35 (37.2)	46 (10.9)	36 (24.1)	67 (13.1)
High-competitive	0.70 – 1.00	28 (19.8)	62 (57.1)	17 (7.6)	69 (58.4)	18 (13.1)	81 (49.5)

Source: Authors' calculations.

Table 9.17
RCA Indices for Commercial Services Exports of ASEAN-5 and India

	ASEAN-5			India		
	1993	1998	2002	1993	1998	2002
Computer, communications and other services	0.07	0.06	−0.10	−0.08	0.19	0.32
Insurance and financial services	N.A.	N.A.	0.01	N.A.	N.A.	−0.03
Transport services	−0.22	0.03	0.11	0.00	−0.18	−0.37
Travel services	0.12	0.00	0.11	0.12	−0.09	−0.43

Source: Authors' calculations.

enhance the mutual competitiveness of both countries, provided proper regulatory mechanisms are in place.

6. ASEAN–Japan

A regional FTA binding Japan and ASEAN would be particularly desirable. This is because ASEAN and Japan have been linked by an extensive web of economic, cultural, and other ties that bind them through human interactions and bilateral flows of goods and money. Japan served as an economic growth engine for ASEAN, as a significant market and source of investment, technology, and financial aid. These links have grown in recent decades. In 2003, ASEAN exported goods worth US$52.2 billion to Japan, and imported US$58.7 billion worth from Japan, accounting for 12.6 per cent of ASEAN's total exports and 17.1 per cent of ASEAN's total imports. The trade intensity indices (Table 9.18) are significantly higher than 1, implying that the bilateral trade flow between ASEAN and Japan is always larger than expected, given Japan's importance in world trade.

Table 9.18
Estimates of the Bilateral Merchandise Trade Intensity Indices

	1993	1998	2003
Bilateral Trade Intensity Index	1.18	1.15	1.18
Bilateral Export Intensity Index	1.50	1.59	1.88
Bilateral Import Intensity Index	2.59	2.63	2.65

Source: Authors' calculations.

Second, ASEAN has been a strategic investment location for Japanese firms. For instance, Kwan and Qiu (2003) found that an ASEAN member receives 2.5 times more Japanese FDI than a non-ASEAN member. Cumulatively, Japan's FDI in ASEAN-6 during 1990–2003 reached US$58.2 billion, accounting for nearly 10 per cent of Japan's total outward FDI and 18 per cent of ASEAN's inward FDI. In relative terms, FDI intensities between ASEAN and Japan have always been significantly greater than 1 (Table 9.19), suggesting that bilateral investment flows have been greater than expected, given the countries' importance in the world as investment destinations.

More importantly, most of the FDI into ASEAN has been vertical in nature, linking parent firms in Japan to their affiliates in ASEAN. This has underpinned intra-industry trade flows (Table 9.20; GL Index doubled to nearly 40 by 2003.), which tend to underpin the complementary trade relationship between the two blocs (Table 9.21 indicates that products shipped specially to the United States became less similar). Across the years, electronic

Table 9.19
FDI Intensity Index between Japan and ASEAN

	1993	1998	2003
Japan's FDI Intensity Index with ASEAN	1.2	3.3	2.0

Source: World Investment Report, Ministry of Finance, Japan.

Table 9.20
IIT for ASEAN-6 Trade with Japan

	1993	1998	2003
Grubel Lloyd Index	20.87	37.06	39.51

Source: Authors' calculations; UN Comtrade.

Table 9.21
Export Similarity Indices for Merchandise Exports of ASEAN-6 and Japan

	1993	1998	2003
To the World	40.4	42.7	42.6
To U.S. market	34.8	32.4	26.9

Source: Authors' calculations; UN Comtrade.

microcircuits, electrical components, data processing machine parts and other consumer electronics showed the highest volumes of intra-industry trade between the two countries.

Compared with goods exports, services products exported by ASEAN and Japan generally share a higher degree of similarity (Table 9.22), thus limiting the scope of comparative advantage.

6.1. Internal Strengths

Japan is widely recognized as a global leader in product development and R&D, supported by a well-educated talent pool. It is able to tap on a sophisticated and sizeable consumer market, which serves as a test-bed for new products. Additionally, Japanese firms have established strong product franchises around the world. Services activities, such as digital media and consumer electronics, telecommunications and IT, are relatively advanced.

Cyclically, domestic economic conditions continue to register robust growth, and the global economy is also showing signs of an upturn after a period of inventory liquidation. Structurally, loan growth and underlying inflation are showing signs of turning positive by year-end, and land prices continue to rise, putting an end to more than a decade of deflation.

6.2. Internal Weaknesses

While the present upturn in Japan is supported by continued progress on the structural front, as well as increasing cyclical momentum on the back of a pick-up in global economic activity, investor sentiment remains clouded by political uncertainty. The Upper House will continue to be controlled by the "unreformed" ruling coalition. This would likely to slow down the pace of reforms. Fiscal consolidation would remain on the backburner for some time. Meanwhile, tax increases seem inevitable, as tax revenues account for a portion of proposed spending in the Budget. It is therefore unlikely that the country's huge public debt, which totals 160 per cent of GDP, would recede anytime soon.

Table 9.22
Export Similarity Indices for Services Exports of
ASEAN-6 and Japan's to the World Market

	1993	1998	2002
Export Similarity Index	63.6	73.8	67.2

Source: Authors' calculations.

While the Financial Services Authority (FSA) has delivered on promises to purge the banking system of excessive non-performing loans, strengthen supervision and tighten auditing standards, the financial sector remains on a fragile footing. Most of the improvement, however, came from the city banks, while regional banks continue to lag. Nonetheless, a strong plus for both creditors and debtors is that the economy is recovering and that many corporations are now seeing their revenues, profits and ability to service their outstanding debts strengthening.

6.3. External Opportunities

Of late, ASEAN officials have remarked that Japan has sought to match China's regional initiatives. In response to the proposed ASEAN–China FTA, and negotiations with South Korea and India for a similar deal, Japan has agreed to enter into negotiations with ASEAN as a group with an understanding that an FTA will be achieved by 2012. A more receptive Japan provides ASEAN with unique opportunity to broker a more comprehensive deal and to broach difficult issues like agriculture and services liberalization.

Services liberalization could propel FDI. Deliberations are under way among senior ASEAN officials to make recommendations for expanding the scope of the AIA to include services sectors, such as education, healthcare, telecommunications, tourism, banking and finance, insurance, trading, e-commerce, distribution and logistics, transportation and warehousing, and professional services. FDI flows to the services sectors will continue to increase in the coming years, particularly in light of the expected improved access to these sectors.

For Japan, an agreement would deepen its already extensive linkages with ASEAN, which encompasses trade, investment, and cultural ties. The deal would provide Japan with a strategic foothold in Asia, with which it can strengthen economic engagement and business base with the rest of the region. Boosting commercial ties within ASEAN at a time when Japan's diplomatic role in the region is increasingly eclipsed by China may also help to reinforce positive perceptions of a constructive engagement in the region.

A closer relationship with Japan can serve ASEAN's interests in science and technology development. However, in order to harness the full benefit of technological transfers, developing ASEAN countries need to pursue more actively human capital and SME development programmes.

ASEAN firms can capitalize on current initiatives in Japan to revitalize its domestic manufacturing, R&D and product development capabilities, particularly in digital consumer electronics. According to JETRO (2004), these initiatives are likely to create investment opportunities in the manufacturing of flat-screen TVs and digital cameras. In services, Japan is keen to develop exportable "soft services", which can capitalize on the growing international appeal of Japanese culture, music, and fashion. This could create significant investment opportunities for ASEAN in software, digital media and cinematic content development

6.4. External Threats

An overarching ASEAN–Japan FTA will also have to grapple with the issue of access for Southeast Asia's agricultural products. Given the sensitivity of agriculture in Japanese politics and ASEAN's comparative advantage in resource-based products, this sector may pose a formidable obstacle in bilateral FTA negotiations. This would also limit the number of opportunities in Japan available to potential ASEAN investors.[4]

To conclude, it should be noted that there is empirical evidence showing that FTAs can precipitate more FDI flows. An ASEAN–Japan FTA would be mutually beneficial, given the complementary nature of existing trade linkages. The deal would provide Japan with a strategic foothold in Asia, with which it can strengthen economic engagement with the rest of the region. Boosting commercial ties within ASEAN at a time when Japan's diplomatic role in the region is increasingly eclipsed by China may also help to reinforce positive perceptions of a constructive engagement in the region.

An agreement with Japan should also include investment provisions that are WTO-plus and of high quality. A comprehensive ASEAN investment framework that includes Japan would help to catalyse economic integration between Southeast Asia and Northeast Asia. Within ASEAN, it should also spur harmonization of trade facilitation and investment rules as well as speed up services liberalization. More importantly, this could in turn open up more opportunities for less developed CLMV economies to draw more outward investments from Japan as well as more developed ASEAN economies. This would also give economic incentive for developing ASEAN economies to pursue human capital and SME development programmes in order to maximize the full potential of technology transfers from MNCs. Japan's bottom-up strategy (from bilateral FTAs with ASEAN countries) can also help narrow the disparity in the economic development of ASEAN countries.

7. ASEAN–Korea

Economies of ASEAN and Korea have grown vigorously over the past ten years and the economic ties between the two parties have become stronger. The close economic tie is confirmed by the historical patterns of their economic growth as the growth rates have been highly correlated with each other. Historically, Korea has maintained close diplomatic relationships with ASEAN members. It has shared the knowledge gained from its own economic development experience with ASEAN members. A large share of Korea's official development assistance (ODA) has been directed towards ASEAN. Through Economic Development Cooperation Fund (EDCF), which is an ODA loan programme, Korea provided US$5 million to support the Initiative for ASEAN Integration (*Annual Report 2003* of The Export-Import Bank of Korea). Finally in 2003, during the Korea–ASEAN Summit in Bali, Korea proposed the possibility of establishing a free trade area between the two parties. The ASEAN–Korea FTA has since been signed and enforced in the area of trade in goods.

7.1. Internal Strengths

The Korean government has successfully developed its economy since 1962 through various developmental planning measures. This "know-how" could be applied to further develop the relations with other countries. ASEAN-based investors can take advantage of it when they attempt to develop business in Korea. They can approach Korean governmental agencies to seek for the industrial or national planning outlines. This could be a good business opportunity to foreign investors. It is, therefore, a unique strength that foreign investors can enjoy in Korea.

During the period of economic development programmes, Korea also developed its infrastructure such as highways, railroads, and telecommunication networks. This played a major role in accelerating the economic growth of Korea. The well-built transportation network makes it easier for foreign firms to choose locations for their investments.

The high level of education is another major strength of Korea. People in Korea have relatively high educational careers, and they adjust easily to new growing industries. The quality of the workers is very high "on average", and these educated workers can easily and spontaneously adopt a new environment that the investors may bring into the business. Moreover, as the labour market for highly-educated workers are large, this gives foreign managers a wider choice.

7.2. Internal Weaknesses

Korea was divided into two countries after the Korean War in 1950–53. The tension between South and North Koreas is still unresolved. This creates political instability and inconsistency in policy implementation.

Political instability in Korea is closely related to the business instability. For example, during the 1997–98 financial crises, the Korean government was at the brink of national default. Upon this possibility, a vast amount of foreign capitals and foreign-owned assets were continuously withdrawn from Korean financial institutions. This almost destroyed the entire economic system of Korea.

Inconsistency in policy implementation is also related to the above problem. But this inconsistency of policy is mainly induced by private sector interest groups such as labour unions and political and social activists. So from a foreign investor's perspective, if they find a policy to be an attractive one for their business, they still needs to be patient to see the "final" consensus among Korean people.

Economically and historically Korea has been dependent on the U.S. market. However, trends have changed recently.

7.3. External Opportunities

Ideally speaking, the current political status of the Korean peninsula could be a potential opportunity to foreign investors if both South and North Koreas reunify its political and economic systems. It would create a larger market. The population size could increase from 40 million to 60 million.

The Korean government also pursues a long-term plan to make the country a logistic hub in the Northeast Asia region, thus connecting Russia, China, Korea, and Japan. Before the occupation by Japan from the early twentieth century and the ensuing Cold War politics in the latter half of the twentieth century, Korea had been historically a middle player between China and Japan. This role can be enhanced by the current plan of the government. Making such a logistic hub is a big business and requires a lot of money during the development stage. Foreign investors including the ones in ASEAN countries should see this as a unique opportunity available in Korea only.

Korea's economy used to be behind Japan's, and Korean economic planners had followed Japanese economic successes and experiences. Naturally the two countries became close neighbours. Recently, due to the faster growing performance of the Korean economy than that of the Japanese, the relationship between the two nations has become more equalized, and it became Japan's turn to learn from the Korean economic successes and experiences. This back-and-forth relationship can be taken as an opportunity by foreign investors. That is, learning Korea is learning Japan, and vice versa.

7.4. External Threats

Nuclear empowerment of North Korea is the biggest security threat to South Korea as well as to the rest of the world. It could evolve into a full-scale war, which might affect other nations around the world. In fact, this threat is evolving towards reality and thus many Asian nations such as China and Japan are cooperating with the United States to engage North Korea in order to mitigate the threat. Investors in ASEAN region should take into account the current international politics and dynamics between South and North Korea as well as among the other involved countries. This is clearly a non-economic burden to the foreign investors as far as Korea is concerned.

Furthermore, China's economic rise also presents a possible threat for the Korea's economic development. In particular, Korea has experienced a loss in competitiveness in the global export markets due to cheaper Chinese products. This not only reduced the profit margin of Korean firms in the domestic market but also in the global market.

Apart from the above analysis, there are economic evidences that support an ASEAN–Korea FTA. It is observed from the analysis of merchandise trade patterns that ASEAN and Korea are both competitive and complementary in manufactured exports. Export competition is evident in the sectors such as computer, telecommunications, data processing, and parts. Import competition is also quite apparent in the sectors of crude petroleum, electronic microcircuits, telecommunication, and motor vehicles. However, apart from these products, the relationship is largely complementary. This evident in Table 9.23 wherein the magnitude of overall export similarity indices of ASEAN and Korea to the world market and to the United States during 1993–2003 is stable between 48 and 50, implying that only half of the export composition is identical. Indeed, there are very few overlapped industries wherein the competition is intense when competitiveness analysis is undertaken at the four-digit industries level (Table 9.24). This implies that a potential ASEAN–Korea FTA is likely to yield mutual gain for both parties, and create greater business opportunities.

Table 9.23
Export Similarity Indices for Merchandise Exports of ASEAN-6 and Korea

	1993	1998	2003
Exports to the World	47.89	49.83	48.15
Exports to the U.S.	48.27	50.67	40.88

Source: Authors' calculations.

Table 9.24
RCA Indices for Merchandise Export of ASEAN-6 and Korea

Categories	Range	Number of Products (% share in total exports)					
		1993		*1998*		*2003*	
		ASEAN-6	*Korea*	*ASEAN-6*	*Korea*	*ASEAN-6*	*Korea*
Non-competitive	less than 0	781 (20.4)	729 (23.1)	817 (24.7)	782 (20.7)	799 (29.6)	774 (19.6)
Low-competitive	0.00 – 0.49	173 (43.6)	139 (26.9)	157 (30.5)	131 (34.1)	172 (33.2)	135 (49.9)
Mid-competitive	0.50 – 0.69	43 (16.3)	59 (34.8)	35 (37.2)	39 (23.4)	36 (24.1)	37 (12.2)
High-competitive	0.70 – 1.00	28 (19.8)	20 (15.2)	17 (7.6)	18 (21.7)	18 (13.1)	13 (18.4)

Source: Authors' calculations.

The degree of competition between the two countries in the service sector is also not that highly significant when analysed with respect to disaggregated service sector exports in Table 9.25.

Nevertheless, the investment relationship between ASEAN and Korea has a relatively good history. Kwon (2004, p. 86) has a summary of the historical relationship as follows.

The first Korean overseas direct investment to the region was established by the Korea South Development Corporation to develop forests in Indonesia in 1968. Korean FDI reached full scale in the 1980s, and since the mid-1980s, Korean firms have looked to Southeast Asian countries as a source of inexpensive labour as well as abundant natural resource.

So, Korea's motivation of investment has been cost-driven. This becomes very clear, if the data from Export-Import Bank of Korea is observed. Among the ten ASEAN countries, Indonesia and Vietnam were the most significant FDI destinations for Korea among ASEAN nations. As of 2003, 31.1 per cent of FDI and 22.1 per cent of FDI have invested in the two countries respectively. Interestingly Vietnam has become an attractive destination for Korea since 1992. 98 per cent of total investments were concentrated in the ASEAN-6 (Indonesia, Malaysia, Philippines, Singapore, Thailand, and Vietnam), while only 2 per cent are on Myanmar, Cambodia, Laos, and Brunei, which are not yet industrialized at some degrees.

That said, it is observed that the degree of competition between ASEAN and Korea both in goods and services sectors is not significant and thus the sectors do not pose a serious threat in case of FTA negotiations. In fact both parties are found to be competing and complementary at the same time. The recent trend, however, shows more complementary relations. This implies that there will be greater scope of mutual gains of trade by concluding

Table 9.25
Export Similarity Indices for Services Exports of
ASEAN-6 and Korea to the World Market

Sector	1993	1998	2002
Computer, communications and other services	31.93	30.28	28.84
Insurance and financial services	0.68	0.67	1.62
Transport services	15.88	24.56	27.84
Travel services	23.75	27.82	19.55
Overall	72.25	83.34	77.85

Source: Authors' calculations.

an FTA between the two parties. Similarly, there exist significant potential for expansion of bilateral investment flows in both manufacturing and services sectors in future.

8. Concluding Remarks

Overall, the above analysis seems to indicate that ASEAN stands to gain from entering into bilateral FTAs with these five DPs. Although there is limited degree of competition in some areas of manufacturing between ASEAN and these DPs, there exist far more complementarities. In the area of services, such complementarities are abound. This provides a strong basis for ASEAN in negotiating bilateral FTAs with a focus on expanding investment flows with all these dialogue partners. However, the challenges ahead for ASEAN in FTA negotiations with these individual dialogue partners relate to both realizing the external opportunities arising from its internal strengths, while concomitantly mitigating the external threats that could aggravate as a result of its internal weaknesses. This would require ASEAN to balance its goals of regional economic integration with that of maximizing economic and strategic benefits in a globalize world from its relations with major external trading partners. Creation of an ASEAN Economic Community within a desirable time-frame is an important goal in this direction that ASEAN must strive for, in order to sustain its current competitiveness strengths vis-à-vis its FTA DP members. It is also important to note that this would require individual ASEAN countries to undertake important unilateral liberalization so as to adjust their economies in the post-FTA period.

NOTES

This is a summarized version of Chapter 3 of the REPSF Project Report 04/10 entitled "AIA-Plus: Beyond Free Trade Agreements". For analytical details related to computation of competition and complementarities, please refer to the same.

1. Data is not available for ASEAN-6.
2. It is up to the individual ASEAN countries to define what are these particular problems that need to be set in order and what are the particular aspects of capacity-building that need to be given priority since the conditions and particular problems facing them are varied.
3. These measures are actually some of the aims of the AFTA Plus.
4. Chia (2002) noted that in the bilateral negotiations between Japan and Singapore on the JSEPA, the exports of orchids and tropical fish by Singapore proved a stumbling block that prevented JSEPA from being an FTA that is comprehensive in sectoral coverage and inclusive of agriculture.

REFERENCES

Asian Development Bank (ADB). *Key Indicators for Developing Asian and Pacific Countries.* Manila: ADB, 2004.

Association of Southeast Asian Nations. Website of the ASEAN Secretariat. http://www.aseansec.org.

———. *ASEAN Statistical Yearbook 2003.* Jakarta: ASEAN Secretariat, 2003.

———. *ASEAN Statistical Yearbook 2004.* Jakarta: ASEAN Secretariat, 2004.

Balassa, B. and M. Noland. "Revealed Comparative Advantage in Japan and the United States". *Journal of International Economic Integration* 4, no. 2 (1989): 8–22.

Bhattacharya, B. and M. Ariff. "Study on AFTA–India Linkages for the Enhancement of Trade and Investment". A report submitted to the Government of India and the ASEAN Secretariat, May, 2002.

Chia, S. Y. "ASEAN and Emerging East Asian Regionalism." Paper presented at a seminar held on the occasion of the Asian Development Bank's 35th Annual Meeting entitled Towards Asian Integration: The Role of Regional Cooperation, 2002.

Government of the People's Republic of China. *China Statistical Yearbook 2004.*

JETRO. "JETRO White Paper on International Trade and Foreign Direct Investment". Japan External Trade Organization, Tokyo, 2004.

Kumar, Nagesh, Rahul Sen and Mukul Asher. "ASEAN-India Partnership in an Era of Globalization: An Overview". In *ASEAN–India Partnership: Meeting the Challenges of Globalization,* edited by Nagesh Kumar, Rahul Sen and Mukul Asher. New Delhi: RIS; Singapore: Institute of Southeast Asian Studies, 2006.

Kwan, K. K. and L. D. Qiu. "The ASEAN+3 Trading Bloc". City University of Hong Kong, 2003.

McKinsey Global Institute. "The 'Bird of Gold': The Rise of India's Consumer Market". May 2007.

Sheng Lijun. "China–ASEAN Free Trade Area: Origins, Developments and Strategic Motivations". ISEAS Working Paper on International Politics and Security Issues Series No. 1. Singapore: Institute of Southeast Asian Studies, 2003.

UN Commodity Trade Statistics Database (UN Comtrade).

United Nations Conference on Trade and Development (UNCTAD) Statistics Database.

World Trade Organization (WTO), *International Trade Statistics 2004.*

World Bank. *World Development Report 2004,* Washington, D.C: The World Bank, 2004.

10
Conclusion: Towards an ASEAN Economic Community by 2015

Denis Hew

The vision of an ASEAN Economic Community (AEC) by 2015 is certainly bold and ambitious. Although there are already building blocks in place such as the ASEAN Free Trade Area (AFTA), the ASEAN Investment Area (AIA) and the ASEAN Framework Agreement on Services (AFAS), ASEAN faces a number of daunting challenges in realizing this vision. From the studies presented in the preceding chapters, a number of compelling questions emerge. Among these are:

(i)   whether or not the roadmap to achieve the AEC is realistic given the relatively short timeline set to undertake this endeavour;

(ii) whether the progress made in expediting economic integration, particularly of the fast-track integration of the priority sectors, is on track to achieve its targets and objectives;

(iii) whether ASEAN has the institutional framework to support such deeper economic integration; and

(iv) whether ASEAN would be able to successfully address the economic development divide among its member countries.

There is also the nagging question of what is the ultimate end-goal of the AEC — is it a European-style common market or just a free trade area? To be sure, these challenges need to be seriously addressed in the short to medium term. In this concluding chapter, key issues are discussed reflecting the challenges ahead.

1. Addressing the Stumbling Blocks to Economic Integration

1.1. Tackling Barriers to Trade

Although most ASEAN countries have complied with tariff reductions under AFTA, Tongzon (2005) found the utilization of the Comprehensive Effective Preferential Tariffs (CEPT) has been relatively low due to lack of clear and transparent procedures, a lack of mutual trust between preference-receiving country and preference-granting country, low margin of tariff preferences (between CEPT and most-favoured nation rates) and a lack of private sector awareness regarding AFTA concessions. Furthermore, the less developed ASEAN countries may be reluctant to fully implement AFTA given the huge losses in customs revenue due to the implementation of the CEPT (Tongzon and Khan 2005). Intra-ASEAN trade has not increased significantly since the signing of AFTA in 1992 (see Figure 10.1). Studies in this book on the priority sectors have also found that non-tariffs measures (NTMs) continue to persist and impede greater intra-ASEAN trade. Hence, effectively tackling NTMs, particularly those that are barriers to trade, would be crucial if a fully functioning AFTA is to be feasible by 2015.

1.2. Expediting Investment and Services Trade Liberalization

The AIA aims to reduce or eliminate investment barriers and grant national treatment to ASEAN investors by 2010 and to all investors by 2020. ASEAN is currently considering whether to extend National Treatment to its free trade agreement (FTA) partners, namely, China, Japan, Korea, India, Australia, and New Zealand by 2010. By turning the region into an integrated investment area, the AIA would serve as a natural complement to greater trade integration under AFTA. Given that regional production networks and FDI flows into the region are driven mainly by non-ASEAN investors (e.g., the United States, Japan, and Europe), it therefore makes more sense to extend national treatment to all investors. Hence, the AIA should be open to all investors sooner rather than later. In this context, a new AIA strategy may need to be designed — one which moves away from a regional investment strategy that promotes intra-regional investments to one that creates a platform that

Figure 10.1
Intra-ASEAN Trade Share as Percentage of Total ASEAN Trade

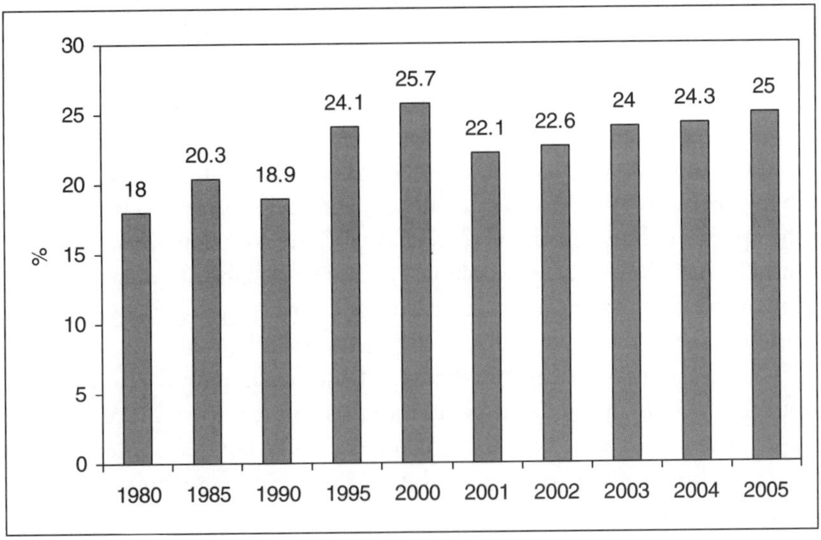

Source: ASEAN Secretariat.

attracts global foreign investments. This new AIA strategy would be more consistent with the AEC's objectives of creating an integrated production base that is plugged into the global supply chain.

To date, progress made in services trade liberalization under AFAS has been slow. Member countries have been very cautious in committing themselves to AFAS and have made little progress in liberalizing service trade at the regional level. In fact, member countries' commitments have not been significantly bolder and more far-reaching under the AFAS than under WTO's General Agreement on Trade in Services (GATS). It would therefore be challenging for ASEAN to liberalize the services sector beyond GATS. Applying the "ASEAN minus X" or "2 plus X" formula may be required to expedite the implementation of AFAS, if the AEC goal of free flow of services within ASEAN is to be achieved. Unlike "ASEAN minus X" where a consensus is needed by member countries, the "2 plus X" enables two member countries that are ready to liberalize specific sectors to proceed first. The "2 plus X" formula was first introduced at the 2003 ASEAN Summit and was endorsed by the Eminent Persons Group (EPG) on the ASEAN Charter as a useful policy tool to expedite economic integration.

1.3. Making the ASEAN Dispute Settlement Mechanism Workable

Despite recent enhancements to the ASEAN Dispute Settlement Mechanism (DSM), it continues to be unused by member countries. It is hard to imagine how ASEAN will be able to cope with trade disputes that will likely increase with deeper integration. Hence, an unworkable DSM could undermine the AEC. To depoliticize the process, the High Level Task Force (HLTF) on ASEAN economic integration recommended the establishment of an appellate body comprising of well-qualified, independent, and experienced professionals as the appeal body under the DSM. That said, the complete depoliticization of the ASEAN DSM process would not always be possible. Even at the WTO where proceedings are more structured and legalistic, disputes among member countries continue to be politically charged (Hsu 2003).

The other concern is whether there will be sufficient resources to effectively implement the enhanced DSM system. In this context, the CLMV countries and even some of the ASEAN-6 countries may not have the technical capacity to fully benefit from the ASEAN DSM. Hence, technical assistance and legal training should be incorporated in the new system.

1.4. Impact of Proliferation of FTAs

In recent years, there has been a proliferation of bilateral and regional free trade agreements (FTAs) in East Asia. FTAs appear to be a popular means of trade liberalization given the slow progress made at the WTO. Besides creating a regional FTA among member countries (i.e., via AFTA), ASEAN has been keen to solidify its economic relationship with its major trading partners. ASEAN currently has FTA arrangements with China, Japan, Korea, India, Australia, and New Zealand (see Table 10.1) and stands to gain from entering into trading agreements with them by creating an FTA hub that would strengthen ASEAN's efforts to establish an AEC.

However, FTAs are generally regarded by economists as the "second-best" option in global trade liberalization. The proliferation of FTAs in East Asia could give rise to a host of technical and administrative complications including mismatches in the phasing of tariff reductions under overlapping arrangements and implementation of different rules of origin under separate FTAs. This so-called "noodle bowl" of FTAs which may actually turn out to be a stumbling block to regional economic integration rather than a facilitator (Baldwin 2006). Uncoordinated proliferation could also lead to inconsistent provisions between FTAs, especially on the rules of origins, hampering the cross-border production networking process, which has been so crucial to the region's economic development (Feridhanusetyawan 2005).

Table 10.1
ASEAN's Regional Trading Agreements

RTA	Status	Coverage Areas	Timeframe for RTA to be in force
ASEAN–China Comprehensive Economic Cooperation Agreement	Framework Agreement signed on 5 November 2002; Agreement on Trade in Goods and Dispute Settlement Mechanism in force from January 2005.	Comprehensive: trade in goods, early harvest, services, investment, dispute settlement and economic cooperation.	2010 for China and ASEAN-6 countries, and by 2015 for the CLMV countries.
ASEAN–India Comprehensive Economic Cooperation Agreement	Framework Agreement signed on 8 October 2003.	Comprehensive: trade in goods, early harvest, services, investment, dispute settlement and economic cooperation.	2012 for India and ASEAN-6 countries; 2017 for Philippines and the CLMV countries.
ASEAN–Japan Comprehensive Economic Partnership Agreement	Framework Agreement signed on 8 October 2003. Negotiations commenced in 2005.	Comprehensive: trade in goods, services, investment, trade and investment facilitation and economic cooperation.	By 2012 for ASEAN-6 countries and 2017 for the CLMV countries.
ASEAN–Australia and New Zealand Free Trade Area	Agreed to launch negotiations in 2005.	Comprehensive: trade in goods, services, investment, trade and investment facilitation and economic cooperation measures.	Expected to be fully in force by 2015.
ASEAN–Korea Comprehensive Cooperation Partnership	Framework Agreement signed on 13 December 2005. Under this framework, nine ASEAN countries (except Thailand) have signed the Trade in Goods agreement in May 2006.	Comprehensive: trade in goods, services, investment, trade and investment facilitation and economic cooperation measures.	Aim to have at least 80% of products with zero tariffs by 2009, and with consideration for special and differential treatment and additional flexibility for the CLMV countries.

Note: RTA is Regional Trading Agreement
Source: Sally and Sen (2005), ASEAN Secretariat.

One possible approach to ensure FTAs are building blocks and not stumbling blocks is to "multilateralize" existing FTAs by adopting a comprehensive regional framework agreement. This would imply that all ASEAN countries should agree on signing only those FTAs that are WTO-consistent, have a comprehensive agenda of liberalization and economic cooperation (with minimum exclusions), as well as also allowing for inclusion of newer members as parties to the FTA on similar terms and conditions (Sen 2004).

2. Narrowing the Development Gap in ASEAN

The greatest challenge to ASEAN economic integration lies in addressing the development divide among its member countries. ASEAN is made up of member countries at very different stages of economic development. This development gap can be manifested in terms of differences in GDP per capita (income per capita) but also gaps in other human development indicators such as incidence of poverty, life expectancy, literacy, public expenditure in health and education. This divide is particularly pronounced in terms of income per capita between the ASEAN-6 countries and the less developed newer members, i.e., Cambodia, Laos, Myanmar, and Vietnam (CLMV). In current prices, income per capita of the ASEAN-6 is five times larger than that of the CLMV. Tables 10.2 to 10.4 provide economic, human development and poverty indicators that highlight this wide economic and human development divide within ASEAN.

Vo (2005) raised concerns that deeper economic integration could lead to huge social costs incurred by the CLMV countries due to structural adjustments and the risk of falling into a low-cost labour trap (where there is little incentive for domestic industries to move up the value chain). Appropriate resources should therefore be allocated to these countries to ensure the full participation of all member countries in the integration process. This would include financial and technical assistance, transfer of technology, education, training facilities and other capacity-building activities.

In this regard, ASEAN launched in 2001 the Initiative for ASEAN Integration (IAI) to address the development divide. Over the years, the IAI has evolved from a platform of mutual assistance between the ASEAN-6 and the CLMV to an expanded framework to involve Dialogue Partners and development agencies. Under this policy framework, the IAI Work Plan, a six-year plan (July 2002–June 2008) currently has over a hundred projects in four areas, namely, infrastructure, human resource development, information

Table 10.2
ASEAN Macroeconomic Indicators

	GDP (US$ billion), 2004	Population (million), 2005	Per Capita GDP (US$), 2004	Share of Agriculture in GDP, 2003	Share of Industry in GDP, 2003	Share of Services in GDP, 2003	Imports/ GDP (%), 2004	Exports/ GDP (%), 2004
Brunei	5.2	0.4	13,879	2.1	58.4	39.5	28.8	98.1
Indonesia	258.0	219.0	1,193	15.4	45.0	39.6	18.0	27.8
Malaysia	118.0	26.2	4,625	8.1	42.1	49.8	89.2	107.2
Philippines	86.1	84.2	1,042	19.8	33.5	46.7	51.1	46.1
Singapore	106.9	4.3	25,207	0.1	31.1	68.8	152.5	167.4
Thailand	163.5	65.0	2,537	10.2	45.8	44.0	58.3	59.6
Cambodia	4.9	13.9	358	36.8	27.9	35.4	40.8	51.0
Lao PDR	2.4	5.9	423	50.2[a]	24.6	25.1	—	—
Myanmar	9.1	56.0	166	42.9[b]	17.3	39.7	20.9	42.9
Vietnam	45.4	83.1	554	21.1	38.5	40.5	—	—

Notes: a. share pertains to year 2002.
     b. share pertains to year 2000.
Source: ASEAN Yearbook of Statistics; Salazar and Das (2007).

Table 10.3
ASEAN Human Development Indicators

	Human Development Index (Rank)	Life expectancy at birth (years) (2004)	Adult literacy rate (% age 15 & above) (2004)	Gross enrolment ratio for primary, secondary & tertiary schools (%) (2004)	Public Expenditure on Health (% of GDP) (2003)	Public Expenditure on Education (% of GDP) (2002–04)
Brunei	34	76.6	92.7	77	2.8	—
Indonesia	108	67.2	90.4	68	1.1	0.9
Malaysia	61	73.4	88.7	73	2.2	8.0
Philippines	84	70.7	92.6	82	1.4	3.2
Singapore	25	78.9	92.5	87	1.6	—
Thailand	74	70.3	92.6	74	2.0	4.2
Cambodia	129	56.5	73.6	60	2.1	2.0
Lao PDR	133	55.1	68.7	61	1.2	2.3
Myanmar	130	60.5	89.9	49	0.5	—
Vietnam	109	70.8	90.3	63	1.5	—

Source: UNDP Human Development Report 2006.

Table 10.4
Incidence of Poverty in ASEAN

	Population in Poverty (National Poverty Line, in percentage)	Proportion of population below US$1 (PPP) a day (in percentage)
Indonesia	18.2	7.5
Malaysia	7.5	0.2
Philippines	30.4	15.5
Singapore	—	—
Thailand	9.8	1.9
Cambodia	35.9	34.1
Lao PDR	38.6	39.0
Myanmar	22.9	—
Vietnam	28.9	13.1

Source: ADB Key Indicators 2005.

and communications technology, and regional economic integration. The IAI Work Plan also involves the development of legal, institutional, and regulatory frameworks and the building of technical capabilities and capacities of the CLMV.

ASEAN leaders at the 2004 Vientiane Summit recognized that deeper economic integration has to be accompanied by technical and development cooperation to address the development gap among member countries. In this regard, the VAP highlighted the strategic importance of narrowing the development gap to realize the ASEAN Community. As part of the strategies to narrow the development gap, the VAP recommends that the IAI be strengthened to address the needs of the CLMV countries and sub-regional areas (such as BIMP-EAGA and IMT-GT). This would include:

- broadening the scope of the IAI CLMV Work Plan as well as developing new modalities for resource mobilization;
- strengthening the framework for sub-regional economic cooperation;
- maximizing the benefits of economic integration and ensuring that these benefits are equitably distributed to all member countries;
- minimizing the cost of economic integration in terms of economic dislocation and disruption arising from market adjustments; and
- assisting less developed member countries in removing tariff, non-tariff and physical barriers to the free flow of goods and services.

In the EPG's report on the ASEAN Charter, it was noted that ASEAN's ability to achieve its long-term economic goals would depend on how the development gap is addressed today. Given the limited financial resources available to ASEAN, innovative ways to source development assistance will be needed to narrow the development gap. In this regard, the EPG recommended that a Special Fund for narrowing the development gap be established with voluntary contributions from member countries. Also, a new innovative funding mechanism should be explored by experts to raise funds for this Special Fund, for example, through a share of sales or excise tax, airport taxes or visa fees.

New strategies to narrow the development gap should, therefore, be focussed on ensuring that the less developed member countries will be in a position to participate and fully benefit from the economic integration process. ASEAN policy-makers should focus on addressing the economic development divide given that the 2015 AEC deadline is less than ten years away. Hence, the IAI and its work plan needs to be aligned in terms of approach, structure and mechanism with the AEC.

3. Stronger Institutional Structure

It is also important to note that deeper economic integration in ASEAN cannot be successfully achieved without the establishment of a stronger institutional structure with a better enforcement mechanism. There is thus a need to streamline, strengthen and enhance coordination among the existing institutions, as well as to design better enforcement mechanisms in order to facilitate and expedite economic integration.

ASEAN still maintains a very loose institutional structure and does not presently operate on the overriding principle of using a formal, detailed, and binding institutional structure to prepare, enact, coordinate, and execute policies for economic integration (ISEAS 2003). The "ASEAN way" of making decisions, i.e., *musyawarah* (discussion and consultation), *mufakat* (unanimous decision), and consensus, is very much entrenched.

ASEAN's weak institutional structure may be one of the reasons for the relatively low impact of ASEAN's initiatives to reduce tariffs and eliminate non-tariff barriers (Schwartz and Villinger 2004). Nonetheless, ASEAN has, in recent years, been moving towards a more structured rule-based system to regulate and enhance economic relations and integration amongst its members. Progressive steps have also been achieved in terms of the content and directives contained in the newer ASEAN trade and investment agreements since the 1990s, with binding rules and procedures now more clearly set out in such documents. Furthermore, the ASEAN Charter, which is likely to be signed at the Singapore ASEAN Summit in November 2007, will pave the way towards a more rule-based system for ASEAN.

For ASEAN to move towards the formation of a viable and vibrant AEC, there may be a need for stronger institutions to oversee and coordinate the administrative tasks of establishing and setting policies, coordinating, implementing, and enforcing present and future agreements and protocols. As it stands, the present ASEAN Secretariat does not have enough resources and expertise to carry out such tasks effectively.

Akrasanee and Arunanondchai (2005) propose that ASEAN needs to adopt a more centralized institutional structure and suggested that two supranational institutions be established to realize the AEC which are: an ASEAN Court of Justice (to be responsible for dispute settlements); and an ASEAN Economic Secretariat to manage regional economic integration. Soesastro (2005) suggested that a major institutional innovation for ASEAN would be the creation of "regional units" staffed by professionals who are independent of governments to manage the integration process. These bold ideas would require a change in the political mindset of ASEAN policy-makers with regards to the concept of national sovereignty. Unless political elites in the region adopt a more flexible stance on sovereignty and be more forthcoming with the notion of "pooled sovereignty", many of these initiatives would only remain moot and academic.

4. The ASEAN Charter

At the 2005 ASEAN Summit in Kuala Lumpur, Malaysia, a ten-member EPG was appointed to examine the possibility of having a Charter and to consider bold and new ideas to strengthen ASEAN as an institution. The EPG submitted their recommendations for the consideration of ASEAN leaders in December 2006. The draft Charter is expected to be ready in time for the ASEAN Singapore Summit in November 2007.

The Charter should provide ASEAN not only with a legal personality but also set out the long-term strategic direction for the region. The Charter would put in place the necessary arrangements to realize the ASEAN Community as well as define the institutions, mechanisms and processes for dealing with transnational issues (Severino 2005). On the economic front, the Charter should unambiguously describe the ultimate end-goal of the AEC. In this regard, the proposed Charter comes at a propitious time as ASEAN currently faces both challenges and opportunities arising from regional economic integration.

When considering economic inputs for the Charter, there is no need to "reinvent the wheel" as key economic integration measures are already outlined in the Bali Concord II and the VAP (Hew 2005b). Although most of the essential economic elements have been identified for the Charter, the main problem lies in its effective implementation and compliance by member countries. In this context, the EPG on the ASEAN Charter recommended that dispute settlement mechanisms should be established not only in economic cooperation but in all fields of regional cooperation, which would include compliance monitoring, advisory, consultation as well as enforcement mechanisms.

As mentioned earlier, it is also important to note that deeper economic integration cannot be successfully achieved without the establishment of a stronger institutional structure. Having a Charter is an important step in that direction as it can provide a more rule-based institutional structure for ASEAN. But, a change in mindset is required if ASEAN wishes to remain economically competitive. This includes reviewing the consensual "ASEAN way" of making decisions that clearly slows down the economic integration process. In order to successfully realize the AEC, the "ASEAN minus X" and "2 plus X" should be applied to the implementation of all economic integration programmes. At the same time, ASEAN policy-makers must be cognizant of the need not to exclude the less developed member countries such as the CLMV countries as the pace of integration accelerates.

5. ASEAN Economic Community by 2015

At the ASEAN Cebu Summit in January 2007, ASEAN leaders agreed to bring forward the deadline for realizing the AEC to 2015. But what exactly is being brought forward to 2015? AEC's end-goal of a "single market" connotes an EU-style common market where there is complete freedom of trade of goods, services, capital and labour. Lloyd (2005, p. 263) noted that the establishment of an EU-type single market is a large evolutionary step for ASEAN. He argues that this would require very deep economic integration as:

> ... the objective of a single market is quite definite in terms of the ultimate coverage of measures, namely, all measures required to remove discrimination against other ASEAN suppliers of goods, services, and factors.

ASEAN ISIS, a consortium of ASEAN think-tanks, suggests that the ultimate form of integration for the AEC is indeed an EU-style common market in which ASEAN would be declared a common market but would have a type of "negative list" of areas where member countries could reserve deeper economic integration for a later stage (ASEAN ISIS 2003; Soesastro 2005). However, as it stands, there is no evidence to indicate that there is any political desire by ASEAN leaders to establish a customs union let alone a common market (ISEAS 2003). A customs union is considered an important building block towards the establishment of a common market.[1]

Given the different degrees of openness and stages of economic development among ASEAN countries, it would be politically difficult for ASEAN to reach a consensus in agreeing to take this step up the economic integration ladder. Hence, the AEC's "single market" is conceptually an ambiguous end-goal.

Nevertheless, ASEAN could still be a highly competitive economic region by 2015. While an EU-style common market may not be realistic in such a short time, the AEC could realize an "AFTA-Plus" arrangement in less than a decade. All ASEAN countries would have implemented AFTA, AIA, and AFAS by 2015. If the challenges related to these three economic building blocks as mentioned earlier are addressed, the AEC would be a fully functioning free trade area with minimal non-tariff barriers. While this is a more limited end-goal compared to the EU-style common market, it would be politically acceptable and feasible given the tight time line. By 2015, ASEAN could also potentially be an FTA hub for the region. The regional organizations' "ASEAN plus 1" FTAs with China Japan, Korea, India, Australia and New Zealand would be fully operational by this time.

In this regard, an AEC blueprint, which sets out the approach, targets and milestones leading up to 2015, would be crucial at this point in time. Like the ASEAN Charter, an AEC blueprint is expected to be drafted in time for ASEAN Singapore Summit in November 2007.

6. Concluding Remarks

Since its inception in August 1967, ASEAN has indeed come a long way in becoming one of the most dynamic regional organizations in the developing world. This dynamism has made ASEAN the linchpin of broader international cooperative frameworks that have since been established beyond East Asia to the wider Asia-Pacific region. These include the Asia Pacific Economic Cooperation (APEC) in 1989, the Asian Plus Three (APT) in 1997, and more recently, the East Asia Summit in 2005. In all these cooperative endeavours, however, ASEAN's declared vision of becoming an Economic Community by 2015 has certainly been one of the most decisive steps in advancing its goal of becoming an integrated market. In fact, the envisioned establishment of a three-pillared ASEAN Community reflects the extent to which member countries of ASEAN are willing to go in building a regional community that is just, prosperous, and secure (ASEAN Vision 2020).

In charting the path ahead, it had been argued that having an ASEAN Charter is not only a prerequisite but more importantly, an important foundation that would define the shape of the AEC. Yet, as mentioned in the introduction of this chapter, numerous questions and issues abound — not least the extent to which having a legal framework can facilitate the realization of an economically integrated market. This is where comparisons with the experience in Europe become inevitable. Among the questions commonly asked are whether the ASEAN Charter can be made to function like the 1957 Treaty of Rome, which had laid out the foundation for the successful establishment of the EU and whether ASEAN's economic integration could follow a similar route? Although the establishment of an EU-style single market is not realistically feasible by 2015, one could nevertheless argue that it should be a longer-term goal that ASEAN should strive to achieve (Hew 2005a). The ASEAN Charter, while not a panacea for ASEAN's current problems, has certainly provided the unique opportunity to lay out the groundwork for this long-term vision.

To do so requires the much-needed political will in addressing the difficult issues of national sovereignty and non-interference. Despite these difficulties, however, ASEAN has shown that by adopting a more flexible decision-making mechanism through its "ASEAN minus X" and the "2 plus X", advancing regional integration projects is feasible. The slow yet incremental progress underscores the fact that there are opportunities to push ahead when policy-makers are willing to cooperate to achieve a common goal. In this regard, the ability to adapt and change existing mindsets to meet the challenges ahead will perhaps be the most important test of ASEAN's relevance in the new millennium.

Finally, while studies on ASEAN economic integration have pointed to the role of the state in pushing for deeper integration, it is worth noting that market-driven trade and investment integration in East Asia has been very active and far more intense. Hence, while the AEC and its building blocks (i.e., AFTA, AIA, and AFAS) are state-led initiatives, market-driven integration in East Asia has already been making the entire region more inter-connected economically. Already about half of East Asia's (i.e., all ASEAN countries plus China, Hong Kong, Japan, Korea) trade is with itself with intra-regional trade expected to rise significantly over the next decade, underpinned by China's strong economic growth and rapid industrialization. It will, therefore, be important for ASEAN policy-makers to ensure that AEC policy initiatives are aligned to the market integration process. Similarly, the East Asia Summit (EAS) agenda should also give top priority to trade and investment integration.[2] In this context, financial cooperation, which is one of the five priority areas of cooperation under the EAS framework, should be aimed at facilitating market-driven integration.[3]

NOTES

1. A customs union is essentially a group of countries where trade barriers among member states are removed, tariffs among member countries are harmonized and a common external tariff policy is established with non-member countries. A customs union is generally considered one integration level above a free trade area.
2. The inaugural East Asia Summit (EAS) was held in Kuala Lumpur, Malaysia in December 2005. The EAS comprise of sixteen members which are all ASEAN countries, China, Japan, Korea, Australia, New Zealand and India.
3. Chairman's statement of the second EAS, Cebu, Philippines, on 15 January 2007. www.aseansec.org/19303.htm.

REFERENCES

Akrasanee, N. and J. Arunanondchai. "Institutional Reforms to Achieve ASEAN Economic Integration". In *Roadmap to an ASEAN Economic Community*, edited by D. Hew. Singapore: Institute of Southeast Asian Studies, 2005.

ASEAN ISIS. "Towards an ASEAN Economic Community: A Track Two Report to ASEAN Policy Makers". Unpublished manuscript, Jakarta, 2003.

ASEAN Secretariat. *ASEAN into The Next Millennium: ASEAN Vision 2020, Hanoi Plan of Action.* Jakarta: ASEAN Secretariat, 1999.

———. *ASEAN Statistical Pocket Book 2006.* Jakarta: ASEAN Secretariat, 2006*a*.

———. "Report of the Eminent Persons Group on the ASEAN Charter", ASEAN Secretariat, December 2006*b*.

Asian Development Bank (ADB). "Preferential Trade Agreements in Asia and the Pacific". In *Asian Development Outlook 2002.* Manila: ADB, 2002.

———. "Foreign Direct Investment in Developing Asia". In *Asian Development Outlook 2004.* Manila: ADB, 2004.

———. *Key Indicators 2005*, Vol. 36. Manila: ADB, 2005.

Austria, M. "The Patterns of Intra-ASEAN trade in the Priority Goods Sectors". Unpublished manuscript. REPSF Project No. 03/006e. Regional Economic Policy Support Facility (REPSF). Downloaded from ASEAN-Australia Development Cooperation website www.aadcp-repsf.org.publications.htm. 2004.

——— and J. Avila. "Looking Beyond AFTA: Prospects and Challenges for Inter-Regional Trade". PIDS Discussion Paper Series No. 2001-10, Philippine Institute for Development Studies, 2001.

Baldwin, R. "Managing the Noodle Bowl: The Fragility of East Asian Regionalism".

Centre for Economic Policy Research (CEPR) Discussion Paper no. 5561, March 2006. www.cepr.org/pubs/dps/DP5561.asp.

East Asia Vision Group. "Toward an East Asian Community: Region of Peace, Prosperity and Progress". East Asia Vision Group Report, 2001.

Feridhanusetyawan, T. "Preferential Trade Agreements in the Asia-Pacific Region". IMF Working Paper, July 2005.

Freeman, N. and D. Hew. "Introductory Overview: Rethinking the East Asian Development Model". *ASEAN Economic Bulletin* 19, no. 1 (Special Focus, April 2002): 1–5.

Hew, D. "Towards an ASEAN Charter: Regional Economic Integration". In *Framing the ASEAN Charter: An ISEAS Perspective*, compiled by R. C. Severino. Singapore: Institute of Southeast Asian Studies, 2005*a*.

──────. "Southeast Asian Economies: Towards Recovery and Deeper Integration". In *Southeast Asian Affairs 2005*, edited by Chin Kin Wah and Daljit Singh. Singapore: Institute of Southeast Asian Studies, 2005*b*.

──────, ed. *Roadmap to an ASEAN Economic Community*. Singapore: Institute of Southeast Asian Studies, 2005*c*.

────── and M. Anthony. "ASEAN and ASEAN+3 in Postcrisis Asia". *NIRA Review* 7, no. 4 (Autumn 2000).

────── and H. Soesastro. "Realizing the ASEAN Economic Community by 2020: ISEAS and ASEAN-ISIS Approaches". *ASEAN Economic Bulletin* 20, no. 3 (December 2003): 292–96.

────── and R. Sen. "Towards an ASEAN Economic Community: Challenges and Prospects". ISEAS Working Paper on Economics and Finance. Singapore: Institute of Southeast Asian Studies, 2004.

Hsu, L. "ASEAN Economic Integration: A Fillip For The Future". In *Trading Arrangements in the Pacific Rim*. New York: Oceana Publications, 2003.

Institute of Southeast Asian Studies. "ISEAS Concept Paper on the ASEAN Economic Community". Unpublished manuscript, Singapore, 2003.

Kawai, M. "East Asian Economic Regionalism: Progress and Challenges". *Journal of Asian Economics* 16 (2005): 29–55.

Lloyd. P. J. "What is a Single Market: An Application to the Case of ASEAN". *ASEAN Economic Bulletin* 22, no. 3 (2005): 251–65.

Nikomborirak, D. and S. Stephenson. "Liberalization of Trade in Services: East Asia and the Western Hemisphere". Paper prepared for the Pacific Economic Cooperation Council (PECC) Trade Policy Forum on Regional Trading Agreements, Bangkok, Thailand, 12–13 June 2002.

Rajan, R., and R. Sen. "The New Wave of FTAs in Asia: With Particular Reference to ASEAN, China and India". In *ASEAN Economic Cooperation and Integration: Progress Challenges and Prospects*. Manila: Asian Development Bank, 2005.

Salazar, L. and S. B. Das. "Bridging the ASEAN Development Divide: Challenges and Prospects". *ASEAN Economic Bulletin* 24, no. 1 (April 2007): 1–14.

Sally, R. and R. Sen. "Whither Trade Policies in Southeast Asia? The Wider Asian and Global Context". *ASEAN Economic Bulletin* 22, no. 1 (2005): 92–115.

Schwartz, A. and R. Villinger. "Integrating Southeast Asian Economies". *The McKinsey Quarterly*, no. 1, 2004.

Sen, R. *Free Trade Agreements in Southeast Asia*. Southeast Asia Background Series No. 1. Singapore: Institute of Southeast Asian Studies, 2004.

Severino, R. C. *Southeast Asia in Search of an ASEAN Community: Insights from the former ASEAN Secretary-General*. Singapore: Institute of Southeast Asian Studies, 2006.

———, comp. *Framing the ASEAN Charter: An ISEAS Perspective*. Singapore: Institute of Southeast Asian Studies, 2005.

Soesastro, H. "Towards an ASEAN Economic Community". In *The 2nd ASEAN Reader*, compiled by Sharon Siddique and Sree Kumar. Singapore: Institute of Southeast Asian Studies, 2003.

———. "ASEAN Economic Community: Concept, Costs and Benefits". In *Roadmap to an ASEAN Economic Community*, edited by D. Hew. Singapore: Institute of Southeast Asian Studies, 2005.

Tongzon, J. "Role of AFTA in an ASEAN Economic Community". In *Roadmap to an ASEAN Economic Community*, edited by D. Hew. Singapore: Institute of Southeast Asian Studies, 2005.

——— and H. Khan. "The Challenges of Economic Integration for Transitional Economies of Southeast Asia: Coping with Revenue Losses". *ASEAN Economic Bulletin* 22, no. 3 (2005): 266–83.

United Nations Development Programme (UNDP). *Human Development Report 2006*. New York: UNDP, 2006.

Vo. T. T. "ASEAN Economic Community: Perspective from ASEAN's Transitional Economies". In *Roadmap to an ASEAN Economic Community*, edited by D. Hew. Singapore: Institute of Southeast Asian Studies, 2005.

World Bank. *East Asia Update: From Cyclical Recovery to Long Term Growth*. Washington, D.C.: World Bank, 2003.

Index

PERTAMINA, 160
Philippines
    elimination of NTMs, 121
    integration with ASEAN, 81
    investment arbitration, 161, 162
    tariff rates, 73
policy recommendations
    CLMV countries, 52
political and security cooperation, 1
portfolio investments, 166
poverty
    CLMV countries, 39
    incidence in ASEAN, 217
preferential trade agreement, 67, 76
price
    definition of, 19
price-raising effects
    service restrictions, 124
Priority Goods Sectors, 9
priority sectors, 3, 9, 76, 118, 136
    CEPT rate, 66
    horizontal IIT, 78
    impediments, 136, 137
    ranking, 84
    Thailand, 73
private sector development, 55
privatization
    state-owned enterprises, 55
production base
    creation of single, 2
    integrated, 3
profit repatriation, 10
profits
    repatriation, 155
    taxation, 156
provincial laws, 21

R
RCA indices
    ASEAN commercial services
        exports, 197
    ASEAN merchandise exports, 196
    commercial services exports, 186

merchandise export
    ASEAN-6 and CER, 181
    ASEAN-6 and China, 185
    ASEAN-6 and Korea, 205
re-exports
    VAT rebates, 126
re-training
    relevant skills, 56
regional and bilateral trade
    agreements, 98
regional cooperation
    scope of, 130
regional economic integration, 212
Regional Economic Policy Support
    Facility (REPSF), 7
regional free trade agreements, 212
regional groups, 14
regional investment
    disincentive, 10
regional market
    single, 22
regional trading agreement (RTA), 4,
    9, 13, 17, 96
    economic integration in, 22
    membership in, 99
regionalism, 95, 96
    impact on liberalization, 99
    multiple memberships, 97
    proliferation, 175
regulated standards, 117
relationship with IIT, 83
Republic of China, 145
retail prices
    impact of NTMs, 92
Revealed Comparative Advantage
    (RCA), 9, 75, 180
    by priority sector, 77
revenue
    calculation, 45
    effect of CEPT, 47
revenue collection
    Cambodia, 39, 40
    Myanmar, 42
    Vietnam, 43

Contents of Accompanying CD-ROM:
AADCP-REPSF Phase I Research Program

The following is the complete list of reports under AADCP-REPSF Phase I. For some reports, only the abstracts and/or executive summaries are included in the accompanying CD-ROM.

No.	Project No.	Title	Authors	Date of Report
1	02/001	Developing Indicators of ASEAN Integration — A Preliminary Survey for a Roadmap	David J. Dennis Zainal Aznam Yusof	August 2003
2	02/002	Options for Managing the Revenue Losses and Other Adjustment Costs of CLMV Participation in AFTA	Jose L. Tongzon Habibullah Khan Le Dang Doanh	October 2004
3	02/003	Reforming Trade in Services Negotiations under AFAS	H. S. Kartadjoemena	June 2003
4	02/004	Liberalizing and Facilitating the Movement of Individual Service Providers under AFAS: Implications for Labour and Immigration Policies and Procedures in ASEAN	Chris Manning Pradip Bhatnagar	March 2004
5	02/005	A Proposed ASEAN Policy Blueprint for SME Development 2004–2014	Choompon Asasen Kanchana Asasen Nataya Chuangcham	July 2003
6	02/006	Liberalization of Financial Services in the ASEAN Region	Jenny Gordon Ross Chapman	May 2003

No.	Project No.	Title	Authors	Date of Report
7	02/007	Liberalizing Capital Movements in the ASEAN Region	Alex Erskine	July 2003
8	02/008	Preparing ASEAN for Open Sky	Peter Forsyth John King Cherry Lyn Rodolfo Keith Trace	February 2004
9	02/009	Liberalization and Harmonization of ASEAN Telecommunications	Christopher Findlay Roy Chun Lee Ma. Joy V. Abrenica Florian A. Alburo Deunden Nikomborirak Somkiat Tangkitvanich	December 2004
	03/001	Issues and Options for the Work Programme to Eliminate Non-tariff Barriers in AFTA		withdrawn
10	03/002	Preparing for Electricity Trading in ASEAN	Michael Porter Hardiv Situmcang Edward Willett Sandra Gamble Ross Ramsay Amy Auster	March 2005
11	03/003	Harmonization and Integration of Customs Valuation Policies and Practices in the ASEAN Region	David Widdowson Mark Harrison Pantipa Prammanee Santichoom Srirunpetch Daniel Dawes Mike Spong	August 2004
12	03/004	A Background Paper for the Strategic Plan of Action on ASEAN Cooperation in Food and Agriculture (2005–2010)	Alan Oxley Selwyn Heilbron Kristen Osborne Steven Macmillan Rolando T. Dy Senen U. Reyes Florence E. Mojica Marie Annette S. Galvez Ditas Macabasco	July 2004

No.	Project No.	Title	Authors	Date of Report
13	03/005	Maximizing the Contribution of IP Rights (IPRs) to SME Growth and Competitiveness	Stuart Macdonald Tim Turpin Amelia Ancog	September 2005
	03/006	Background Papers for the Next ASEAN Plan of Action to Enhance Economic Integration (2005–2010)		
14	(a)	Global Economic Challenges to ASEAN Integration and Competitiveness: A Prospective Look	Peter Lloyd Penny Smith	September 2004
15	(b)	An Assessment Study on the Progress of ASEAN Regional Integration: The Ha Noi Plan of Action toward ASEAN Vision 2020	Cielito F. Habito Fernando T. Aldaba Ofelia M. Templo	October 2004
16	(c)	Resource Mobilisation for the Implementation of the Vientiane Action Programme: A Background Paper	Jenny Gordon John Humphreys Robert Warner Teresa Hearne	November 2004
17	(d)	Monitoring and Impact Assessment Mechanisms for the VAP: A Background Paper	John Martin	December 2004
18	(e)	The Pattern of Intra-ASEAN Trade in the Priority Goods Sectors	Myrna S. Austria	August 2004

No.	Project No.	Title	Authors	Date of Report
19	04/001	Promoting Efficient and Competitive Intra-ASEAN Shipping Services	Steve Meyrick Keith Trace Richard Filmer Jeremy Brown John A. Lee Jose Tongzon	March 2005
20	04/002	Harmonization and Integration of Customs Cargo Processing Policies and Practices in the ASEAN Region	Andrew Cuthbertson Jenny Gordon Adelardo C. Ables Florian A. Alburo Loreli de Dios Ma. Joy V. Abrenica	January 2006
21	04/003	SME Access to Financing: Addressing the Supply-side of SME Financing	Yeah Kim Leng Julie Ng Lee Tin Hui	July 2005
22	04/004	The Economic Research Network for ASEAN Partnership	Andrew MacIntyre Vo Tri Thanh	February 2005
23	04/005	ASEAN Telecommunications and IT Sectors — Towards Closer ASEAN Integration	Ma. Joy V. Abrenica Adelardo C. Ables Roy Chun Lee Somkiat Tangkitvanich	June 2005
24	04/006	Regulatory Models for ASEAN Telecoms	Rod Shogren Roy Chun Lee Annette Lancy Jeff Fountain Jong Kwan Lee	September 2004
25	04/007	Movement of Workers in ASEAN: Healthcare & IT Sectors	Christopher Manning Alexandra Sidorenko Philippa Dee George Manzano Yongyuth Chalamwong Pradip Bhatnagar	June 2005

No.	Project No.	Title	Authors	Date of Report
26	04/008	Strategic Directions for ASEAN Airlines in a Globalizing World: Overview	Christopher Findlay	August 2005
27	(a)	Competition and Consumer Protection Policy	Deunden Nikomborirak	October 2005
28	(b)	Development of Principles for the Implementation of Subsidies and State Aid	Rafaelita M. Aldaba	August 2005
29	(c)	Ownership Rules and Investment	Mahani Zainal-Abidin Wan Khatina Wan Mohd Nawawi Sazalina Kamaruddin	November 2005
30	(d)	The Emergence of Low Cost Carriers in South East Asia	Yose Rizal Damuri Titik Anas	October 2005
31	04/009 (a)	Developing the ASEAN Minerals Sector: A Preliminary Study	Christopher Short Yeon Kim Allison Loise Ball Karen Schneider Graham Love	January 2005
32	(b)	Enhancing ASEAN Minerals Trade & Investment	Jane Mélanie Marina Kim Sam Hester Peter Berry Allison Loise Ball Karen Schneider Paul Burke Le Hoa Au Duong Adam McCarty	December 2005

No.	Project No.	Title	Authors	Date of Report
33	04/010	AIA-Plus: Building on Free Trade Agreements	Denis Hew Rajenthran Arumugam Hur Jung Rahul Sen Hadi Soesastro Shin Jang Sup M. Sornarajah Toh Mun Heng Ray Trewin Jose Tongzon	December 2006
34	04/011	An Investigation Into the Measures Affecting the Integration of ASEAN's Priority Sectors (Phase 1)	Christopher Findlay	April 2006
35	05/001	ASEAN Tourism Investment Study	Wayne Crosbie Yeah Kim Leng Catherine Ng Julie Ng Shuba Kumar	September 2006
36	05/002	Relationship between the AJCEP Agreement and Japan's Bilateral EPAs with ASEAN countries	Toh Mun Heng	January 2007
37	05/003	Australia and New Zealand Bilateral CEPs/FTAs with ASEAN Countries and Their Implication on the AANZFTA	Robert Scollay Ray Trewin	June 2006
38	05/004	Ten Years of AFAS: An Assessment	Vo Tri Thanh Paul Bartlett	July 2006
39	05/005	ASEAN Tax Regimes and the Integration of the Priority Sectors	Ian Farrow Sunita Jogarajan	October 2006

No.	Project No.	Title	Authors	Date of Report
40	05/006	Expanding Trade in Business Services in ASEAN	Gwendolyn R. Tecson Andrew Stoler Deunden Nikomborirak Ma. Joy V. Abrenica Florian A. Alburo Agustin Arcenas Loreli de Dios Ma. Nimfa Mendoza Titik Anas Haryo Aswicahyono James Redden Barry Brogan	June 2007
41	05/007	Desirability, Feasibility and Options for Establishing ESM within the AFAS	Malcolm Bosworth Dionisius A. Narjoko	December 2006
	06/001	An Investigation Into the Measures Affecting the Integration of ASEAN's Priority Sectors (Phase 2)		
42	A	Overview	Christopher Findlay	April 2007
		Non-Tariff Barriers to Trade in the ASEAN Priority Goods Sectors	Loreli C. de Dios	October 2006
		Review of Regional Trade and Available Tariff Rate Data	Rina Oktaviani Amzul Rifin Henny Reinhardt	May 2007
		Impediments to Trade in the Priority Services Sectors	Ryo Ochiai	December 2006
43	B	The Case of Electronics	David Parsons Assisted by Mawardi Maghfuri, Bintoro Ariyanto, Rina Oktaviani	June 2007

No.	Project No.	Title	Authors	Date of Report
44	C	The Case of Textiles and Apparels	William E. James Peter J. Minor Kakada Dourng	April 2007
45	D	The Case of Logistics	Robert de Souza Mark Goh Sumeet Gupta Luo Lei	April 2007
46	E	Region-wide Business Survey	Catherine Eddy Rowena Owen	May 2007
47	F	Overall Findings and Recommendations	Christopher Findlay	May 2007
48	06/002	Impact Assessment of the Visit ASEAN Campaign	Noel Scott	May 2007
49	06/003	A Background Paper on Energy Issues for the 2nd East Asia Summit	Robert Curtotti Angelica Austin Andrew Dickson Lindsay Hogan Peter Drysdale	November 2006
50	06/004	ASEAN Fiscal and Monetary Policy Responses to Rising Oil Prices	Peter Downes	May 2007